SMALL BOAT, VAST OCEAN

SMALL BOAT, VAST OCEAN

My Years in
Solitary Buddhist Retreat

Diane Rigdzin Berger

BUTTER LAMP PRESS

Small Boat, Vast Ocean:
My Years in Solitary Buddhist Retreat
Copyright © 2023 Diane Rigdzin Berger

"Like a Boat Drifting," from *Poems from Ish River Country, Collected Poems and Translations* published by Shoemaker & Hoard, 2004, used by kind permission of the Robert Sund Poet's House, www.robertsund.org.

ISBN: 979-8-9866945-0-4

Library of Congress Control Number: 2022918392

Butter Lamp Press
Seattle, Washington

Cover Collage by Diane Berger
Book Design by Sandra Moreano
Author photograph by Gus Berger

Printed in the United States of America

9 8 7 6 5 4 3 2 1

For Gus and Sophia
who graciously allowed me to step out
of family life
for this oceanic inner passage

Contents

INTRODUCTION

Three years, three months, three days. A long time to go away from friends and family, away from society altogether, to dive into the realm of deep psyche, and further, into soul and spirit. In our Western tradition, but only rarely these days, religious hermits, monks and nuns in cloisters, those who take vows of silence or stay in the mountains, do so in order to become quiet enough to contact the nether reaches of what it means to be human, contact then followed by transformation. Or that is the hope. Christians who wish to open to God hope to become more like Jesus. Shamans who wish to connect with spirit hope to become more effective healers or visionaries. Buddhists who wish to open to their *intrinsic nature* hope to become enlightened. Beautiful wishes to benefit others.

I would sometimes explain to the curious: this three-year retreat is a traditional form in Tibetan Buddhism. There is a guide, a place, a small community, a curriculum, and boundaries. The purpose is to have a chance to practice the array of Buddhist meditations and liturgies in a concentrated way, in order to give this inner "medicine" a chance to do its work on oneself. Without undisturbed retreat, especially in today's world of serial distraction, most of us can't fully delve into the path, much less realize the goal.

My own retreat leaned slightly unorthodox. It had an eccentric orbit, touching down for months at a time at one place or another—nine stays at five different places. All were in the Pacific Northwest, and most were not at retreat centers, instead at the homes of kind friends or family with unoccupied houses where I could stay for an extended time and do solo retreat.

This style of roving retreat, while not unheard of in Tibet, is pretty unusual in the West. Most Western retreatants go into long retreat with a group in a retreat setting and stay put for the prescribed time. They receive guidance from teachers who enter into their space; and they see or speak to no one outside their small community, while all their needs are arranged for them by a liaison. But for me, while I had many of the requisite elements for retreat, I was lacking a ready retreat center, or the funds to pay my way into one. My customary response to any perceived obstacle, though, would be to say: Well, there must be a creative solution, so how can I accomplish x, y, or z? In this case, the solution was in finding free or inexpensive places to stay, places that would be conducive to, even inspiring for, spiritual journeying. And further, for the lack of retreat community, I would substitute limited social contact.

So, retreat housing, check. Authentic *lama* as guide, check. Years of experience in Tibetan Buddhism, check. Dharma meditation and practice in back pocket, check. Support of *sangha* and friends, check. Permission of family, check.

As obstacles melted away, as intention advanced to forward movement, it became clear that it would happen. A date, auspicious for beginning a spiritual endeavor according to the Tibetan calendar, was chosen. And I felt increasing certainty and joy with each passing day toward its approach. Ready for launch.

And yet, how did I get there? And why?

———◇———

A dream.

I was beckoned down a pathway to the edge of the ocean, where I gazed in wonder at its immenseness and grandeur. A deep male voice boomed out, commanding me, "You must cross this ocean. You must do so by walking. And you must leave your people." I woke up in a terror, sobbing and calling out to my mother, because I was just a little girl of five. And then the dream reoccurred many times, for years.

The last time it came, it was no longer a nightmare. I was fourteen, and by then I was ready. I stepped out and began the journey. After some steps I looked down and saw that my feet were walking on the surface of the ocean! Realizing the impossibility, I sank down up to my neck. Instantly waking, not discouraged, but with a sense of triumph, I knew that my dream-self finally knew what to do.

To my waking self, however, the dream was still a mystery. It had been a source of some trauma early on, then wonder. Clear, recurring dreams like that must mean something, but what? Even at age five I knew that I'd been standing on the eastern edge of the Pacific Ocean facing west. But where was I supposed to be going? Japan? China? Was it to be taken literally? I had no idea.

Finally. I was allowed to stay on the small island alone, no running water, no electricity, no roads, no stores, no phone. I was seventeen. I had just dropped my mother off at the harbor where she could pick up her car and take a ferry back home to the city. Aiming our small outboard back over the sea, I returned to our family's summer cabin on one of the outer islands of the San Juan archipelago.

I nestled back in for those few days, sometimes rowing the length of the island in our small dinghy and back again. This was unlike the long, sleek shells that I'd competed in at the Women's Nationals that spring, but no matter. Pulling the oars against the dark currents, watching my progress along the shore, the splash of the wavelets, union with the sea happened in this way. I walked the madrona-shaded paths that run along the island's perimeter, sitting for long spells on the far eastern cliffs, my gaze caressing the surface of turbulent icy waters below, the rocky reefs and adjacent island shores, the blue and clear sky. Eagles were returning to the tree tops in those days, as well as seals to the reefs, and the sea lions and otters, so I was made happy by sightings and language of those friends. I did not know how to meditate yet, but the presence of stillness, the potency of the moment, and ardent connection to the natural world sometimes set me pensive, and sometimes filled my mind and heart with joy.

One early evening, sitting on the cabin's deck gazing out to the sea, in this state, it overflowed. I sprang up, filled with ah ha!—my heart about to burst with connection to all, the beauty of awareness! I found myself running down the path toward the far point of the island, singing, calling, tears streaming down my cheeks, Pure Joy. There was no boy, no mind-altering substance. Just the realization of a truth, one with no words, no explanation.

Years later, reading about *satori*, I remembered that evening alone on the island, and knew that this is how it can happen, to anyone. If not a lasting state of realization, I had tasted a moment.

> *Satori is the sudden flashing into consciousness of a new truth hitherto undreamed of. It is a sort of mental catastrophe taking place all at once.*
>
> –D.T. Suzuki, An Introduction to Zen Buddhism

In my twenties and thirties I felt an urgent longing to find my spiritual home. It wasn't only because of those recurring dreams, but something deep inside was prodding, pulling me. The quest was a rich time, delving into books, religions—traditional and new age—and deep talks with teachers and other seekers. And I built up a store of confirming inner experiences.

Then, in my mid-30s in 1989, through a series of "coincidences," I was introduced to Tibetan Buddhism. Instantly and with great joy I knew I'd found my home. Soon I was attending retreats in California and France, organized by the international Rigpa Fellowship. For seven years I practiced on a weekly basis with their local Seattle group, while my knowledge of this ancient tradition grew. I sometimes made what I called "half-day retreats" lasting from one to five months, undertaking the practices on my own at home. After one retreat in France with the renowned lama Dilgo Khyentse Rinpoche, who embodied a vast enlightenment I had before only imagined, my faith in the tradition never wavered.

Wanting to give my fourteen-year-old twins a broad experience of the world, in 1996 I decided to take them on a one-year journey. We began in Europe, backpacking along ancient pilgrimage trails in Belgium and France. We had a setback in southern France when I badly twisted an ankle, so we readjusted our plan, taking trains into Spain, Italy, and finally the Netherlands. It was a rich time. We read and discussed European history and philosophy at night in our tent or hotel room, and followed up at city sites and museums during the day. At the end of our Western travels, as per his plan, Gus returned home to school, and Sophia and I continued on to the East.

The adventures that unfolded over the following eight months in India and Nepal could fill another book. But for now, the important story is that we met a Tibetan lama who would have a significant impact on the remainder of the trip and beyond. After landing in Mumbai, we made our way to a small Tibetan settlement in southern India. The Rigpa organization had a connection with a monastery there, and because I'd written ahead, we were expected. We stayed there a week or two, Sophia learning cricket from the younger monks and studying her math, while I meditated in the temple.

It was here that we met Tulku Tsultrim Dorje, who had gotten stuck in India and deeply wished to return to his home in Tibet. In our meetings, the compassion transmitted by this individual, whom I initially took to be an ordinary monk, was breathtaking, conveying that he was in no way ordinary. It was later, when I learned he was the reincarnation of an enlightened master, that it all made sense. Inspired by his great compassion, I decided to help him find the resources needed to head back north—eventually to eastern Tibet where he could return to his life's mission: to rebuild the monastery of which he was the head.

There was not to be a direct route in getting Tulku Tsultrim back to Tibet, of course. First stop, Nepal, and even that came with challenges. After we succeeded in getting him there, at least closer to Tibet, I began to volunteer for him, chiefly by fundraising for that monastery rebuild.

But more was needed than could be found in Kathmandu, and the obvious answer was to bring the *tulku* to the United States. After Sophia and I returned home at the end of our year of travel, I began the process of arranging for Tulku Tsultrim to visit Seattle to find out if he would like to stay on. And stay he did.

In the beginning, we concentrated on fundraising for the monastery, for which we created the nonprofit Kilung Foundation. We did well enough so that when Tulku Tsultrim made that first, longed-for trip back to Tibet (after an absence of seven years in India, Nepal, and then the States) he was carrying with him funding for beginnings of a monastic college. When he returned to the States, requests for his teaching of Buddhism were increasing, so we created a sangha and eventually opened a small center in Seattle. Students joined locally, and as well, he received invitations to teach in other states and abroad; and he gained a new title: Dza Kilung Jigme Rinpoche. We added other projects in Tibet: a bridge, two schools, housing for monks, and renovation of the ancient temple.

While continuing to teach school part-time, I managed most aspects of the foundation: organizing, scheduling, event planning, writing, fundraising, and directing volunteers. I sat in on Rinpoche's spiritual consultations as interpreter until his English improved. I began to teach meditation and Buddhism classes when Rinpoche traveled, and often accompanied him on trips, including to Asia. I organized and led tours to his region of Tibet, and one to India.

It felt like a fruition: finally I'd found satisfying work that utilized my talents, knowledge, and experience, all for a worthy cause—humanitarian work that was benefiting the world and sharing Buddhadharma with other Westerners. I threw myself into it with great joy. On top of that, I was attending scores of Rinpoche's teachings and retreats, and continuing to develop spiritually.

Then, after fourteen years, a shift was taking place on several planes at once. And it was time for me to make a change.

———◇———

Over the course of my life, that girlhood dream became clear with both literal and symbolic meaning. It glimmered awake when I first embraced Buddhism. Later, with all that unfolded in India and Nepal, the dream felt quite literal: traveling to the East and meeting many Buddhist teachers, some enlightened. The symbolic meaning opened when I brought Kilung Rinpoche to Seattle to begin teaching in the West. And it deepened when, on October 17 of 2011, I shoved a small boat off from the shores of *terra firma*, onto the great ocean of long retreat, and after the journey, arrived safely on distant shores, end of retreat, May Day 2015.

During this crossing I wrote often, creating a loose body of work, a reflection of my inner journey, which I have gathered together into this book. Because the writing was spontaneous, reflecting the nature of the experience, it has the feel of collage—expository writing, depth writing, letters, essays and poetry, and snippets of experience, offered in chronology.

Original writings from the retreat are in normal text; writings done in the present during the creation of this book are indented and in italics.

There is a glossary at the end for those unfamiliar with the specialized language of Tibetan Buddhism. Each term is italicized in its first use.

I'm intentionally oblique about what practices I did and most "mystical" experiences, protecting the innermost sphere of the retreat, while sharing the outer, and much of the inner—the realm of the psyche. This reticence follows tradition. It's said that revealing too much dissolves the potency of the experience, which continues to unpack itself over a matter of years after retreat's end. Crossing fingers, in fact, that what I have revealed here will be, on balance, more beneficial than the other way round.

———◇———

The medieval alchemists of Europe sometimes depicted an inner hermetic process with a drawing of an adept in a large steaming tub, the subject himself directing an acolyte to pile more and more logs on the fire beneath. In other words, turning up the heat on the deep psyche to hasten the process of inner transformation, symbolically turning lead into gold—showing that the process is clearly not for sissies. Similar imagery in Tibetan Buddhism to "stir up the depths of *samsara*" is this same process, deemed necessary on the path to enlightenment. If becoming enlightened requires deep systemic change, something's gotta give.

Long retreat in solitude is one way into this process; it's said to be normal for most long-term retreatants, within Tibet and out, to have something difficult come up, some theme which may cause psychological anguish. It's around that point that one makes a "descent of the psyche," in the Jungian sense, into a journey that one is compelled to make, into one's own darkness—even turning this darkness into fuel—in order to transform one's inner core into golden light, a light which turns out to be one's birthright. From a Buddhist point of view, this core, when revealed, is compassionate and vast enlightened mind.

Indeed, I had my painful point. It was delivered in the form of the ending of my second marriage, which, for some time, had been in slow-motion crumble, culminating in a recent divorce. The decision to go into retreat was catalyzed by this tectonic shift, but the shift was not itself the root cause of my entering retreat. I had idealized three-year retreat for many years, and had wished to accomplish it one day. So, when it was clear I needed to make a major life change, three-year retreat emerged as option number one. However, in my naiveté I hadn't yet heard about the proverbial retreat stewpot, the crucible that retreat would certainly turn up—utilizing my breakup, or some other, painful point.

In the opening months of retreat then, without forewarning or expectation, I got to experience how this mechanism of retreat works: As more time is spent in solitude within the sacred container, the heat turns up beneath the caldron... and the inner demons also turn up. In this case they had neatly laid out my assignment before me, apparently unbidden, unwelcome, a torment distracting me from settling into retreat and, gosh darn it, my Buddhist practice! But in time I came to understand it for what it was: an essential task in the quest, and I became unflagging in my efforts, not to turn away, but to heal.

So, I set out across a vast ocean in a tiny boat, like the trusting youngest son in a fairy tale, with the simple goal of reaching the other shore. I knew and hoped the journey would change me, but with a kind of simpleton's mind, wasn't prepared for what the great ocean might have in store. This is the story of that passage. May it be of benefit, to you and, by extension and multiplication, to all.

PROLOGUE

The greater the tension, the greater is the potential. Great
energy springs from a correspondingly great tension between
opposites.

—Carl Jung

"I offer all my forgiveness."

These words emerged in my offering practice recently, my own addition to
the traditional lines of the liturgy. Mandala offering, a tactile ritual that lends
itself to rich metaphorical possibilities, is practiced to develop generosity and
non-attachment. My hand scoops a colorful portion of tiny, polished semi-pre-
cious stones out of a large bowl in my lap, my mind multiplying them into the
myriad appearances of the universe, imagined as all the finest elements of life,
material and unseen. I place them in little piles on the back of a polished copper
dish, offer them up to the Buddhas and *Bodhisattvas*, and ultimately to one's
own intrinisic *Buddha nature*. And then as everything must eventually go,
sweep them away into oblivion... only to do it again, and again. Lifetimes and
worlds forming and collapsing, without end.

The new line came from something unexpected—a phone call out of the
blue, a man wanting prayers for his marriage.

*People often called looking for Kilung Rinpoche, the Tibetan lama. When
he was away, sometimes for months, they would talk to me. I had been in
informal training with Rinpoche for more than a dozen years, acting as his
interpreter, sitting in on his consultations, aiding him in multiple ways.
That, plus previous counseling background, and years of experience in Buddhist study and practice, gave people a natural inclination to share and ask
me for advice.*

The man on the other end of the line was gregarious and full of life, and himself. A new-age leader of shamanic wilderness experiences, not a Buddhist, he said, but he had heard that Rinpoche's prayers were potent. He talked and talked about all kinds of things, his distraught wife, his philandering, and suddenly began to speak about the power of forgiveness. It hit me like a thunderbolt and I realized I, myself, need to work with this. Later that day in my practice I began by inserting it into the offering ritual, "I offer all my forgiveness," and I just sobbed, allowing the tears to come freely. Then I added, "I offer all my forgiveness *and love.*" More tears. Each time the crying didn't last long, but how refreshing. Each time my back stopped hurting, and this pervasive sadness began to lift. I brought in the Buddhist deities as witnesses to a kind of pledge I was making, this resolve to heal myself, to take this step away from blame— toward forgiveness. I thought of Shakespeare's quote *"The quality of mercy is not strained..."* and a wish to find that state. I also thought deeply of my son, whose art photo is on the wall facing me as I practice... feeling his love, that all is not lost, that I can afford to go out into the world, not completely all alone, or abandoned.

> *My own marriage was dissolving, that was clear. A feeling of abandonment, of lost sacrifice, and blame would rear its head suddenly at times, a fiery dragon on the loose. Anyone who has gone through divorce knows the anguish, the palette of contrasting emotions, the drama, and how that torment can drag on... and on.*

And yet... I seem to have met a *dakini* last night who gave me some advice and oracle-like predictions. She said I would have to go alone, that I was, in fact, entrusted to do so. She said something quite outlandish, that I had been a Buddhist lama in my last life. That I have much to do and will soon be at it. That I have all the "juice" from the ancient *lineage* of Buddhist teachers. That I need to go into solo retreat, but it doesn't have to be in a special place or near a lama. That I need to learn to be alone in this.

> *What do I do with this, I thought at the time? This American lama hadn't known about my girlhood dream, nor about my aspiration to do long retreat. I put it away and forgot about it, but something had been seeded.*

JULY 28 – JOURNAL

Up here at my family's island cabin at the moment, taking a little time to rest, meditate, practice, think. Two Buddhist friends, Diane and Cutty H., are with me and last night we started reading aloud a commentary on an old Tibetan text. Later I had a dream which took up where our reading left off...

Dream: There was a book, huge, heavy, ancient and mystical, which seemed to be the one we'd been reading earlier that evening. It morphed into another book with old illustrations. In the room were interesting characters with long white beards, elder wise men, to whom I was showing this rare and precious book. When we flipped backward in the book, the images disappeared, replaced by new pages with images of old anthropological drawings of cultures from around the world. Everyone in the room was impressed with the book, but the magic of it wasn't entirely out of the ordinary for any of us. I awoke happy.

After a week I found a boat ride for my friends off the island with neighbors, back to their jobs in Portland, and then I had one more retreat week on the island, solo. Continuing with the old text, every day before dusk I walked to the quiet north side of the island and sat for an hour of meditation, gazing out over a long expanse of sea, toward Canada. Resting with the conundrum of nonduality, and the mind as the originator and projector of one's perceptions, I played with the scene before me as a bubble, or as a flat screen, rather than the diminishing horizon of classic perspective. A profound sense began loosening up, and of ultra-presence. My gaze dropped to the surface of the water just below, riding on the peaceful swells of the depths, and in that exact spot a huge, lone seal suddenly emerged, turning over with balletic grace, and disappeared again. I met his appearance without surprise, as if nothing is ever a surprise. Merged with this animal cousin and the present moment, I knew intimately his movements, beyond time. A glimpse. Joy.

FEBRUARY 15, 2011 – JOURNAL

There's an analogy from a teaching I've been reflecting on, of a deer who is thirsty, sees the mirage of a pond, runs toward it, but the pond keeps eluding and the deer keeps running after it. In the same way we keep pursuing illusory phenomena. This imagery has been speaking to me, in my current state of depression and looking for external solutions—even a plan to go stay with friends for some days as a diversion to help shift this inner state. Still, it seems there's no harm in seeking a balm—though not ultimate, yet compassionate action extended to oneself.

APRIL – NOTES FROM A TEACHING OF KILUNG RINPOCHE

Rinpoche shared frankly about his three-year retreat in Tibet begun when he was about fourteen. He said the first year was a period of settling in and moving toward the next year. The second year he began to feel settled, describing his experience as "Now I'm practicing, and it's happening more deeply. Even still I'm not perfectly gaining confidence. But now I understand deeply that it's happening." In the third year, "Now it's happening; it's the inspiration year... even though as a teenager I was very distracted at times."

By May Day, 2011, an inner crisis was brewing, leading me to the sense that it was time to come to a decision. I went to stay with my mother and her husband for a few days, to get some space and bounce ideas off a sympathetic and reasoned audience. After long discussions about possible life changes, including practical considerations, I decided on my long-held aspiration of formal three-year retreat as the best option. What a relief to have made a decision. But importantly, I felt strong determination to take the current upheaval as unique opportunity, and turn it into my next adventure—of life and of the psyche, with aspirations going well beyond the self.

Months of preparations followed. I needed to find capable volunteers willing to take on the many positions within the nonprofit foundation and Buddhist sangha that would become vacant with my long absence. I hadn't been running the whole operation quite single-handedly, but in the end it required twenty-three different people to fill all my former roles.

Rinpoche and I pulled together a small group of longtime sangha members to request their blessing for the organization to support my retreat financially; there was unanimous agreement. By the end of May we made the official announcement to the sangha. Things quickly fell into place.

At the end of June, I emailed my family a progress report: the first-year locations were all in place, all in Washington state. First would be on Bainbridge Island at the unoccupied home of my former mother-in-law; second, I would be housesitting on San Juan Island for my mother and her husband while they spent the winter months away; and the third location was outside the town of Raymond on Willapa Bay in the second-floor apartment of a sangha member. All three places had beautiful views, quiet, perfect for retreat. I was enormously grateful.

Three months to go. Work for the sangha and foundation continued, including organizing teachings and retreats, and training my volunteer replacements. There was the personal, such as paying off last bills, arranging for storage of belongings, and selling my car. I dealt with my private sadness by flying off to Washington, D.C., in July to attend the awe-inspiring Kalachakra empowerment of HH Dalai Lama. But all in all, my mood was optimistic, eager to plunge into the adventure ahead.

OCTOBER 10 – SPEECH

Given to Sangha at Going-Away Party

Gratitude to everyone: All the immense support for this enterprise, more than I ever imagined. I am touched. A cross-fertilization of inspiration—others are inspired and I'm inspired back.

And it's been humbling. This seems counterintuitive, but it's true. Perhaps it reveals something about my own self-concept of worthiness, or lack thereof. But it feels somehow more like poetry, like those Japanese prints that show an immense landscape of tall, craggy mountains, with a tiny person walking along. To be that human, relatively small and singular in the scope of things, but participating in something profound, universal and ancient. The support and enthusiasm that everyone has shown reveals each one's participation, as a community endeavor. So, it's not just me doing three-year retreat. Somehow it is all of us together—all of us walking up the mountain path, staff in hand, bundle on back, aspiring to the awesome landscape of enlightenment.

Even non-Buddhists have been inspired by my plan to enter into this retreat, and in some cases to the point of helping support this in the same ways Buddhist friends are doing. One friend from college looked at his wife and said, "Marla, I want to go on a three-year retreat, a kayak retreat." He looked half-serious, and his wife didn't bat an eyelash, just said, "You go ahead, Andy." They insisted on driving me on one leg of my journey between retreat locations. Another couple, Buddhist sympathizers, instantly jumped in to help financially. And an old high school friend spontaneously offered her cabin in the Montana mountains for part of the retreat.

It seems there's something here that's striking a note for all kinds of people. How fortunate I feel to be the bearer of a shred of inspiration to the greater community, or to participate in a cultural opening that's appearing at this moment.

Among the responses from people have been queries: Do I feel excitement? or trepidation? The other day a response came from within me that finally resonated. I replied, "You know, I've been a Buddhist for twenty-two years, and this, for me, is 'settling in.' " I feel I'm finally going to be able to settle into the practice, settle into the path. There's neither excitement nor trepidation there, but a great sense of further deepening and connecting. As most of us have been, I've been flying around for years, accomplishing, busy-busy, taking teachings and retreat time where I can, which have resulted in glimpses, and then which dissolve over time. And now with gratitude, I'm entering into a time where I can actually practice. It feels really quite simple.

Of course there's a trap inherent here. One could set up expectations, feel obligated to accomplish something, sense pressure from self, and perceived pressure from others. In this retreat preparation time I so far seem to have fended this off alright, keeping self-expectations humble. Trying on the idea of "journey without goal."

I totally appreciate, and in some ways have been wistful about, the Tibetan wisdom of quietly disappearing from view into secret retreat. No obligations, except between self and teacher. "Less excitement and talk—more *tendrel*, auspicious interconnection," says Tibetan wisdom. But my situation has called for the current American culture of openness. So, as an antidote to western sharing and anticipation, I'd like to offer to the sangha this image of "settling in," which to me conjures equanimity, calm, cozy, warm, heart-mind-connected, and humble—a middle-way approach.

In 1998 I brought an accomplished Tibetan *Vajrayana* master to Seattle. Kilung Rinpoche came out of his cultural matrix, braved the secular and foreign energy of America, and decided he was actually up for staying and taking us on. Every time since then that I greeted him at the airport, *khatak* in hand, I thanked him from my heart for returning to the West. It's never been obligatory that he return here. This is important—how rare and fortunate Rinpoche's presence here is, and I recommend to keep this in the forefront of your minds.

In my departure, I'm also leaving many of you with the fortunate opportunity to work closely with Kilung Rinpoche, to "serve the lama," more directly than before. I often thought of my own experience and opportunity of working with him as imprinting, like a duckling imprinting on its mother duck. You might ask yourself the question, "If the Buddha were here now, would I be so open to him—his essence, energy, and behavior—that I would study him, emulate him in a state of alert attention, that a kind of imprinting might take place?"

Once, my daughter asked the question of Rinpoche: "What kind of advanced training could one take in order to teach the dharma and perhaps become a lama one day?" She was thinking of Buddhist study programs. Rinpoche's answer, "Serve a lama." Now, you have the opportunity to do just that.

Chapter One
Bainbridge Island, I

Ideally what are you retreating from? You are supposed
to be retreating from the past and future. That is the
ultimate boundary of your retreat. Not your door. Not your
geographical area. Ideally you are supposed to be in the hut,
and this hut is the present moment. But of course this is not
that easy, especially for those who are not used to it.

—Dzongsar Khyentse Rinpoche

OCTOBER 17, 2011 – SETTING OFF

*Everything jammed into my friend Jeanne's car—suitcase, boxes of sacred
books and altar items, sitting cushions, whatever I thought I'd need for three
years of retreat. Rinpoche and I squeezed in, and with Jeanne at the wheel,
we drove off, downhill to the Whidbey Island ferry, crossing over the Salish
Sea for a quick twenty minutes' trip to the mainland. There would be a second ferry crossing that day, to Bainbridge Island, and then after tucking me
into retreat, Jeanne and Rinpoche would retrace the path back to Whidbey.*

*Calm and collected, we went upstairs to the ferry's galley for tea. Re-
turning to the car, Jeanne suddenly realized that her keys, missing from
her purse, had been left in the ignition, safely locked inside! A ferry worker
was called over, no luck opening the door with a slim jim. The lines of cars
disgorged onto the Mukilteo side, while the three of us helplessly looked on.*

*Jeanne was beside herself, apologizing and inwardly steaming. I quietly
chuckled at the unexpected and surreal scene of us standing on the car deck,
watching as the ferry made its return trip to the island. I was supposed to be
leaving Whidbey, not approaching it. But there was a karmic message in
there for me, I thought: I would return one day, welcomed by the community of Buddhists there. Recalling the Tibetan belief that if you accidentally*

leave something behind when you depart a place, it is an auspicious sign
that you'd be returning in the future, reunited with friends or family. So, I
wasn't disturbed by this unexpected ruffle in the plans, but took it in stride.
No blame.

The ferry people had called in a locksmith from Mukilteo, who met
us on our return-return trip, unlocked the car in minutes, and we were
off—down the freeway, through Seattle, onto our now-fourth ferry crossing
of the day. Then we drove up Bainbridge Island, to my former mother-in-
law's house where the three of us unloaded my things into this large and
sprawling, empty house, and readied me for embarkation on a voyage of
major import.

Margi's house was a quiet refuge high on a bluff, surrounded by green
and a storybook garden. The formerly sweeping view had become obscured
by the thriving trees and shrubs, but there was a beach close by for walks.
The house, big, dark and cold at night, often felt haunted by not unfriendly
spirits. But it was familiar, a house I had been going to since I was twen-
ty-one. That familiarity held so many warm and happy memories, I felt
I was in the arms of family. So it was a wonderful place to start out, es-
pecially considering being so suddenly out of my old context. I sometimes
called Margi, in her mid-90s, at her retirement home to remind her that I
was staying at her house and to thank her. We had beautiful conversations
and I would read her own poetry to her. At her house I had many subtle
experiences of meditation, dreams, signs in clouds. It was more than a good
beginning, and Rinpoche thought so, too.

OCTOBER 17, 2011 – JOURNAL

Exhausted after the long period of preparations. So many aspects to write
about, now tucked into bed, as I'm tucked into retreat. My sister-in-law Barbara
had met us at the house. Together we made the altar and sitting area beautiful.
A special retreat sign in Tibetan script was installed on the outside of the house,
facing east. Then Jeanne and Barbara left us, and Rinpoche made prayers to seal
me in—invoking all the energies and entities possible to keep obstacles out, and
to accomplish all the aspirations of the retreat. In serious concentration, we
prayed that the endeavor would benefit all beings, and all would be auspicious,
all the way through to the end.

I was aware of the loving kindness between us, and the excitement and joy
begun yesterday that had spilled over to that moment. It had been late last night
on Whidbey that he had given my first retreat instructions, saying these first

two weeks I am to Rest! So, this is a little holiday with practice. Even still I need to make some practical preparations. Rinpoche had checked the Tibetan calendar and identified today as auspicious for beginning retreat because the combined elements of earth and water are harmonious for increase and development. Other signs also good, he said.

Because of how busy things have been I've barely let myself perceive it, like a dream. But this is big. So much happiness at being here, but also grief at leaving. Many friends, dharma students, and family felt some grief over this. I had said to them: I will be in close contact through prayer.

Tonight after everyone left and I was putting things away, I was aware that the shrine room is infused with power after Rinpoche's blessing, so I sat down for some meditation, a short session because exhausted. But now, that's all for one night. Looking forward to tomorrow and all to come.

OCTOBER 18 – JOURNAL

Last night, difficult dreams and couldn't sleep with negative thoughts about escaping the situation. Awoke after 9 am after having slept through an hour of alarms. I was depressed all day, but determined not to succumb, knowing it to be temporary. Finally after dinner I sat for a powerful practice in which the melody eluded me, so I made up my own version, using the English translation, in a loud, forthright singing voice... and everything lifted.

OCTOBER 19 – JOURNAL

End of third day—already! Last night was good. Today I feel surprisingly busy and full, and haven't even begun the real practice schedule yet. Tonight I wrote many thank-you notes to supporters. Rinpoche spoke strongly to me about not pushing myself in the beginning of the retreat, but I can see I've already been doing that. Perhaps I'll take it even easier the next several days.

OCTOBER 20 – SCRIBBLED NOTES

Noticing details in outdoor meditations:

A chevron of three birds ascending,
Followed immediately by another of same.

Two dive-bombing birds,
Fall from the sky like rocks.

Tiny particles, filling the air,
From the looming, dancing birch in a big wind.

OCTOBER 21 – JOURNAL

Morning meditation in a sky of swift clouds, headed north, against a blanket of grey much further beyond. Cloud spontaneously coming by—a Hindi OM letter, dissipating quickly. Followed by a face, taking up the whole sky. Two large piercing eyes and a stoic mouth. One eye remained long enough to set awareness into it, awake.

Evening walk just before dusk, along the beach, headed back home, north with the wind now, and the scudding waves. Up ahead, a passel of otters—counted seven, all about the same size—popped out of a hidden path in the marshy reeds, and headed for the water like dachshunds of the sea. Oh, what a delight! I hung back until they were securely in the waves, and then I restarted up the beach. Their circle of play, and catching dinner no doubt, took them in the same direction as me, we all getting swept north with the wind. Still a long walk back to my landward reentry point, and after awhile it seemed we were keeping apace. Finally I made my turn up over the beach logs, looking back at them, sending messages of sweetness and protection, of which, I was aware, they probably had no need. However, they did seem to notice my departure, bobbing their heads out, eyes trained on me. If I were them I'd want to keep track of this two-legged, for she knows where our home lies hidden.

OCTOBER 22 – JOURNAL, DAY 6

Last three days mostly ups and downs, alternating between peppy (yes, peppy!), sprightly and FINE... sometimes bliss state from practice, or engrossed in some project, and, you guessed it, depression. A kind of rocking boat, riding the waves which have not settled down yet. But the good part is that the depression segments, while deep and poignant and difficult, are in the minority, and mostly responsive to practice, self-therapy, patience, and love. Also to applying specific thought and perspective.

> *One essential element for a retreat location was having a willing someone who could shop and deliver food to my abode. For one thing, I was now car-less, but this extra measure was primarily to eliminate extraneous interactions with the outer world, enhancing the hermitage atmosphere. I was fortunate in that each of these retreat places had willing and able friends living nearby.*
>
> *For the first location on Bainbridge, Tracy, with Barbara as a backup, had the post of "retreat attendant." I would send an email each week; one of them would shop and then deliver the groceries, for which I would reim-*

burse from my retreat funds. Creating this grocery list was head-scratching in the beginning since I have little cooking imagination, made worse without the grocery aisles and seasonal produce displays in front of my eyes. After awhile, though, I settled into a list-making routine, referring to my previous lists for ideas, and accepted the resulting, fairly repetitive diet. Anyway, staying healthy took precedence over gustatory enjoyments, and for that I relied on cooking with fresh, basic ingredients: vegetables, fruit, granola, whole grain bread, chicken, yogurt, cheese, olive oil.

I would often get into a comfortable cooking rut—some peasant-food casserole, a stir-fry or soup that came into my head, making a large batch and extending the leftovers another three days. Sometimes I'd repeat the same dish for weeks. Or, large Greek salads every day during the summer months. Actually, as the retreat took effect over time, it didn't really matter, the food: Whatever it was, I genuinely derived great enjoyment.

And, these delivery days brought a fellow human into my sphere. In the beginning this contact was highly important for me, and so we would usually chat a bit in the process of unloading groceries, discuss other needs that may have arisen, or just share how life was going on both sides. These interactions provided a check-in, too, to assure the attendant of my physical and emotional health.

This system went well throughout the retreat. In a few cases I even was helped by friends of friends, people I hadn't met before. Everyone was thoroughly committed, and I deeply appreciated their gift of time.

Two days ago, as part of her regular grocery delivery, Tracy gave me a bodywork session. For decades this has been her profession, enhanced by her ability to "see" and move energy in others' subtle body systems. She noted that my forehead *chakra* was blocked, and perceived this was due to my trying to rewire, or put into a new framework, the last fifteen years of my life.

After she left I put this into a self-therapy session, using something called tapping. The session rewarded with insight: I began with the thought that's been clear to me for years, that helping Rinpoche was so significant and we accomplished so much, it was the reason I was born. The new piece was that that has been Part 1. Now Part 2 is beginning, where it seems, through this fortunate circumstance of three-year retreat, I'm to continue manifesting something beneficial, but on a new trajectory.

OCTOBER 24 – JOURNAL

After being depressed a couple days ago, a meditation arose spontaneously.

I had opened the classic 19th-century handbook by Patrul Rinpoche, *Words of My Perfect Teacher,* to a random page, and there was the section on impermanence—not just any page in that chapter, but the passage on the impermanence of relationships and position. The reading struck me profoundly—partly that it was gifted to me, the precise antidote for just that moment.

Then, a little further in the chapter came these words: *This convergence of mind and body is impermanent, this body is on loan...* Not a new idea, it comes from Patrul Rinpoche, but sometimes these things jump up and grab you. In that afternoon's contemplation on the *Four Thoughts*, one of which is on impermanence, this arose in my mind:

> These eyes with which to see are impermanent,
> They are on loan until my death,
> They are part of this precious human body,
> But they don't belong to me.
> There is no me.
>
> These ears with which to hear are impermanent,
> They are on loan until my death,
> They are part of this precious human body,
> But they don't belong to me.
> There is no me.

...And so forth, nine stanzas covering each of the five senses, plus "this consciousness with which to perceive and to bloom *cognizant luminosity* is impermanent..." and finally the last three verses covering the upper chakras of head, throat, and heart-mind.

> *Later I sent it to Rinpoche, who replied: "It's very good and you can use it... very much like 'emptiness shunyata.' But at the same time make sure it's not in nothingness; luminosity and cognizant quality are also there—beyond words! ;-)"*

NOVEMBER 5 – JOURNAL

I've been using these verses in meditation, saying each part slowly, contemplating their multiple levels of truth. As you say the first line, for example, you are looking with your eyes; so you can experience the appreciation of that sense organ and the ability to see; can experience how much attachment you have to it; then try to imagine you don't "own" it, and how impermanent it is. It's affected my meditation profoundly—with heightened clarity, etc.

Now close to end of Week 3. So many realizations, deep transition. Realization #1 – I should have taken a one-month holiday before starting retreat. But the solution has been to take it easy; not holding back on contacting family; Tracy and Barbara came once for a *sadhana* practice; Barbara has been here several times for visits. So, I've needed lighter isolation at this point to deal with this seismic transition. And Barbara has been essential, like a therapist.

Right from the start my sister-in-law, Barbara, filled a role that initially I didn't know I would need: confidante, quasi-therapist, fellow Buddhist practitioner, someone trusted who had known me for many decades. In fact, she had been an informal spiritual mentor for me since my twenties, before I had found my Buddhist "home." Later, the favor was returned when I introduced her to Tibetan Buddhism. But at this point our deep conversations came about spontaneously, and after a few weeks of this we both realized the great benefit for my retreat experience, and in fact, psyche-survival. So we formalized it into a weekly conversation which continued over the first two years of the retreat. I thought many times that I wasn't sure I could have made it through without her.

Realization #2 – This "Part 1 Life Mission" has now been accomplished! When I shared this with Rinpoche, not having been raised on a popular diet that included 007, he didn't quite get it, but the sense beneath it, he got completely. He said my being on this retreat is now like his life mission.

Realization #3 – Today I had a transcendent sense of the lineage and connection to *Guru Rinpoche*. Everything felt easy and vast.

Every day a full morning of practice, beginning with meditation sitting up in bed. Then opening the altar, then outdoors for *Riwo Sangchöd*, then *prostrations*, then the Four Thoughts. Also other parts of *Ngöndro*. Later, a walk and tai chi. Now expanding the menu, see what happens next.

NOVEMBER 8 – POEM, written on the full moon in a soft twilight sky after receiving in the post the gift of Rinpoche's prayer shawl.

Wearing My Lama's Robes

He sent them today,
His smell still wrapped up in
Warm maroon and soft wool.
A big shawl to fill,
Like shoes,
But this is one size fits all,
Full of undulating grace,
Falling like the folds of a Michelangelo
On the body of a bodhisattva.
This buddhist wrapping transmits
More love and warmth than is possible
In words to comprehend,
Since the love of one bodhisattva,
Who did wear this,
Is larger than my imagination.
Only by inspiration and multiplication
Can i come even close.

NOVEMBER 10 – ESSAY

Looking at Renunciation

In these first three weeks of retreat, renunciation has been on my mind. I keep hearing and reading that having strong renunciation is one of the key ingredients in being able to keep up a long retreat. Incongruously, I don't think of myself as much of a renunciate, and yet I feel strongly motivated to do this retreat. A conundrum. So, every time that word comes around, I've been paying attention. For example, Dzongsar Khyentse Rinpoche, in his Ngöndro commentary, writes that Westerners shun renunciation, and I thought, yes, that's me.

One young lama, a Tibetan who had completed long retreat, advised me last summer that I have to have strong renunciation for samsara in order to get through the not-inconsequential trials of three-year retreat. I replied without skipping a beat, "I don't have a problem with samsara. But I know where I'm headed." Ever since then, I've been thinking, what did I *mean* in that moment? And what did *he* mean, exactly? I *don't* have a problem with samsara *per se*, but I *do* have a problem with the eight samsaric dharmas, and am strongly motivated to be free of them. Is that renunciation? Is it a western version of renunciation?

My problem with ascetic, run-of-the-mill renunciation seems to be in the delight that's always come easily to me in small things. Like when discovering the existence of teabag squeezers—really?! Or being simply awestruck at the sight of a Japanese maple awash with acutely sublime colors of peach and yellow, so brilliant, as if a light bulb is lighting up the leaves from inside. Or sharing hilarity over a joke with a friend that doubles us over. I mean, how can this kind of delight and also renunciation for samsara share space inside of one retreater? This delight, often feeling like a form of joy, is, as we know, included in the Four Immeasurables—love, compassion, joy, and impartiality.

Does that mean delight might just barely squeak inside the boundaries of three-year retreat? Will this get me into trouble with my psyche down the road in this retreat? Or will it be an intrinsic component of the path of transformation?

If both can live side by side, as in good Vajrayana paradox, then where is the renunciation located in this retreatant? Okay, back to those eight samsaric dharmas. I start to squirm when I read them, because they're all pointing at me. And guess where they turned up in my retreat? When I opened up the unabridged version of the *Longchen Nyingtik* Ngöndro. They're invoked at the end of my favorite section, which, look at the title: "Song of Renunciation." Maybe we're finally onto something.

Here are relevant examples: "Though appearing calm and speaking softly, I haven't got rid of the attachment and aversion boiling inside..." Or, "Though I am distracted in my meditation, I let myself get stuck in mental gossip and concepts..." Then this line zeroes in, "O Lama, free me from these eight samsaric dharmas." The footnote lists them:

Hope for happiness and fear of suffering
Is that me? Shall I count the ways...
Hope for fame and fear of insignificance
Here's where the squirming begins...
Hope for praise and fear of blame
Okay, who isn't there with me in those...
Hope for gain and fear of loss
Shall I start weeping yet? For I have been weeping...

If I renounce these, *strongly*, is that renunciation? the kind that will carry me through this long retreat? I'm guessing it is. Because here my motivation is strong—the wish to transform in myself these most human of traps. "Quickly set me free from this dismal self-imprisonment!" implores the last line.

But what most strongly compels me to do this three-year retreat? That's another chapter, but briefly, two thoughts: The first comes from a line in our practice about fulfilling the opportunity of this life, of realizing our full human potential, more vast than we usually are aware. And the second is the aspiration that my actions may *truly* be of benefit, the wish to bloom *Bodhicitta*. I have a sneaking hunch that all of these—delight, embrace of life, earnest goodwill, and a peculiar Western brand of renunciation—can co-exist on this path to Enlightenment.

NOVEMBER 15 – JOURNAL, WEEK 5

Barbara filled me in on Carl Jung's term *complexio oppositorum*(!). It means "enduring the tension of the opposites." I'd heard of this a couple years ago from a Jungian therapist friend. She said that I'd been bravely maintaining that balance. So yesterday I read further on it—definitely interesting, although quite academic and technical. Sacrifice is in there, too, which it said is always self-sacrifice. Letting that one steep.

This transition is quite a process. Today for the first time, I just sat on a beach log, facing out toward the water, meditating. Surprising not to have done this till now. Partly, today was warm after cold weather these last weeks. But mostly I've been a little too purposeful, keeping up with my schedule... in order to possess? or to accomplish something, or to maintain momentum. On my walks, I've been walking; then coming back to sit on my cushion because the schedule says to be there, etc, etc. I can feel this decompressing process quite literally. And so now I'm purposely trying to head a bit toward purpose-*less*, yet keeping a certain discipline or lack of laziness. Fine line. Still in process, not really arrived yet.

Schedule, Phase II

6:45	Wake up and practice
7:30	Ready for day, Breakfast along with Reading
8:45	Opening altar, Riwo Sangchöd outdoors
9:45	Prostrations
10:15	Ngöndro
1:00	Lunch along with Reading
2:00	Walk, Tai chi
3:00	Meditation of different types
4:00	Break with possible communication
6:00	Dinner
8:30	Sadhana practice
9:30	Bedtime and Reading

NOVEMBER 17 – JOURNAL

Two nights ago I was awakened with a word that came in forcefully—*AHIMSA!* It was vivid, a dream message. I soon fell back asleep, but before I did, while still barely lucid, thought: What does it mean? The word was familiar and I knew it was Sanskrit, but when I asked for the meaning, the dream answer was ridiculous: "Oh Susanna!" Next morning, while puzzling and chuckling over the cryptic reference to the old American folk song, I looked up ahimsa: non-harming. Oh yes, of course. I interpreted it as a message to become vegetarian.

For retreat I had significantly cut down on meat consumption, but normally followed the Tibetan habit, or need, to eat meat. Living above the tree line has required that as a group, Tibetans evolved over millennia to be most healthy as omnivores, "agriculture" for them meaning raising animals with few vegetable options. Philosophically they believe since all living beings are equally valuable, all containing Buddha nature, it's preferable to sacrifice one large animal which will feed many, rather than the opposite. Further, they hold that a vegetarian diet necessitates killing of countless tiny creatures through all the various means of cultivating soil, harvesting, etc. Many committed vegetarians find this to be mere rationalization, especially for anyone living at lower altitudes with the means to eat a vegetarian diet.

In response to this dream I did become vegetarian, but after some months began having health problems. My naturopathic doctor recommended adding meat back into my diet, so with Rinpoche's approval, I reverted to my former ways. But still, taking ahimsa, non-harming, as a broadly underlying directive. As a Buddhist, this was not new, but the dream compelled me to examine myself for the next level.

NOVEMBER 21 – JOURNAL

Retreat going well and inner state good. Becoming sensitive to social contact, which tires me out easily, as if becoming an introvert. Still I wish to talk to family. Every day there's some business or phone call to attend to, and I'm now ready to be through with that.

Before the retreat began we knew I would have to continue advising Kilung Foundation and sangha organizers for the first six months of retreat. There were even papers I had to write in the first weeks to complete some work. People sought my advice from time to time, fortunately diminishing over this period.

My afternoon and evening practice times are still not gelled, not like the morning sessions, which feel amazing—entering with ease, aware concentration, and confidence. By afternoon I'm actually tired. Tonight I was in bed by 8:30 and have set the alarm for 6:30—a minor miracle after a lifetime as a night person, in recent years often working until midnight or 1 am.

There's a big storm outside now. Noisy wind, sound of powerhouse, big gulps of air galloping through the trees, up from the beach, coming from over the inland sea. Every day I go down to the beach, meeting the sea, lifting drops of salt water from its edge with my fingers, sprinkling them into the air, an offering.

The wind, salt, water, mountains, clouds, trees—all now part of my day, this communing with the elements—important. A sensitivity has extended to these walks. The waves seem alive, a whole world of tides and sand and pebbles and logs, always changing, like the movement of the clouds.

On a Halloween evening walk, the tide was high just as the sun had set, and the wind was bringing the waves upward with the incoming tide. I felt aggression in the waves in a way I'd never experienced before, as if they wanted to catch me and drag me into the sea. It was almost shocking to experience the sea as if personified—Poseidon in a black mood. I hurried back along the narrowing beach to home in the darkening evening.

More recently, an opposite seaside moment: The sea between the island and Seattle was flat calm and the tide wasn't very high, still slowly ebbing. As I began to walk along, suddenly a wave hit the beach, not so big, and it went from near me in a perfect, gradual roll moving ahead fifty feet or more along the beach. It was the sound that drew my attention, with such clarity and beauty, as these minute wavelets moved in a perfect, gradual progression, water playing gently against smooth pebbles. Then I watched a succession of these waves, watched and listened. The edges of this huge body of water, Puget Sound, gently cresting and creating patterns of movement of earth, progressions of sound. Like a breathing, resting beast, at peace.

NOVEMBER 27 – JOURNAL

Among my "light" nighttime reading, just finished *The Fisher King & the Handless Maiden* by Robert Johnson, which I found affecting. I've been trying on the Jungian idea of seeing all the characters in the story as aspects of my interior. In "The Handless Maiden" the father (my adventurous, masculine side) makes a difficult bargain with the devil, of which then the daughter (my tender, feminine side) must reap the consequences, resulting in her suffering. Now, I seem to be living the healing part of the tale where the daughter must spend time alone. The moment of climax comes when she has an experience of profound compassion that sweeps away her fear and compels her to act. And the long time in solitude in the forest helps her to be ready for that moment. Here I am.

NOVEMBER 28 – JOURNAL

I also just finished *She* by the same author, Johnson, written in the late '70s, an analysis of the Psyche and Eros story of ancient Greece. Relevant parallels run throughout. One of them speaks directly to the perils of my retreat, *ergo* quest. Psyche's fourth quest is to enter the underworld—of course one can get stuck in Hades, so it comes with dangers. You have been made strong by previous quests, yet still you need a spiritual guide. Psyche is instructed not to do her normal helping of others who may request it, but to keep to her own task. Johnson describes this as a deep spiritual quest, not for most people. He writes, "... a woman must not do good indiscriminately at this point in her life. Collective good particularly is forbidden. The reason for this is the fourth task requires *all* of a person's energy and resources." Journey at night, I think, really subterranean.

Sand Manuscript

The sea wrote on the beach again.
Obscure message for someone, me?
Most days it leaves long meandering empty lines of sand
Edged by borders of pebbles, hard for the foot to navigate.
Hard-packed trail of sand invites paw prints, boot prints.

Most days it goes like this, from down to up:
Margin of water continuously lapping, scouring, scribbling,
Border of pebbles,
Sketchy line of sand,
Border of pebbles,
Broad corridor of sand,
Margin of salt-saturated logs to signal: Ends here, look below.

But today, there were messages left by the sea.
The tide had been busy carving circles and shapes between the lines,
Leaving distinct o's and diagrams,
Piles of pebbles in cryptic script
Upon sandy manuscript.

This was the beach for me,
But a message in mysterious language,
Alphabet, even.
Cyrillic and Tibetan I have known, but this was script written by
                                                                dakinis,
or those who live in the angel realm, or of fairies,
Braille for the feet walking the beach, but mine beyond blind.

Perhaps by enlightenment one would come to know,
If the tide hadn't, too early, erased the secret.

Chapter Two

San Juan Island, I

> When you walk past my window,
> Bless me
> For the light is still on.
>
> The light is on—
> In this dark night,
> Like a speck of fisherman's lantern.
> You may suppose that my little cabin
> Is a small boat tossing in the storm.
> Yet I'm not sinking
> For the light is still on.
> *—Shu Ting*

DECEMBER 7, 2011 – NORTHERNMOST OUTPOST

All packed, having rewound my retreat belongings back into their bags and boxes. Barbara had come to spend the previous night so we could get an early start for the Bainbridge ferry. Leaving the house as empty as when I'd arrived, but hopefully enhanced with the warmth of retreat, Barbara's little car now jam-packed, we putted off into the cold, dark December morning. To maintain retreat boundaries as much as possible on this long travel day, we stayed down in the car for the half-hour crossing on the crammed commuter ferry, quietly chatting in our automobile cocoon. Always so cozy being with Barbara, treasure time, lingering in the twining of her warm gravitational pull.

We met up with my old college buddy Andy at a Seattle shopping center parking lot, and transferred all my things over to his truck. He loudly guffawed, "What's all this? Are you supposed to have so much stuff on retreat,

Diane?!" I laughed. Yes, somehow I carted around a small household on retreat—not like the 14th-century Tibetan saint Longchen Rabjam, who for years had only one piece of tattered fabric total for both clothing and blanket in his Himalayan cave. Whereas I had clothes for all seasons, bedding and linens, a box of sadhana texts and another of Buddhist books, a box of files and tools, a tub of food and kitchen things, a tiny laptop, and sitting cushions. And this array grew over the three years.

I'd always been sheepish about my tendency to over-pack on long-distance journeys, ignoring the usual advice handed out in travel columns; but then grateful once arrived anywhere to have what I needed. Later when I saw how the Tibetans pack—not skimping at all, in fact double what I would have stowed away—I began to end the self-reproach, and just do my thing. But now, on retreat, shouldn't this be different? Well... not in a cave, nor settling into one place for the entirety, it's just what it is. That's what I decided.

I hugged Barbara goodbye for now, with loads of gratitude, and Andy and I drove up the highway, to the ferry to San Juan Island. We spent the many hours of the trip deeply engrossed in Buddhism 101 since Andy, a non-Buddhist, is interested in philosophy and compassion, and as a journalist, is trained in the art of incessant questioning. After my two months of near-solitude, it was refreshing and I loved every minute.

Arrival: My mother and her husband, Tom, welcomed us to Cattle Point. Their elegant, comfortable place on the beach, with a constant dynamic flow of the elements, would be my home for the season. Though we didn't know it then, this would turn out to be my hermitage for three out of the four retreat winters.

The house has the ideal meditation view: unimpeded sky sweeping from north to east to southeast. Straight on are other islands, and in between is a narrow passage of swift-flowing sea, constantly changing in color, texture, direction, and velocity.

The wildlife was constant, and the storms amazing, the waves sometimes crashing, the wind sometimes keeping me awake at night. I awoke every morning in the main bedroom, looking out onto a small crease of light, red or yellow, at the eastern horizon above the water. Sometimes I jumped out of bed to start my morning fire puja, trying to race the sun before it came up.

That house doesn't have spirits, that I'm aware of. It has clear energy. At night, though, while doing wrathful practice in front of the big picture windows, the pane of glass would bend and shake in the wind. That was a bit freaky and I'd then close the blinds. The subtlety of meditation was often there that first winter, but it seemed slightly reduced from before, maybe from the distraction of the intense emotions that arose during that time.

On that arrival evening after we offloaded his truck, Andy stayed for a companionable dinner, then headed back to his life of work in the metropolis. In a couple days my folks would be leaving the cold, dark, dank Northwest, headed south in their RV to the California desert.

I, on the other hand, had always reveled in my native winter. The dark turn of our northern latitude encouraged a going inward that I relied on, like menstrual periods, leading to exploration of deeper recesses of psyche and soul. I always thought of it as the annual winter steeping and holy descent. Now it would be combined with the life of a Buddhist renunciate, to see what would turn up.

DECEMBER 9 – JOURNAL

Now settled into practice, just barely. After my folks left yesterday I went into gear making my little sanctuary. Two altars, one in the center of the bookcase with my treasured deity *thangka* heading things up. In front of a big, low window is the second altar with offering bowls and mandala. Strands of xmas lights weave throughout both altars, reminders of invisible five-colored *tiglei's*—orbs of energy containing whole Buddha realms said to inhabit holy places—and of course Christmas, when needed. In between the two altars is the book box; when turned on its side it becomes a traveling bookshelf of sacred books, singing the sound of dharma.

All of this took so long, finding things needed, it was 4 pm and getting dark by the time I was up on a ladder outside, hammering the retreat "certificate" to the house—centered above the "shrine room" windows, with its fresh green cedar bough and fluttering green ribbon. Then still outdoors facing the eastern sea and sky, I performed my own version of Rinpoche's previous supplication to the buddhas and bodhisattvas, to protect and nourish my endeavor, for the benefit of all.

By this time the bright moon was rising, and this on top of the auspicious moment called out for a short Riwo Sangchöd puja. Then dinner, laundry, making up the bed. Exhausted, I collapsed for the night at 9:30 with an aching back. Ahh.

This morning had a full practice, a little slow in body and mind. Happy to be here, and delighted with "shrine room." The sky today is cloudless, brilliant sun with only blue, reflecting on calm sea. Cold, clear, clean, quiet, winter, all welcoming for practice and this long retreat.

DECEMBER 10 – JOURNAL

Today's weather report: Concentration easily drifting into useless, low-key, inner conversation and memories. Connections foggy. But not unhappy, contented except for the "practice not great" thoughts. I think the transition from Bainbridge to here took away quite a bit.

DECEMBER 11 – JOURNAL

Most difficult day yet, questioning self in retreat. But moment of grace came in the form of an unexpected visit from Dechen, first visit of my retreat attendant here. The visit totally turned me in the right direction. And then another moment of grace later—realizing my own intrinsic spiritual value.

The Demons of Doubt—I must try to remember when they return that that's all it is. And that it's a common problem on retreat. Today they seemed to have visited in the form of "This is the last straw!" I have to be patient with myself. Grieving is still natural, and forgiveness is still in process.

DECEMBER 12 – NOTES FROM A PHONE CALL WITH BARBARA

Mother of God as a pure vessel. Barbara paraphrased from Meister Eckhart: Our soul is like Mary's—pure, empty, utterly open, humble, selfless. When we restore these qualities, God can't help but pour into this vessel. Divine birth will then take place in us—total fruition.

The Virgin Goddesses don't need anyone outside themselves to complete them. Artemis/Diana, for example, had lovers, but this meaning of "virgin" is that she is whole, complete, in herself.

Barbara's advice: Keep present with *Vajrayogini*, utmost female buddha and torchbearer of the feminine principle in Tibetan Buddhism, all day (and night). Dabble in practices of female deities to see if there's one that I feel especially connected to and of help. She says I'm doing magnificently!

The message is a feminine one, that I have value, spiritual value, on my own, independently. That I am worthy of retreat. It's so obvious that I would be going through this, it's stupid! But the realization of self-value came through in this moment of grace yesterday, truly needed, not something to be gained by simply repeating a phrase over and over again... *I AM worthy, I am WORTHY*... like in a therapy session. But Bam! It was there! It came to me after remembering some significant experiences of teachers and other spiritual beings seeing and confirming my value over the course of my life.

DECEMBER 14 – JOURNAL

In the dawn sky, a bright vertical light blazed straight up, about 10 degrees south of the coming sunrise. I was in the middle of early morning practice and immediately thought of the sword of Manjushri, the Buddha of Wisdom, who brandishes a flaming sword to cut through ignorance.

Later a buddhist friend said it could be the Archangel Michael's sword of courage, helping us to go into the dark and come back out into the light. Yes, I need that courage, I thought.

DECEMBER 19 – JOURNAL

Last night I listened with great joy to Handel's *Messiah* while eating dinner and doing dishes. This seemed to magnify the increasing *joy* over the last few days—of practice. This Western sacred music then fed evening sadhana practice with a vivid sense of connections.

Dream

I had bought a house, on behalf of my family. Even though I hadn't seen it yet, I somehow knew the house was special. So there it was, on a hill, large and spacious, an "old Seattle" home with character. I went inside and there was the previous owner, a young man from India, early thirties, and distraught at having to give it up. He had graduated from a good university and had bought the house with confidence that he'd get a great job. But the job wasn't forthcoming, the house payments too big, so he lost it. I was compassionate toward him; and letting him know this was my hometown somehow helped him feel better. Then he joyfully took me around to see this incredible house.

The main floor was okay, large rooms with big windows giving way to city views. Then we went upstairs, which led literally to tops of mountains! We pushed open some of the clerestory windows up there, and looked out to see that the roof was embedded at the top of a gleaming mountain. There were crystalline glacier formations, sparkling with sunlight, reflecting off snowdrifts. Magical! Roof peaks of other extraordinary houses, just barely visible above the snow, were all around. They were made of crystals, jewels, special metals and materials, stained glass, in fanciful ways. It was a whole community, almost a fairyland. I was enchanted with this treasure of a house!

The symbolism of the house as a picture of the psyche, with the highest level being one's spiritual facet—in this dream, ascending to treasure, the parallel to my current endeavor and aspiration is unmistakable.

A few days ago I put some photos of lamas and dakinis from Samye Chimphu on the altar. Samye Chimphu in Tibet, the mountainside filled with retreat caves and rarified practitioners, a place where I had done a week of retreat nine years before, and returned with a new sense of my own spiritual value. This photographic reminder has helped broaden and shift my focus.

DECEMBER 23 – JOURNAL

Rinpoche came here for a two-day visit. We had a splendid visit in every way. I was only a tiny bit sad when he left, but actually was good, pensive, and no problems.

DECEMBER 24, CHRISTMAS EVE – JOURNAL

Out for my daily walk, a great cumulous cloud day. I saw in those sky clouds: a phallus, really, an anatomically precise penis; a huge yak with pig-like nose; a beautiful, long-legged bird; and the word "IS." Thought: that says it all.

There's a good chance that people have, for many thousands of years, been finding meaning in cloud formations—faces, animals, and nameable shapes. As with appearances in dreams, or symbols in divination, we humans have been accepting these as gifts, interpreting meaning, and then sometimes utilizing them to find our way in life.

Before retreat, my own cloud image "sightings" were fairly rare, even though I certainly spent time looking at the sky: meditating while sky gazing, or soaking in countless sunsets. There was one memorable time, though, when a group of us were receiving a Tibetan Buddhist empowerment at the house of one of the members. Most of us were facing a large picture window with an expansive sky view. The lama had powerfully and unusually intoned a series of Sanskrit syllables, invoking mythic protector deities of Tibet. Just then my eye strayed out the window, and there, in a sky full of cumulous clouds, were three gigantic heads of Tibetan protectors, wrathful with bulging eyes. It was so distinct, I wanted to call out to everyone, "Look!" But in the hushed sacred setting, that didn't seem the thing to do, so the clouds slowly morphed, and I hoped I hadn't been the only one to see this phenomenon. Was it confirmation of the lama's veracity, or further, an energy-manifestation of the actual deities? I didn't know. Afterward, I mentioned it to the lama, who, unimpressed, did not find it at all unusual.

In Tibet, signs are often found in the skies, and sometimes even expected to be found. Rainbows, for example, or unusual cloud formations, are often seen at the time of the death or rebirth of an enlightened master.

On the day that our organization conducted the opening ceremonies for a large bridge crossing a river in Tibet, the whole community watched for hours as unusual rainbows unfolded across the rainless sky. The Tibetans wondered out loud, why the phenomena happening just for a bridge? One of the lamas answered that it was a matter of the motivation, in this case the great compassion that had led to the bridge being built in the first place—not to aid commerce, but to save lives of nomads and their animals.

I had listened in on conversations between Kilung Rinpoche and other lamas in Tibet as they discussed imagery in the clouds, or while examining unusual stones. But this isn't a buddhist practice, as such. I believe it to be an aspect of Tibet's indigenous and enduring pre-buddhist culture, utilized by the spiritually adept, as in dream symbolism, to find the way, or for affirmation or some kind of assessment. This kind of divining is rarely taught directly. Instead, one utilizes one's intuition, sensitivity, and wisdom to interpret the message. And it doesn't hurt to be slowed down, aware, and deliberate enough to notice the sign in the first place.

Finding symbols in clouds was never hinted at as an assignment—neither before nor during retreat—and I hadn't set out with any expectation of receiving messages via this means. But it did seem I was gifted with them many times. I usually took an appearance in its most simple form: as confirmation for the journey I had chosen. Or, as obscure poetic metaphor, confident that the appearance itself would do its work on my subconscious in the way it was meant to do.

DECEMBER 25, CHRISTMAS DAY – JOURNAL

A pod of orca whales came in through Cattle Pass from the straits. Thank you! my mind called out to them.

Dechen came for a small Christmas-birthday party, because today is her birthday. We had small gifts for each other which we opened in front of the fire. She gave me some pastels and a small notebook for sketching, which I hadn't thought of doing before. We talked about our love for opera—she told the story of *Turandot*. Then we made hot milk with cardamom and maple syrup.

Last night and today I've spoken to nearly everyone in my family, sharing Christmas greetings. I feel tired after it all, and primed to dive more deeply into practice now. Everything else feels a bit shallow. Seems a good phase since it *is* time, after all. I'm about to make another schedule shift with less communication.

DECEMBER 27 – JOURNAL

Storms, big winds lately. Didn't sleep well last night. A little girl on Whidbey was killed on Christmas Day by a falling tree on her family's car, her dad now in serious condition. We had met this artisan when he delivered the iron firepit bowl he'd made for our sangha.

Then, last night, December 26, Thinley Norbu Rinpoche passed away. We're so sad. Some of us wanted to see him, again or for the first time, including Kilung Rinpoche. In fact, he and I had just made a plan a few days ago to make this happen, so Thinley Norbu was present in our minds.

During *sang* offering this morning, outside, the air was humid. It looked something like rain but there was no rain, not a drop. What I saw was *very* faint, a shimmering veil of teeniest water drops, yet not a fog, it was a rain of blessing—that's what I thought. This was before I'd heard the news. Then I remembered the morning rain and thought, that's one of the practices that Thinley Norbu was famous for, "Shower of Blessings."

The day Rinpoche and I had discussed a possible visit, Thinley Norbu's book had also coincidentally come in the mail, *A Cascading Waterfall of Nectar.* Today I opened it randomly for a teaching divination. It was on the subject of guru devotion, and dedicating every virtuous action, no matter how small. Both excellent for me, and needed. It's time to begin *dedication* for each day's efforts, just after I settle my head onto the pillow at night.

DECEMBER 31 – JOURNAL

I've been subtly impatient with my meditation progress, feeling that I'm supposed to be in, or trying to get to, the next valley over. It's a place I've visited several times before, but like in a dream, as much as you try you can't quite gather together to get over there. Yesterday and today this imagery has been coming. Then today's Longchenpa reading, "*At the very center of the panorama of this uncreated nature, the entranceway that frees one from developmental effort is wide open.*" Ah la la! Felt like crying when those words appeared.

But I'm sure I'm a silly one: other practices are going strong and meditation arising out of that also strong.

Jeanne came today to do some parallel retreat along with me. Lovely to have her here. We'll settle into practice tomorrow, beginning with sang offering.

JANUARY 1, 2012 – JOURNAL

Jeanne and I, separately from our retreat rooms, watched as an eagle seemed to have been drowned by a seagull! Eagle went into the water, seagull sat on it. Eagle butterfly-stroked the length of Goose Island and into the main channel of Cattle Pass. Swim to shore! I thought. I had to stop watching after awhile to return to practice. Long time later I peered through binocs out to the pass and thought I saw it finally submerge into the swift current. So, so sad. But it had been raiding the Goose Island seagull camp. So maybe an air guard of the harassment squadron had caught a wingtip, knocking him out of the sky to the sea. Then, through the binocs, I picked up a view of minke whales going south out the pass into the straits.

JANUARY 2 – JOURNAL

Something truly extraordinary this morning. I heard a sea mammal calling, unusual and repetitive, a seal-like, plaintive cry, and close. I got up from practice and stepped out the door. Seeming as close as the bushes in front of the house, but wanting to investigate, I took the binocs, and gently, gingerly, walked out on the lawn; then realized the sound was skating along the water, bouncing uphill from the shoreline. I continued down toward the edge of the grassy low bank, expecting to see a large seal stranded, or a sea lion, right below on the beach. But suddenly I noticed in the water off a bit to the south, what looked like a huge new rock outcropping, black, in the shape of a cone volcano, as if a new micro-mountain had erupted as part of the reef there. What in the world was that? *Way* too huge for any of our local creatures, but yes, it was indeed the mourner.

With the binocs I could see it was calling, calling to the land, toward our neighbor's house perhaps. It went under, came back up, so big—beyond big. Knowing this to be special, I decided to interrupt Jeanne from her meditation.

It was so loud she had heard it, too, from the guestroom behind the house. When we got back out to the lawn, we could still hear it, but nothing was now visible in the water. Suddenly we saw that he had moved onto *land!*—onto a rocky ledge about 100 yards away. He was of mythic dimensions, as big as a small whale, or a big truck, or a retreat cabin. I'd never seen anything like this in my life, in all my years of being up here in these islands. He was a seal-like creature, the granddaddy of them all.

He was still calling, calling, three precise, distinct notes, to the land. Then we saw a large, black dog on the low bluff just above the seal, with a man who stood mutely back. The dog, with a Christmas ruff around his neck, was agitated and prancing around barking, unleashed, approaching closer and closer the edge of the bank. Then too close, for the sea animal jumped back into the water. So agile, so quick! He then took one last leap out of the water, calling one last call, and was gone.

Astonishing. Like a dream. If a mythic creature comes into your retreat, calling, some story, some message is there.

Elephant seal, quite sure. Male. Thank you.

Yes, indeed it was a male elephant seal, only rarely seen, if at all, around these parts.

JANUARY 9 – JOURNAL

After the seal experience, two synchronicities:

First, I had been reading as my bedtime book the Jungian *Women Who Run With the Wolves*. The night of the elephant seal, I was to begin a new chapter and story which happened to be a tale of a relentlessly calling giant male seal. Author Clarissa Pinkola Estés' interpretation: Seal is soul. The giant seal was calling his daughter back home into the depths, his daughter a seal disguised as a human woman. The story reveals the importance of alone time. Alone = all one = becoming whole.

And second, Jeanne and I listened that same night to a dharma talk of a western lama. She happened to use the term "mythic proportions," so similar to the term I had written earlier that I pricked up my ears. She had been referring to the Vajrayana as a path of mythic dimensions that we have entered. She also spoke in grand and powerful terms about the feminine principle. In the context of my elephant seal experience, I'm taking this in, listening carefully. The lama was also calling, a siren call. I'm planning to listen again, to distill the essential message for me at this time.

This experience of the elephant seal continued to reside with me strongly for a long time, causing me to steep deeply on the symbolism and meaning, like one does after awakening from a profound, lucid dream. I couldn't but think he was calling to me in retreat, or maybe I had called to him. I had always been connected to the water and life on the water; and on retreat had been doing Riwo Sangchöd, the incense offering, outdoors every morning, rain or shine, or blowing—while looking out to the sea.

What if I had been able to walk over to him before the dog forced him back into the sea? Could I have blessed him in some way, if that's why he was calling? Even more, could I have received his blessing? Perhaps I did. It powered my retreat in a new way. I felt I'd shifted over into a different realm, one of dream and myth, a diving board from which to explore further depths of psyche and soul, while magnifying this Buddhist path.

JANUARY 10 – JOURNAL

The full moon, not yet risen, at 6:30 pm, went outside, stars brightly glittering. Looking east, a lovely shooting star, longish. A gift.

Bright full moon in clear, calm sky, rising a little later, just before 7:30.

Moon's effortless procession guides my inner pulse. What need of clocks?

JANUARY 13 – JOURNAL

First day of rest in these three months. Sounds like a long haul, but the first part was a relaxed schedule, so no need. However, the schedule has evolved with my capacity, so for the last two weeks I've been "on the clock" all day with only one unstructured daily break. Lately I had come to feel quite tired, even starting to envy people who were sick, thinking a day in bed sounded awfully good—always a dismal sign. When I shared that with Rinpoche he said, "You should take breaks every two weeks or so. Don't wait until exhaustion sets in." I thought, "Oh you're kidding! I didn't know breaks were on the program!"

So, what did I do with my rest day? No watch on arm, no alarm clock. Still, I awoke at the usual time, 6:30 or so, dozed back to sleep a few times and enjoyed no pressure to get up. But another gorgeous sunrise was gathering, so I started sitting-up-in-bed practice at 7:30, then rushed into clothes in order to greet the sunrise with Riwo Sangchöd just after 8. Glorious morning of thick frost, white, slippery, crystalline shimmers. The sky was all pastels—unusual, even the sky was covered with a gauze of whitewash, but at the same time clear, few clouds.

Breakfast in living room, relaxed, with a Dilgo Khyentse book, happy enjoyment, altar already opened. The reading and happiness inspired prostrations, tossing the mat down and plunging in, without the usual prayerful preparations, for just twenty-seven, lovely and connected. Then laundry, cutting fingernails, and tried to call Mom.

I even started dragging stuff out for—chocolate chip cookie making! In thawing out butter, it got neglected during lunch, so I wound up with a small catastrophe all over the stove. Thought, where is my mind now? On this relaxed and happy rest day after three months of practice, am I now looking at the results: space cadet? Then more: an irritation of activity. So I left cookie ingredients, dirty dishes, and butter disaster where they were and took myself out for my daily walk.

The delicious relaxation of the morning had melted away with the butter. But a forest walk, even if purposeful, does wonders. Coming back to a kitchen needing to be put back in order, my sense of humor already restored, and sense of proportion—I thought, what's a cup of butter in the scheme of life?

Then, cookie making! I set up the computer to replay the recording of the previous talk on the Sacred Feminine while mixing cookie dough. The new little speakers that Rinpoche gave me for Christmas worked great.

Cookies made, now in bed, writing, enjoying, wishing for a second day of relaxation soon.

JANUARY 15 – JOURNAL

Yesterday I fell. While out on a walk in a big windstorm, I foolishly went out on a rough rocky promontory overlooking Cattle Pass. It had been so pastoral a few days before and I had found a cozy spot to sit in the sun there. This day the wind was coming from the other side of the island, so the waves and wind weren't hitting our beach, only peripherally. But they were blustering over this point, buffeting my body so I couldn't walk straight. All at once the wind wound my long skirt around one shoe, the gushing air pushing my body as I gingerly stepped on rough ground. Over I went, landing on a left shin and right hand. Lucky: no broken bones, avoided knee, and thick leather gloves protected my hands.

Here's the benefit of practice: I didn't feel afraid, didn't cry or call out. I experienced the impact fully—the earth contacting my leg, like the edge of a dragon's spine, granite unyielding. The leg's skin, soft, loses in that confrontation. This intimate contact with earth and rock, suddenly familiar from the many like-collisions of childhood, which would send me wailing to mother, or going off forlorn, or even angry. This time no fear or anger in the way, hyper-real, the rock teeth edges, the sense of familiarity, and big pain. First, picking myself up, checking: good to be able to stand, apparently still in a piece. Simultaneously, mind struggling with pain, working to overcome instinct to hyperventilate. Watching pain subside quickly to a manageable point. Sitting down for a bit, still buffeted by cold wind, overlooking crashing waves below. Sounds of gulls mixing with granules of granite crunching as my body found a comfortable resting position. This sound of earth and body, also familiar, comfortable like old shoes, was beautiful to my ears. Watching, listening, and then my body spoke, saying, take me home, see if we can hobble. And we did.

Injury report: Leg badly bruised, thin outer layer of skin scraped off, bright red patch with swelling. Arm torqued by impact. From fingers to shoulder, needs lots of rest. Can pull okay, but not push at all. Many things, even subtle or easy moves, can't do. But it will heal.

When I had returned it was time for afternoon practice. Part of me wanted to call someone for moral support. But instead I tended my wound, propped self comfortably on couch and had a lovely practice. I called Rinpoche later for sympathy. All fine. Today healing is progressing. Slow day.

> *Throughout the following months my arm was slow to heal. I hadn't wanted to leave retreat for a trip to the hospital, believing there to be no breakage since there was no swelling, fingers operable. But months later, still achy, I visited an orthopedic specialist who said I had probably fractured the arm, but in such a way that the injury required only simple rest to heal, and so I was fortunate to have taken the right non-action.*

JANUARY 18 – JOURNAL

Big, big snow. About eight inches, a lot for Cattle Point, quite beautiful. This morning, out to sweep porch so I could get to woodpile and also do Riwo Sangchöd. Wind blowing in every direction, although mostly from the north-northeast. A cloud of fine, light, dry, *cold* snowflakes were blown onto my cheek. I felt every flake, like ice-tiglei crystals, kissing my cheek, ultra-real.

Practices good today, still things going a bit slow—body parts healing. Yesterday had hard moments. Today when I read that there have been many self-immolations in Tibet, my heart open, I easily burst into tears.

JANUARY 20 – LETTER TO SANGHA, EXCERPT, AFTER THREE MONTHS AND THREE DAYS

... In my going-away talk in October, I spoke of this retreat as "settling into the practice," and after the initial adjustments, this settling has definitely begun. The tone changes every day, in constant variation, like the changing of the weather, and yet there is cohesiveness of the dharma and the practice, stability of the daily schedule, and blessings of the lineage, the buddhas, bodhisattvas, dakinis, and *dharma protectors.*

On an inner level, I sense compulsiveness dropping away. The compulsion to engage, to accomplish, to communicate, and most interestingly, the compulsion to avoid. By this I mean avoidance of the self, leading to that mysterious "need" to fill in the empty spaces with distraction. This is where the addictions of samsara come in, and for most of us, not what we would consider destructive, yet compelling; for me (in my previous life), things like watching movies, searching the internet, playing solitaire, checking the weather report, chatting, making plans, etc.

At the beginning of retreat, I particularly noticed at mealtime and in the evening this hungry compulsion to fill in the gaps. Rinpoche advised to go slow with this adjustment, not indulging in the usual distracting habits, but to replace old with more neutral new ones, for example, reading a book at meals. He was right. In this gentle way, this compulsiveness has diminished substantially, and I'm now even quite happy to be spending all my time alone. It seems as if one who formerly leaned extrovert is now contentedly living the life of an introvert. For all of this I'm deeply grateful—the result is that a peace is settling down over the terrain, air and breath are circulating more freely and with more subtlety, even with the ups and downs of interior weather changes...

As I sent this letter, I was aware of a Pollyanna-esque tone, as it hadn't mentioned the depth of psychological challenge. I had left this out intentionally: One reason was that it was better for others to relax about me, any worry "out there" being a potential obstacle for progress and natural unfolding of retreat "in here." This was in accordance with Buddhist and Tibetan belief and practice.

There was another reason, though, that I gave Rinpoche generous credit and appreciation. I was aware through comments that had drifted into my sphere that some sangha members had heard about my relaxed start to retreat and, applying a hard-edge approach to "what retreat should look like" and therefore what my retreat should look like, were questioning some aspects that they had heard through reverse grapevine, such as that I wasn't in silence yet. To them, it seemed that I lacked discipline. It gradually dawned on me that the handful of doubters were male, leading me to reflect on male phenomena—their wish to be tested by external forces, which, it turned out, could be applied even to Buddhist men. Such a long human history of military, monasteries, boot camps, exertion of discipline, hierarchy, invented and participated in by men. I wanted none of it. The juxtaposition led me to hold Rinpoche and the approach of the Vajrayana in increased appreciation. This letter, I thought, might redirect some of this hard-line attitude by reminding readers of their own confidence in Rinpoche, which then might be magnanimously extrapolated to me and my retreat.

What others think. In ordinary life, my usual strategy was to just move on to the next engrossing activity and let discomfort from disagreements pass away with time. But now in retreat, more sensitive, no distracting activities, I could see more acutely how affected by the eight samsaric dharmas I truly was. Here even in retreat, I was still enmeshed in fending off criticism, shoring up my standing with others. I could see it, but still I wasn't willing to lay myself out on a boulder undefended in the middle of the village square. Which of the thirty-seven practices of a bodhisattva was I missing here? Or how about Lojong: *Be grateful to everyone—and take* that *to its logical and full extent.*

JANUARY 21 – JOURNAL

Woke up around 3:30 this morning, without enough sleep, kind of depressed without cause, except for the achy arm. Lay down on couch for a short afternoon nap, no sleep. Watched out window. In sky saw a heart in the clouds, upside down. Immediately two eagles flew over house. Then a big rainbow appeared over Goose Island right out front. I leapt up, ran outside. This changed everything—I hadn't been forsaken by the universe! There's still hope.

Evening's practice vivid! My head on fire, whole body HOT. The fiery conch-like mansion of my skull was having a party, everyone dancing! Then a great well of love surged forth, and I sent it in all directions for beings. Thank you.

JANUARY 25 – JOURNAL

Last night I finished the tome *Women Who Run With the Wolves*, leaving me wildly enthused, as the book points to the path I'm on and always have been on. It brought to mind the rich period when we, our family of four, took a year and lived on this same island when the kids were in kindergarten. I wrote, and did inner depth work, exploration. A beautiful time for us, although Skip had to commute. I was so young! Thirty-four. Mystical experiences—the orchard, Mt. Climus, the language of the cedars, family snow walk one full-moon night. That year I learned to knit, to play the harp, and began a set of quasi-yogic exercises brought by an Alaskan shaman.

This book, its core material, its commentaries, and where this led me, reminded me not to neglect "me" on this, my current journey (while understanding there is no me)—to not be a cog on an ecclesiastical wheel, a theoretical retreatant on a prescribed retreat belonging to someone else. But to remember who it is with the ultimate responsibility for my enlightenment. And to continue reflection, dream watching, wonder, watching, awareness of the big picture, how I fit, and to continue writing, while on this retreat. To make this retreat my own.

1987-88

It was seeded, the wish to take a break from the suburbs, from a sense of being penned in, the freeways surging at that time with new transplants from California, and a conventional life shepherding our twins from play-group to preschool to shopping center to family visits. My journalist husband was willing to give it a go, and so the seed sprouted.

By lucky happenstance we soon found a house tucked in the woods on the far west side of San Juan Island, and so we took the plunge, renting out our suburban home, arranging for Skip (my first husband) to stay with friends during the weeknights, and made ready to spend a year on this life adventure. We moved our little family to the end of a long lane bordered by towering cedar trees, corrals next to the rustic house, all at the bottom of a steep hill our son named Mt. Climus, for obvious reasons. The kids were signed up for afternoon kindergarten and a bus ride home. I spent the days roaming the woods and fields, writing, and exploring nontraditional spiritual paths. I sank into the earth, or the earth absorbed into me. We had chickens and eggs, met interesting neighbors, the kids made friends, got teeny leeches while playing in the pond, and climbed often with me up the small mountain next to our place, swinging their short five-year-old legs over the lichen-covered split-rail fence, up the steep hike to our favorite sitting spot. It had some big madronas up there where the kids pretended forts while I sat on the mossy granite ground and gazed out to the north and west, a view of sea and islands and Canada.

We heard that an old, abandoned, labyrinthine orchard was just a couple fields over, and so that fall we four would make a weekend afternoon of it. Carrying a basket through dry grasses, prying our way between rusty fencing, we entered an enticing and ghostly realm. The apples and pears were in stop-frame-avalanche from rickety branches to the ground. Bees were having a feast day everywhere.

In the extra-present state I was in, it felt as if the orchard were an an-cient, living palace, each section, one after the other, with its own unique quality and purpose, like rooms in an elaborate house. As we wandered, as if in a fairy tale, being drawn further and further on, we sometimes lost track of each other. Or, the tell-tale question identifying this as an enchant-ment: had we passed this way before?

If the amorphous "rooms" had life, then the walls, the trees, were trans-mitting something beyond the juicy crunch of old, unfamiliar varieties. They were gnarled and lichen-covered, some with falling branches, long neglected, yet alive, offering their multi-colored orbs as gifts. Maybe "palace" wasn't quite the right idea— instead temple, for it seemed a holy place, brimming with spirit, or spirits, I couldn't tell which. But it was thick, a sphere where the unseen is nearly seen. I wished to worship here, but didn't quite know how, except by simply being, witnessing, breathing, absorbing, in gratitude, and perhaps conveying something beyond words to those two darling children of ours.

Then we conveyed a basket of apples home to our kitchen, a tiny portion of the bushels on the ground and branches, left for the wild animals, and perhaps for other islanders who knew of this secret sanctuary.

To say "delicious" only partially describes that year, with ripple effects that long trailed after us. Immediately upon moving back to our home I noticed that I was no longer frustrated with the hustle bustle and mundane quality of life in the suburbs. An oversimplification of how I found acceptance in our return was: this is here and that is there. The suburbs (or metropolis, the freeways, the shopping centers, that life) would always be the way they were; but now I had experienced on a cellular level that there was something different elsewhere, something that I could go to that offered nourishment of a deeper kind. Quiet and solitude, and the doorway to an even deeper quiet—I now saw that I could create the outer circumstances to bring that into being. I made peace.

JANUARY 30 – JOURNAL

Today Mom and Tom returned from their trip for about a week, and then will be away again for two weeks while I stay on here. When going off for evening practice, I thanked Mom for being a good sport about my retreat, and supportive. She said, "Oh yes! I'm so proud of you!" Surprised me! I should take this and run with it, let it fuel my practice.

FEBRUARY 5 – JOURNAL

They left today for Mexico. I felt sad just after they took off. Why? I think it's a basic loneliness of this situation, being in retreat. It seemed to confirm my nature as... an extrovert? as a human? I was reminded of the 19th-century yogi Shabkar, who sometimes referred so openly to his own sad moments when parting, sometimes even to the point of tears. Surprising in Tibetan writing, but humanizing, one of the reasons I found his autobiography so inspiring. This evening I just needed to readjust my bearings: now it's night and everything's just fine.

Having my folks here was both wonderful and a distraction. Wonderful to have company. They allowed me my practice schedule, and were caring. Being with them showed me that the practice has helped me become more patient, open, and loving. But it was also distracting. Mom, an unapologetic extrovert, spoke whenever I appeared during my silent periods, although she was good about not expecting me to engage. During my meal breaks we had close, warm talks, so things were much more social than normal. My practice sessions were fine—okay or better. But the subtlety of inner experience lessened, especially while off the cushion.

FEBRUARY 6 – DREAM

Dream, or rather, night message. Suddenly in the middle of dreaming, a flash of light with Rinpoche popping out and showing me the number 54. I woke up momentarily, remembered, and returned to sleep. What meaning? 58 would have been the *wrathful deities;* 53 my birth year. So, I don't know.

Months later I wrote in the margin: Half of 108! Auspicious in the Tibetan numerology system, but still, why the message?

FEBRUARY 9 – EMAIL TO RINPOCHE

You wrote *"rigpa"* as "pigpa" ("Try to stay in pigpa.") so thanks for the laughter. Yes, I'll do something for Longchenpa's anniversary, too. Maybe I'll take his text down to the beach and read it in a singing voice to the birds and seals.

FEBRUARY 10, LONGCHENPA'S ANNIVERSARY – JOURNAL

Just recovered from another meltdown. It started during a phone call day before yesterday with my former second husband (SH). I started crying and couldn't stop until after Riwo Sangchöd the next morning, yesterday. I did some cathartic self-therapy while facing a mirror. Anger also coming, I scared myself by seeing reflected a demon-like face and energy. A vertical vein in my forehead became prominent, and I thought: Jeez! Maybe I should ratchet it down a bit.

I've been subtly depressed for a month, since he and his girlfriend moved in together, and that she's pregnant. The latter news was softened by a premonition in the form of a bliss-filled dream. However, thoughts have been popping up in practice, and practice becoming increasingly distracted with so much negativity—about all kinds of things—and long periods of following the thoughts with self-conversation and zero awareness. I've also been more and more self-critical.

Yesterday sobbing and angry while standing in the kitchen, I glanced over toward the sink, when the large knives point-down in the draining rack suddenly seemed to take flight, flashing and dancing, as if animated by a demonic poltergeist. Not hallucination, only imaginal, but because it came spontaneously from my subconscious, it frightened me, and I thought, oh my god, this is getting extreme. My sobbing deepened and I found myself calling out for Help!

I realized I need more support, but Mom is in Mexico, Barbara away to the ocean. And I wouldn't want to burden them with this level of heavy disturbance anyway. So after serious consideration, I decided to call my good friend Diane H., Buddhist and psychotherapist.

But before that, a dakini appeared at the door. Dechen, who usually came only by appointment, mostly with groceries, was suddenly there, with her halo of white wavy angel hair, looking radiant and concerned. She apologized for just dropping in, saying perhaps she should go. I took her by the arm and dragged her over the threshold. We stood in that same kitchen over tea, having a heart-to-heart. Not wishing to worry her—or anyone—I didn't share the knife imagery, but I did speak of my distress and blazing anger. She countered by telling me of her lifelong relationship with sometimes explosive rage, which, by comparison, put me at ease, buoying my confidence—that I would be okay, for retreat and for life. Grace embodied.

Still, the need for professional help was clear, so this morning, after further hesitation, I picked up the phone and made that call to Diane. We talked over an hour. She was so happy to hear from me, and to become my retreat therapist.

Diane had some immediate practical suggestions, but her main concern which struck me: she wished I wasn't in isolated retreat during this grieving period. With no obvious solution to that, I said, yes it's indeed sometimes hard, but I'm definitely committed in here till the finish, hoping that this contact with her will help.

Diane H. had an interesting, almost technical way of explaining: that isolation keeps one in the mindset of the past, rather than doing what people transitioning out of a broken relationship usually do: they go forward with their lives, interact with new people, and actually replace, in the brain pathways, past experiences with new ones. In isolation, this mechanism simply isn't available, and one stays stuck in the grief or worse. Then, even the adage of time being the great healer doesn't have a chance to do its work. Her advice was to turn my attention outwardly somehow, to see that there's a world

outside my former world, and more than that, in order to know it in my
cells, I should interact with it to some degree.
    This professional level of conventional wisdom, probably found in
self-help books if there were any for hermits, was, for someone on cloistered
Buddhist retreat, a light waving in the darkness, saying, the way out, over
here! So I took Diane's advice seriously as doctor's orders.

I felt so much better after our talk. Today practice is also better, distracti-
bility in the normal range. Then, an excellent and frank talk with Rinpoche. I
conveyed much of the session with Diane H.: her professional opinion of the
difficulty of transitioning while in so much isolation, and that she and I had
settled on the task of finding ways to make this work while staying in retreat.

Rinpoche and I immediately decided on one of Diane's ideas: making a
regular time for lama consultations. He also liked the idea that when I move to
Raymond, I should dine weekly with my hosts, and include some regular practice with Brent. He also advised lightening up my schedule a bit in the evenings
while I get through this particularly tight spot.

And, in addition to a therapy appointment with Diane for next week, I can
call her if and when a big need comes again.

FEBRUARY 12 – JOURNAL
    Feeling improved, with better concentration, but I can tell things are below
the surface, not too far down.

FEBRUARY 22, LOSAR, TIBETAN NEW YEAR – JOURNAL
    A rocky boat ride with all this variety. Up and down. Sometimes unbearable
pain, other times tender and poignant. Then there's anger at the incineration
level. Guilt comes, enough to make me curl up and give up. Happiness, just
slight. But otherwise it seems the theme here is *Intensity!* Everything under a
magnifying glass. Funny, I don't feel generically lonely, but Diane H. feels the
isolation is fueling this. Well, something is fueling it! Because I do feel a mess:
ultra-sensitive, easy to cry, be put off-balance, obsessive thoughts.

    I'm just now at the four-month point. Wow, a lot of lovely practice expe-
rience, reading, and reflecting—all accompanied by a puddle of psyche. Is this
just a phase? Or the general direction? In another few months after staying with
Brent and Kathy, perhaps I'll have a better sense. I don't feel crazy, but certainly
don't want to go that way.

    Last night after a difficult phone call with a family member, another puddle of upset resulting from my own intense projection. I turned to the evening practice session, with a mind to transformation. It helped. I was able to concentrate somewhat with some vividness and grateful connection; and I took solace in my friends, the *one hundred deities.*

Dream

A huge sewage overflow in the neighborhood had backed up into our old family house. My dad was there. He and I were knee-deep in the basement assessing the situation, trying to figure out how to solve it. I was struck by the fact that it was more watery and less sludge than expected. I'd imagined it would be putrid, full of shit, but it wasn't even smelly. Dad and I were dismayed, but not hopeless. Instead of a catastrophe it just seemed like life: resolvable.

The dream offered its fairly hopeful message on this Losar morning: Samsara is an ocean of suffering, but that's just how samsara is. No need to go to the darkest place when something arises. Take care of things. Don't fabricate or look for the worst. You don't have to do it alone, at least not completely. Water = tears. You know what to do with that: Open the drain and let it out.

Chapter Three

Raymond, Washington

> When it is left to itself, as a vast sky,
> utterly transparent and serene,
> the poisonous, painful bindings that are mental constructs
> loosen by themselves.
>
> *—Shabkar*

FEBRUARY 29, 2012, LEAP YEAR DAY – JOURNAL

Three days into my new home with Brent and Kathy, today was the first complete practice day, and it felt good. I've been especially cheery ever since presented with the "project" of packing back up on San Juan. Plus the visit with my folks upon their return was one of the best, warmest visits with them that I can remember.

For the first leg of the trip, Jeanne came to get me. Wonderful talking in the car, we drove about halfway, to south Whidbey Island, where I stayed the night at her house. The next morning, Sunday, I had an in-person interview with Rinpoche. After chatting the first hour, we were short on time for the main subject of retreat, but great to be together.

My old friend and travel companion, another Diane, came all the way from Bainbridge Island to pick me up for the second leg. More wonderful talk on the trip south. We stopped off on the way for a short visit with my dad and stepmom. Oh my, so much socializing! I was totally spent by our arrival in Raymond that night.

Brent and Kathy warmly welcomed us into their old-style farmhouse, dinner waiting. Later we carted all my things up the stairs into the small apartment, where Diane B. spent the night on the couch, and I would make my third retreat hermitage.

The low, sloped attic ceiling created coziness and charm, together with vintage wood paneling and the beautifully crafted floor. A complete kitchen was part of the large main room, adjoined by a small bedroom and its own bathroom. And when day came, a whole wall of south-facing windows revealed the wide-open vista of the Willapa River delta, and the sky. Expanse of sky, essential ingredient for meditation, at least for me on this retreat. I felt blessed to have it show up again and again on my journey.

We were greeted that evening by an early spring bloom of ladybugs in the attic. Auspicious little creatures, bu-lama in Tibetan, meaning "insect guru" because of their red color and famously gentle nature—at least toward their human cousins. Over the next weeks they sometimes poured out of the attic crevices. I would scoop them up singly or in multiples, lifting them out an open window onto the wind, wishing them well, om mani peme hung, *for the next phase of their life.*

The house sat just above the river plain, a huge, flat, saltwater-freshwater delta that feeds into the significant Willapa Bay, which opens to the Pacific. Even though Raymond is situated thirty miles from the ocean, salt water travels there slightly uphill twice every day on the tide, making its own sub-marine river, while actually lifting up the lighter-weight fresh water above it. Twice daily, then, the estuary in front of the house would become slowly glistening, filling in every size of meandering mucky streambed, and saturating all the spaces in between. When the sun shone from a particular place in the sky, these pathways of water became ribbons of mirror, winter's muddy brown becoming riveted with scrawling signatures of metallic silver, subtly dynamic, visited by waterfowl of different kinds.

Kathy became like a sister to me, and Brent a good friend. They took me into their home, took good care of me. Being so near to others every day really helped stabilize my emotional state. In the beginning I was still rocky and sometimes shared those feelings with them. Their empathy and presence was just what was needed at that time.

Having wished Diane a fair journey back to home that Monday morning, now exhausted, I slowly and methodically turned to unpacking my dharma things, and creating the sacred container for the next six months.

I spent the entire day Monday preparing the altar. Brent actually built a large, low shrine table same day! While on a recent trip to India he had also bought a couple of lovely ritual objects for me that had to be prepared with intensive cleaning. Then there were things that had to be found and borrowed from their house, small dishes, etc. Plus rearranging the furniture with Brent's help. I'm not sure why, but this took many hours. Finally I made the opening puja in the winter's near dark. Because of my state of exhaustion, they gave me dinner again that night, accompanied by very welcome talk.

The ritual of opening the new space for retreat. Ritual, something sacred repeated, cycling around again. Like circumambulating a great stupa, I was circling around my retreat, honoring all who would protect the intention of it, and in the very center, the retreat itself and its potential. This I did each time I moved to a new locale, first closing, temporarily, at the old place, then reopening at the new.

While Kilung Rinpoche had done this all in Tibetan at the beginning point, I now did it mostly in English, and the words did not come easily, at first. I had only a few of my notes from Rinpoche's verbal instructions, no sadhana or text to follow. There was a surprising shy aspect, too, not really knowing how to address the buddhas and spirits so directly, no script buffering, or to lean on. I felt naked and tongue-tied, as if they could see me at my core. At the same time I felt connected to the task, compelled, almost urgent. The combination of everything seemed to add to my fatigue. But when finished, a deep contentment spread out over the landscape. Ah.

Yesterday, Tuesday, Brent and I did our first Riwo Sangchöd together. Great to have a practice companion! Afterwards though, walking a bit like a zombie, I just came inside and sat down on the couch, unmoving, and stared for awhile. Then began unpacking my personal things, moving in, cooking, wrote thanks to all who helped, talked to Mom. And rested. Now today, *so* improved, much, much better.

Brent and Kathy are a delight—and kind. We're all enjoying each other's company. They've been so helpful, are eager to get to know me, and vice versa. But also letting me have as much space as I want or need.

Today auspicious sighting of an elk herd of forty! which they'd never seen before so close to the house, and such impressive animals. Peacefully moving through. I watched them from my bathroom windows, with binocs newly lent to me—essential equipment for estuaries, Mom and Tom had thought.

Second sighting: three eagles swooped by the second-story windows, then perched in the nearby trees. Also unusual, my hosts said. They seem to feel these are good signs of my arrival for retreat here. And all the ladybugs in the apartment, prematurely awakening from winter slumber.

Being here feels quite different from the last two places. There's a subtle edge of "far from home in unfamiliar territory," akin to a homesick feeling from girlhood. But fortunately, Brent and Kathy are warm and welcoming, and I'm old and experienced as a traveler in the wide world. But this is different from a traveler passing through, and I know my recent vulnerabilities of emotions. I seem to need a nest where I'm not subject to others' emotions or judgments too much. I'm confidant, though, that I'll feel quickly at home. Comfort level already rising.

MARCH 1 – JOURNAL
Snow!

MARCH 2 – JOURNAL
My *mala* broke today. Outside on grass. Found all but one bead.

108 beads of lotus seed, beginning their life ivory white with tiny dark speckles of a songbird's egg, now deepened by time and warmth and use into the color of golden oak.

Just after our incense offering outside on the lawn, rain draining down from the morning sky, tiptoeing carefully around footprints of sticky mud in sparse grass. Suddenly realizing my mala was slipping from my neck down the inside of my jacket, I froze mid-stride, grabbing what I could of the falling strand, beads disappearing into the thick soupy mud. I found all but one. One seed planted, from India and my own Buddhist origins and intent, to this retreat, to Brent and Kathy's land. A sweet offering.

Later on one of his Oregon shopping trips, Brent picked up a replacement bead made of wood, right size and color. It's still on the mala, glimpsed on the rare occasion that I spot it among the other 107.

MARCH 6 – JOURNAL
Everything good. I'm embarking on a major component of the retreat curriculum today, a sadhana, but in a gradual way. Thinking back years with this practice—as a total neophyte participating in big sangha groups; or later as *chöpen, vajra* performer, for Kilung Rinpoche; or in a triad of fond friends, sometimes we three "partying" for hours into the night, quite fun. This, though, is a whole new ballgame. The extensive liturgy with all the detail parts included, but now on my own. And, lots and lots of mantra accumulations, hours per day.

I'm also adding another practice to the sitting-up-in-bed early morning session. So I really have to rise earlier, and I think the new sadhana will inspire that.

MARCH 9 – JOURNAL

Sweet happiness pervades my practice and days. I'm being so well-cared for by my hosts. This is gold to the heart. I realize it's still the honeymoon period, but all bodes so well.

At the end of each sadhana session I feel just plain Happy! No big visions, but deep happiness. After five straight days of blue sky warmth, the soppy low clouds and rain returned. I put on a hat and raincoat and jeans and hiked up the hill, into the woods just a bit, doing mantras with dripping wet mala in hand. Standing under the protection of thin young firs, feeling *at home*.

Far from others, in this secluded, wet forest of my girlhood, I spoke to the spirits and reminded them of who I am, the same one doing *smoke offerings* every morning, the same one who came from this place. I put my spine along a half-fallen skinny alder leaning back forty-five degrees, and just stayed like that, hat brim over glasses, shielding the raindrops from out of my eyes, resting my back, my body, resting the mind, being *home*, skies grey, forest wet, nature green... I cried for half a moment, of happiness.

My mother would pry my younger brother and me away from the small black and white tv in the family room, and send us outdoors to "go run around and play." We would cross the open grass to the edge of the woods and enter our realm: towering firs and cedars, their dark, rain-streaked columns, and green needles dripping incessant drops on our young heads, armpit-high stands of nettles to be avoided, special boulders as landmarks, hidden hollows, old stumps where we would post imaginary letters of maple leaves to the bears, and retrieve answers the following day.

We were four years in this magical land, the foothills of the Olympic Mountains, a place where the soggy grey can press down on people: too heavy, depressive, discouraging—a common complaint. Or it can seep in, molding a deliberate way of thinking, a considered way of perceiving, quietly encouraging deep steeping of a rich inner life. The low clouds diffusing the light, saturating colors to a sublime point, mirrored by countless teeny water globes hanging off ladies-in-the-bathtub, or devil's club, or salmonberries. Somehow I was of the latter camp, being nurtured by the sog and the grey, always grateful for that shaping.

Being with Brent and Kathy in this new environment, and on the edge of a town, I think it's working the needed magic. A new context *is* arising, beginning to replace the "old view" of my life with SH. When I think of that whole department, already there's not the same hook—followed by hammer and chisel! I'm still subject to emotions, but a big shift has taken place. And I can once again concentrate on practice.

Next challenge: exerting a little more discipline on talk. It's been important to spend some time in this way with my hosts, getting acquainted and bonding, plus plain-old setting up. But I can see my tendency to find joy in being with people, not in itself a bad thing, of course, but the temptation to extend short interchanges plays.

And in realizing vast bodhicitta I still have a long, long way to go, but there's also some result: increase of kindness and seeing the positive everywhere.

Dream

I was on retreat, and for some reason wandering in a busy town. The whole sangha was there, some trying to protect me from all the hullaballoo, and some showing me all the amazing things to see. A kind of circus was spread throughout the town and all these bizarre and amazing characters were roaming about, or performing on street corners. It felt over-the-top to be exposed to this for one on retreat. I sought protection with a good friend, thinking, somehow I have to find my way back to retreat!

MARCH 12 – JOURNAL

Snow again today! Sticking!

MARCH 14 – JOURNAL

I had a wonderful session with Barbara in which the question of where shall I go next, after Raymond, came up. There had been the possibility of a place a bit close to SH, which I'd already rejected precisely on account of that proximity.

Barbara offered this story of her father, Knute, talking about healing to his three kids when she was a girl. He had studied it in depth as a surgeon and pathologist, and was quite fascinated with it on a cellular level. He taught the children that when they had a cut, the cells would automatically begin to knit back together. It would happen naturally, starting at the deepest levels, working outward toward the skin—quietly. Then there would be a scab, whose job it is to protect this inner process.

Barbara's point was that in the case of broken-heartedness, the same thing applies. For me, getting this distance now, without reminders, is like having a protective cap so that healing can actually take place, deeply, naturally, with time. And I'll need this space for a good long while.

Not sure where going next. It's okay though.

MARCH 30 – JOURNAL

Rinpoche recently said, "Very good to take a day off anytime I feel. It's part of the practice strengthening method." The Practice Strengthening Method— magic words. So today is a day off, the last one two weeks ago. Seems a good amount of time between. I've been up and down and mostly okay.

A week ago SH told me that they had had their wedding ceremony, and would soon be on a honeymoon. Trying to lighten the message somewhat, he added that he wanted me to hear it directly from him. However, this brought a difficult couple of days, where I got some help from others, including from Barbara.

Then, a moment of grace, a breakthrough experience on the cushion. I realized that I am not the pain-hurt and the hurt is not me! Then, out came: I'm triumphant! It sounds trite written in words on a page, but it went further: I began to stop identifying with the pain, or wanting to disappear permanently from the globe. I realized it's the pain that can and wants to disappear, not the essential me. And suddenly out popped the essential me, at least at one level, a level of emotion and psyche, of happiness and okayness.

> *These thoughts continued in a letter to my mom: "This experience was accompanied by a clarity of central self, homing in on "home," which is independent of emotions, and related to this Buddhist notion: this home contains one's own inner-teacher—an inner wisdom which exists at the ultimate level of one's being, a "location" where we can find our innate buddha-nature. It also brings buddhism and psychology together in that the feelings are temporary, not the true, core self... And I've really been pretty darn good ever since."*

But today, even though my day off, a bit depressed. Why? I don't really know, maybe just lonely. I'm feeling my practice is mediocre, still have negative thoughts about SH that creep in, even though all, *all* the work. Sometimes I feel it's not going to heal in this container of retreat, and that the wound will prevent making significant spiritual progress.

Rinpoche still has confidence. I don't know why. But here's one thing I'm only recently hearing about: all long retreaters have their issue, and so this is mine. Some days are beautiful though, and that continues. I'm still not yearning to be in a different specific place or secular circumstance.

I have a small project that Rinpoche asked me to do: editing a talk given by one of his Danish disciples, also a teacher, on the *Nyingma School* and Rinpoche's lineage. Not always easy to interpret the translated Danish, but a nice challenge, satisfying.

Days off make me realize how short a day is, although even normal retreat days go quickly. I'm eager for bedtime to come, to lie down with a book and rest, and it comes always sooner than I expect, a gift at end of day.

I feel quite attached to my practice lately—the counters on the mala in new places every day, watching the progress, reflecting on the turning of the wheel of time. When I get to starting the *sadhana* in the late afternoon, I'm already tired of practice, kind of wishing I was already done. But then the deep familiarity of the practice floods in, and the effects of it, and sometimes a sense of *samadhi*. That's when I feel the deepest and greatest connection of the day, the greatest result and reason to be here. Then, the ritual offering that follows is short and sweet, mildly celebratory, enjoyment.

I need to stretch out more during the long periods of mantra recitations, stretch out in the sense of relaxing my mind into "happy vacation." I feel comfortable within the mantras, but sometimes find my mind has wandered around in self-conversation too far, or too long. Yet all is okay.

APRIL 1 – JOURNAL

Today lovely. Engaged in the present, with few extraneous thoughts or self-conversation. Happy to be practicing, and not even terribly focused on "three-year retreat." Just moving along, like it's supposed to be, feeling lucky that everything is in place.

I did a more elaborate *tsok*, offering puja, this afternoon and *really* enjoyed it, feeling confident. I can't imagine doing all these practices without the years of experience as chöpen, and observing in Tibetan temples. I'm grateful for that, because now there's fruit of big enjoyment, and unearthing treasures, old and new, tucked into the ancient rituals. I've felt strong connections, though no big visions, but sensing the unseen and shifts of perception.

Yesterday, out for a walk with practice, found a new, idyllic place to sit for meditation where two streams come together. Spoke to Dad this evening. It's social, but seems as though a little of this is helping my emotional stability. Most of the day, every day, is silent and alone, but happy. Doesn't feel alone, because practice is not only busy, but in another way, not alone: often absorbed with the deities. Thanks for this great day—needed.

APRIL 6 – JOURNAL

Small items: Spring is one. Or, Spring is won! About a week ago, looking out at the estuary, I thought, it's totally brown, different colors of brown, I wonder if it gets green—the salt water comes from beneath and pushes the creeks up, flooding the whole Willapa River plain. Maybe all this salt water makes brown. Then one day it happened: Green! The whole place, pretty magnificent, and green it now is. And when lit up by the sun, quite emerald.

A second small thing: When I first came here, one morning the sun was shining brightly and everywhere was a heavy dew. I looked out at the big weeping birch just outside the front window. It was covered with glistening dewdrops, each one lit up by the sun. But something special—each was a brilliant rainbow color, and twinkling like xmas lights. It was a welcoming gift. I'd never in my life seen it before, that I remember. Each so distinct, large, definite. I stopped and appreciated it, moving my head slightly to change the angle and bring out different colors. Red, yellow, blue, green, amber, clear, purple-y!

After that, I watched for the same phenomenon in that tree, but no, not until yesterday morning during incense offering when they appeared in the glistening grass. It reminded me that because the sight of these tiny rainbows, or any rainbow, is just a coincidence of water and sunlight and angles, rainbow potential is there constantly. It seems such a message of auspiciousness and grace, and then these are in potential anytime, too. We just have to stay awake, or to remember. The practices also remind, by occasionally mentioning rainbows and marvelous displays.

Today Brent and I went to look at a possible site to build a small retreat cabin where I could finish out my retreat. It's atop a knoll, a magical place along one ridge with streams on either side. You can still hear car traffic, but it's completely private, hidden.

Brent left me there to feel it out. I sat on the ground to meditate. A snake visited, slowly approached straight on and watched me, head held up. We gazed like that, for a long time. A hummingbird flew over my head. Four vultures flew overhead.

We're thinking. I'm thinking.

APRIL 9 – JOURNAL

Recently during a practice session, a kind of samadhi led to a subtle experience: While gazing at the altar I became aware of the relationship between all the objects. Difficult to find words for it, but I'll try. The relationship wasn't just spatial, but it was partly spatial. It wasn't complex, like human relationships, but enlivened, the objects imbued with energy. And this energy gave them a relationship ability. I realized that all objects in the universe have this, not only living beings. This is whether or not they are touching or interacting in a way that ordinary perception understands, a kind of equilibrium not limited by human intervention or even intention. So where things are placed in relation to others takes on more meaning. Hence, beauty in nature, but this extends to all things. I "saw" this, as a witness. It was very subtle. The energy wasn't visible to me in the normal sense of seeing, although the objects had extra vividness and depth. I felt happy.

Today on the knoll, I brought my text and did sadhana practice. In this place you can still hear the sounds of traffic, often a little loud, and of children's voices from across the road. Even a little of Weyerhaeuser a couple miles distant. So, more thinking to do about whether it would work for a retreat cabin. Still, the ridge is a lovely place.

I can hear Weyerhaeuser right now from my apartment, puzzlingly loud for 9:40 pm, great pounding and hammering, like an infernal foundry evoking a hell realm envisioned by Hieronymus Bosch.

But the frogs have become much louder these days, thankfully.

APRIL 16 – JOURNAL

Yesterday came an email from a sangha friend who happened to mention seeing SH and his wife walking together in a happy scene with a baby goat. Yikes! Visualizing this whole picture really threw me and I cried all that afternoon, and on and off today, even during practice sessions. But then came another gift of grace while in practice, with a thangka of Guru Rinpoche before me, and presence, and this thought: I'm headed elsewhere, to a better place, not hanging around moping and sad and living in the past, not any longer. Then blessing came in, and the horrible stuck fog simply lifted. It's really gone, at least for now. I feel buoyant, light.

Even while in the midst of greatest upset I had two thoughts. One, that my friend who sent the message, an extremely kind person, would have been genuinely pained to know I'd reacted so strongly, or even at all; and also, that the comment came along in that moment to shake me up, to give me a vivid picture of things *as they are*, so I can move along, hard work as it is. Diane H. had advised just letting things arise, not to suppress. So, gack! they did.

MAY 23 – JOURNAL

I've been excellent, busy! far-flung, and social, given the normal field of retreat. But all was with lama permission; the main foray had been worked out with Rinpoche months before retreat even began.

Twice there were dentist visits to Seattle. Then Rinpoche came to Raymond for a two-day stay along with my friend Bruce. And then the big trip: to Albuquerque for my son Gus' graduation from university. At first I had dismissed that major trip out of hand, thinking, "Impossible: retreat boundaries." But after further consideration, in a meeting with Rinpoche months before retreat began, we discussed the importance of attending my son's rite of passage, and I received his permission to take the break.

My friend Karen generously drove me both ways to make the plane connections. Travel, days of saturated family interaction, ceremony and celebration. Upon my return, a big collapse, utterly drained!

The next morning while waking up I heard the call of an exotic bird nearby, over and over. Mystified, my mind kept asking, what avian creature is that? Suddenly it came to me: It was the rooster across the road, the least exotic bird imaginable, and not only that, it had been crowing every morning at the neighbor's since I'd come to Raymond! Taking my misfiring synapses as a serious hint, I spent many hours in bed to rest, just reading and dozing. Still, I was happy I went. It meant so much to Gus to have his mum there, and wonderful for me to see him fulfill this significant goal, long-time coming.

In the last week since my return, I've been happily engaged back in practice. Actually, the practice quality went up several notches—in the range of beautiful. Perhaps a boost from the solar eclipse coinciding with the beginning of the month of *Saga Dawa*. Or was it refreshment: a release of over-concentration followed by a re-dedication upon return? Whatever the cause, finally I feel connected with the mantra recitations, visualizations, deities. Yesterday the experience of bliss was almost painful! I guess that's when the word "exquisite" comes in. So, the time away and being in this house with others hasn't hurt a bit.

I'm currently rethinking building a retreat cabin here. The idea, which even Rinpoche had advocated, has been to create a secluded retreat space that would allow me to stay here on this land. Wonderful to be here, but the atmosphere in the house is a secular one, and as I'm moving through the psyche process toward balance, it's clear I'll be ready soon to return to a more solitary, retreat-like setting.

But to really focus on practice and settle down to things "as they are," it seems unwise to allow the distraction of a Project, potentially a huge complexity, where much of the construction management would end up in my court. On the other hand, not building will mean moving again to obtain a more removed and as yet unknown situation. But something must be available somewhere.

I once read about the potential pitfall of going into long retreat without knowing every precise location in advance, this snag leading to too much retreat time in thinking, researching, and arranging to find the next landing spot. Apparently I'd fallen into that hole. An email sent to several friends looking for the next retreat spot ultimately turned up nothing.

JUNE 23 – JOURNAL

I looked outside and perceived at a long distance a descent of rain, as a subtle rainbow, but not normal. The wide bands were perfectly vertical, of various colors, not the usual rainbow configuration. Not vivid, but subtle, lovely. Both ordinary and not. No excitement, just observation.

Something quite miraculous had been unfolding, and on this day it bloomed. I had been dipping into a beautiful biography. Over the months of reading I noticed a thought tapping on my shoulder, at first subtle, then gradually more pronounced: SH's new wife would benefit from reading it. At first I managed to dismiss the thought as almost heresy to my resentment. But as I moved through the chapters the thought shifted into a wish, and from the wish into a softening of the heart, which then became actual caring. Feeling as she might be feeling, knowing that their baby was soon to arrive into the world, and sensing my healing interconnected with their healing, I began to imagine reaching out to her. The timing felt critical, saying to myself, "Let's clear this before the baby is born."

Then an idea: Send her a copy of the book. After some time, I brought myself to order a copy. It came. It sat there for awhile looking at me as I continued to ask if I was ready. After a couple of weeks, yes, and not only that, ready to wrap it up. Then, after some time, ready to pen a message, an offering of olive branch. Still, it sat there next to my front door, waiting to address it and put into Brent's hands for shipping. And on this day of the rainbow mist appearance, it went out the door, and on its way.

I knew I had broken through something beyond difficult and debilitating, in a monumental way, while respecting internal processes. There was no edge to it, no external or artificial urging, but it was natural and true. And I was relieved.

What I wasn't expecting was that hours later I received an equally disarming, and true, letter from her via email. She had also waited for months, through her own suffering, and on that same day was simultaneously ready to extend herself to me, in openness and kindness.

I was stunned, and five days later replied by email:

I really appreciate your letter, and all that is in it. You're brave to write with so many feelings, so openly. It's good that you waited to make this connection with me, because earlier I wasn't ready to hear from you. So it seems your hesitation earlier was based on your astute intuition. And now the timing was amazing... Thank you again for your message, showing your kind heart.

After this, resentment for her never reappeared. There was no single cause for this miracle. It hadn't come through pushing or wishing, but it needed to come, was born out of a long and difficult passage. Tears, therapy, shifts in thinking, intention, realization, prayer, patience, space of retreat and pressure cooker of retreat, blessing, and then grace.

JUNE 25 – JOURNAL

Since returning from Albuquerque, practice has begun to awaken. Almost half the sessions are connected, some powerful. I then realize right when closing the practice each day that I can barely remember the experiences just had, because it's as if I've stopped cataloguing them, collecting. But here:

The descent of rain two days ago.

Vivifying of the imagery—Vajrayana's specialty—and the new ways things are appearing (as visualization, not visions), accompanying physical sensations, with a sense of vastness, and perfection in samadhi.

Many experiences are coming with some frequency, all different, and I'm now feeling there's no point in wishing for a repeat of this or that. Instead proceeding with confidence that this is a natural process that will result in whatever the next stage is supposed to be. So, previous grasping after more experiences is loosening significantly, undoubtedly helping the whole thing along, too.

I began prostrations and tai chi again, months after I fell on the cliff. Even so, my arm is still healing.

The weather has been cold for June, grey, rainy. Of course I love it. Here in

Raymond, beautiful, often with breaks in the clouds, the dynamic elements on fast-forward.

I found a porcupine incisor in the wood, didn't know what it was, a mysterious, curved bone, slender and delicate. Brent knew and had a small collection in a box to show me.

Kathy made a soufflé for my birthday dinner, and rhubarb-strawberry sauce on ice cream. They gave me a beautifully crafted, hand-woven basket from Ghana.

JULY 3 – JOURNAL

Taking a day off for Tibetan *World Peace Day*, Brent, Kathy and I drove to the Willapa Wildlife Refuge for a walk and picnic. On the way to a one-mile hike, a boardwalk leads alongside a marsh with art installations. Ever the nature guide, Brent pointed out newts swimming in a pond. All was quite a delight.

Then the trail took off uphill through beautiful, forested ravines and hillsides. It came out onto a labyrinth! We lit incense, poking the sticks into the earth alongside the path, and began the meditation walk. Acutely aware that we had entered into this ancient Western mandala—Christian even—while simultaneously as Buddhists in walking contemplation, my sense of the sacred was magnified. Tracing around and around, each of us silent planets on separate orbits, circling around each other, brushing past. Kathy's trajectory fastest, Brent and I mumbling mantras, taking deliberate slow steps, we finally came to the end. We headed back for a picnic.

There were hardly any other folks about, no one at all on trail or labyrinth. So it turned out to be really fine, I think, to emerge into such a quiet world for a day off from retreat.

I dreamt last night of a rescue organization—for alligators! I somehow got roped into working for it, with my family and others involved. There were all these baby alligators who needed bottle feeding and *cuddling!* Weird. Bring on the analysts!

JULY 4 – JOURNAL

Today the baby was born. A girl. Lots of feelings here, but not severe; I was actually quite okay. My first response was happy that it went well. Then I went into afternoon practice and was flooded with many thoughts. Probably most interesting was the feeling that I wanted to end retreat early, not out of depression or frustration, but to engage in *life*. This new baby reminds me that life is moving on "out there." For example, my son and his wife want to start a family and I'd like to be involved. On top of the "out there," I again feel stagnant "in here." The practice has returned to lackluster. But even today, more experiences arose later in the afternoon... and then this sense of quitting disappeared.

I wept many times today, of small things, mostly because of exquisite beauty, and this afternoon because, for the first time, a set of deities felt like personal friends and allies, companions.

JULY 10 – JOURNAL

I had a helpful dream involving the location of *fleas*. In real life I'd been on a flea-ridding campaign for days, and hadn't remembered the dream until I found where they had been hiding. In the dream my mother and I were picking fleas off the stitching crevices of my quilt. According to Tibetan practice, if you hang your bedding up outdoors, the fleas will jump off. This had worked for me once in Tibet, so I tried it on the clothesline here. But apparently it doesn't work that well in Raymond, Washington, because when I went to take the quilt off the line, I found two fleas in exactly the location shown to me in the dream. The quilt then went directly into the washer, *om mani peme hung*, the American way with fleas.

JULY 15 – JOURNAL

Depression has descended today for no apparent reason. A few days ago I took the afternoon to work on a sacred text, an activity making me so happy. A purpose! A "project"!

> *Rinpoche had asked me to put my editor's mind to a liturgy that the Danish teacher had translated from Tibetan to English. Now the translation needed us both: Rinpoche to check the accuracy, and me for the English. Sometimes we worked together via internet. The work of editing liturgies I hardly consider to be work at all, teasing out nuance, making sure esoteric meaning and poetic sensibility are retained. The latter is the most tricky since liturgies must eventually be spoken, the readers needing to find inspiration and ease of speech in the words. And because it's translation, this "poetry" has to be accomplished without overt rhyme and meter, but much can be done on a subtle level. This is rich and intuitive heart-work. This particular text was related to one of my favorite deities, too, fueling even further the draw for this diversion, and I worked on it a little at a time over five months.*

Now it's been about six weeks that my practice has been flat. I'm coming into the last stretch of accomplishing my retreat sadhana and it feels as if I'm even backsliding into ordinary-ness. So, hopeless and purposeless, a perfect combo for depression. At the same time I realize that in the buddhist scheme, I'm actually supposed to go through this. Giving it all up, viewing hope (and fear) as an addiction, and more essentially, seeing futility in the endless cycle of samsara. Rather than sinking into depression though, something else is somehow required, I can feel it. Accepting things as they are...? Sitting and staring out the window...? Relaxing into it...? Pretending I'm on vacation...? Realizing emptiness...?

And, a complex dream came this morning where I carried a sense of failure and shame.

Soon after I wrote this, I fell asleep, which I rarely do, sitting in my comfy chair, must have been an hour. Just before the nap I had felt not only depressed, but a never-before-experienced grinding in my stomach and heart, a kind of despair. I had looked at a *dzogchen* text as inspiration for meditation, and it seemed meaningless, both in the sense of "without importance," and also that I could barely grasp it.

Then, after the nap, I awoke refreshed and in a completely new place and exceptionally relaxed. I picked up the text again, actually recited it to myself first from memory, the first couple of lines, and they were suddenly imbued with beauty and grace. Right away I effortlessly entered meditation. Not full of mystical experience, but connected, so relaxed that it just flowed. Few ordinary thoughts, no sense of timing it or wanting to limit or extend or push anything. Just following the instructions for form, sound and thought—without grasping or conceptualizing any of it—as it was meant to be. Afterwards I did offering practice—with a renewed sense of enjoyment and relaxation, and connection to the deities.

Up down up down...

JULY 16 – JOURNAL

A beautiful and happy day, continuation of yesterday post-nap.

The idea of *kenosis* was offered today by Barbara in our weekly talk. It's a technical term, Greek, in Christian monastic contemplative tradition to mean a state or process of emptying out so that one can then fill up with God. This process isn't easy: full of self-doubt, failure, confusion, questioning everything down to the nubs, shaking up all the underpinnings. Even the guiding self-assessments aren't working. "What the f--- am I doing?!" It could feel like depression. The idea of kenosis is that nothing is wrong. Rather, it's a legitimate process or stage in the spiritual journey. It does seem apropos at the moment. She said, "Maybe this humbling is required." I replied, "And how else do you get there?"

This came to her after our last week's conversation. She had first come upon this concept long ago from a Father Joe who helped her in her own moment of spiritual crisis; she said it helped just by knowing it was a "thing." Perhaps it's also what I need to keep going.

She also talked about the Jungian idea of the Self with a capital "S," a Self much larger than the usual self, which includes the unconscious and the shadow (dark) side, the parts we have always rejected, the failure and shame parts. The wisdom part is there, too, so it's the whole Self. This kenosis, then, can be a doorway to embracing all parts of oneself—with compassion.

JULY 17 – NINE MONTHS IN RETREAT

JULY 24 – JOURNAL

Last week I received the baby announcement. The baby is a beauty, but it threw me into another tailspin, crying, etc, for a day. The following day I took a break—nice, though on flea patrol again. And cleaned the altar, as if making a renewed commitment to my chosen vocation. In the evening Brent and Kathy invited me downstairs for dessert and a movie during which we enjoyed great cathartic belly laughter. Since then better. Yesterday was a lovely practice day, connecting and sensing.

This morning I awoke with a vivid dream: Kilung Rinpoche was giving me a retreat consultation, which then shifted to his teacher giving him a *transmission*. It was beautiful, relaxed, heart-full, a magical dance. Then a western lama, a tulku, came for transmission. He was overly confident, and a little goofy, and lacked a lot of knowledge, so the attending monks had to help navigate some basics of protocol and courtesy. Rinpoche and I watched all this almost as entertainment.

JULY 26 – DREAM

Another dream last night, again with Kilung Rinpoche, Dodrupchen Rinpoche, and also Thinley Norbu. There was a long part in a house with many rooms where I was on retreat. My son was there, among others. Then it shifted to hydroplane racing (when have I ever dreamt, or even thought, about hydroplane racing?) on a big lake, like Lake Washington or Italy's Lake Como—the shores were urban, planted with tall trees, beautiful, and elegant. It was a blue-sky day, with crowds of pleased people. Two of the hydroplanes were being driven by... Dodrupchen and Thinley Norbu rinpoches! It sounds preposterous, but of course serious in the dream.

As they were driving around the lake, it was less a race and more a procession or display. Then one of the boats broke down, Thinley Norbu's. He wasn't in danger. Many attendants were helping him.

The hydroplane theme may have come from seeing two jet skis on the river below my meditation perch yesterday. They were going quite fast, one with a big rooster tail and one making daredevil maneuvers, leaving a deep, curvy wake on the river, his signature.

Today I'm going to complete a million mantras. Still more to go, but this monumental numeral feels like an achievement I never before thought possible. The remainder will take another twenty days to make the accumulation goal, still only an increment of the overall retreat curriculum's commitment.

AUGUST 5 – JOURNAL

A kind friend, a mystic, recently sent this, from 13th-century yogi Godrakpa, as meditation infusion:

> *Mind is insubstantial like empty sky,*
> *Thoughts are unestablished like breezes in space,*
> *Body is impermanent like spring mist.*

AUGUST 14 – JOURNAL

I finished the sadhana today, all the mantras. Another sadhana coming, and we're still unsure which one.

Now that's completed, I'm taking a little break, up to Seattle for some rest and significant meetings. One is to see Dad, who is dying. He's 84, hoping to see 85 in October and the presidential election in November. But he's going faster than he'd like and isn't happy about it at all.

For the other visit Barbara will take me to meet with SH and family. I've come to realize I need to do this, to see with my own eyes, to move me along even further into healing. No fantasies, no fabrication. I think (hope!) I'm ready for this.

AUGUST 18 – JOURNAL

Gus, his wife Crystal, and I set out from Bainbridge Island in their little blue car, for a day with Dad. It turned out to be a most wonderful visit, a precious gift. We three sat with him more than six hours while Loretta went out for a much-needed caregiver's break. We had many talks, in spite of his easily losing his train of thought. He would drift out as if suddenly visiting the realm of sleep, or putting just a toe into *bardo* territory, the realm between lives. In spite of that, he retained his mental sharpness, one of his lifelong hallmarks.

When conversation wasn't easy, I brought out musical memories, one by one, like jewels out of a pouch, to share with Dad. He recognized and received each anecdote with joy, often adding his own embellishments.

Such a lot of talking for him, he took at least two naps. I helped him twice go for short walks with his walker. He asked Crystal how her job was going, and was so proud of her, expressing happiness that she had married into our family. It was clear it meant a lot to her and Gus, especially because Dad usually doesn't effuse, but today he did. It was a love fest, gentle and sweet, and we all were joined in deeply treasuring our time together.

At the end he said, "Why do you have to go?" At that point we were all tired, and I turned to Gus and asked, "I don't know. Why do we have to go?" But it was time. I went to Dad in his wheelchair, knelt down, and said goodbye. I wasn't expecting not to see him again. We looked at each other. He said, "I love you. I *really* love you," with great emphasis. I said, "I *really* love you." And that was it.

I volunteered to spend a night with him, several of us signing up to take different nights so Loretta could get some sleep. When I heard my night had to be delayed several days, I felt he would be gone by then.

AUGUST 19 – JOURNAL

So much packed into one leave of absence. Today Barbara drove me for the visit with SH and his new family. It was rather momentous and intense, and, as it turned out, exceeded expectations.

"She" was not, as I'd assumed, a frivolous, immature person, but a deep, serious, good-hearted one, with a kind of purity, and kind. I actually liked her, and further, felt relief that I liked her. We had tea, gave presents back and forth, and chatted. I had some individual time with SH, in which I told him that his wife was wonderful, and for a moment tears spilled out. It was surprisingly natural to see SH with the baby in his arms. She is darling and will probably become quite beautiful.

After Barbara and I drove away, I shared my thoughts and feelings, and, as in therapy, let out the inevitable sobbing for some time. We could both see it was big medicine to have come—recalibrating to the new, clearing out the old, beginning a new chapter.

AUGUST 22 – JOURNAL

Dad died today in the early morning. He had said to someone apparently on the other side, "No! It's too soon!" Before he went he gave out a death rattle. And stopped breathing.

My brother called me a couple hours later. I told Gus, and we wept together for awhile. Crystal made us breakfast. When Gus handed me a cup of tea that she made for me in her nice china, I was so touched I cried again.

Later Tracy picked me up for a previously scheduled massage. I was kind of a wreck. Using her psychic skills, she put me back together. Then she took me out to a beautiful restaurant for dinner and ice cream. I'm plumping out from all the eating on this holiday. But is this a holiday—or something else? Dad died.

With last Saturday's visit, it was as if he had been waiting for me to come, because after that he declined *so* fast, he just went. Poof!

SEPTEMBER 3 – JOURNAL

I've been back at home in Raymond for five days and mostly alone since Brent and Kathy have been on a sojourn. Good to be back where I've been able to focus on Dad's passage, conducting death practices for him every morning as part of my usual routine. The practices help the deceased make their way, without so much confusion or fear, through the bardos, the in-between state that we buddhists believe we find ourselves in while we traverse to our next rebirth.

Now that I've recovered from the exhaustion of being out in the world, all the intensity, and then coming back home, I feel more balanced once again. But another big shift is coming. In five days I'll be moving—to the Siskiyous of southern Oregon.

> *Brent and Kathy had invited me to stay for the remainder of my retreat, a huge and beautiful offering, and I seriously considered it. But the container was a secular one. Kathy's office was upstairs, right next to my apartment; faint conversation, comings and goings could be heard in my retreat space. The back door would slam shut. Brent's (wonderful) permaculture farming*

outside could often be heard in the form of the tractor busily roaring up and down outside my window. Friends would visit them. And of course there was the ever-present Weyerhaeuser "music" in the distance, serenading me to sleep many nights. None of these things were faintly abhorrent, nor were they even distracting. (Well, maybe make an exception for strains of iron-striking-anvils-in-hell.) And being within Brent and Kathy's nest had been amazingly timed as healing salve. But these consistent reminders of ordinary life kept me subtly tethered to the land of samsara. I was ready now to push off further yet into retreat experience, onto the surface of this ocean, whether by rowing a small boat or walking, on this grand adventure.

Through the help of a couple of Buddhist friends a place emerged: an obscure retreat center in southern Oregon, obscure but I'd been hearing of it for many years, associated with the Tibetan lama Chagdud Tulku. To get to stay at this most affordable of places in remote forest, one had to be known by the American lama who owned it, or to come with a strong reference. I had the reference, but because we hadn't met before, the lama asked me to stay initially for a short period, and then after a break I could possibly return. So off I was heading for a mutual, three-month trial. Perhaps this was a place I could really sink into.

Dream

I was working with the elements—space, wind, fire, water, earth—in a precise, particular and detailed way. Using my hands I was manipulating them, utilizing them. I was putting, infusing this essence, the energies of the elements, into my malas, and so, into my practice—with confidence and knowledge of what I was doing, how to do it, and why.

A lucid dream, I woke up right away, noticing that my hands were resting right on my malas, which, rather than under my pillow, their usual location, were around my neck because I'd already been awake in the early hours doing practice. As to the how and why of infusing the energies of the elements into a material object, upon awakening, this occult knowledge faded into mystery. But perhaps in my dream state it had indeed occurred, malas now charged up for the retreat's next stage.

Chapter Four

Williams, Oregon, I

All cyclic existence and enlightenment are nothing other than
space itself.
Once you recognize that indwelling state, it is sufficient to not
turn your eyes from space.

Do I look at space with my eyes?
Look from a state of uncontrived natural repose. That's it!
—Dudjom Lingpa

SEPTEMBER 8, 2012 – JOURNAL

Back in Raymond I'd spent days preparing, packing, and, under a time pressure, working with Rinpoche on a translation of text for my next phase of retreat. So even before setting off this morning I was already tired out. Oh, and the weather had been hot, close to 100 one day, sweltering in my attic apartment. Finally on my way, sleep deprived, but happy, while Brent drove the first leg of the southward journey to Portland.

Once in Portland, all my things—that growing amalgam of hermit household—were transferred into Cutty's van. Then Brent and I were treated to a gracious outlay of summer picnic in Cutty and Diane's backyard, shaded on that hot day by the protective canopies of old oak trees. Brent headed back to Raymond, with my gratitude extended to Kathy. My Portland friends and I now took off for the remaining leg, covering the length of Oregon in one afternoon.

Turning off the freeway at Grants Pass, we were welcomed by city banners proclaiming "It's The Climate," which struck us as humorously auspicious, resonant with our growing sense of anticipation. The winding highway led into low, rugged mountains, the Siskiyous, set about by green farms, homesteads, orchards, cows, and smatterings of suburban-style homes of retirees. Williams is more of a corner than a town, and we drove through it in a blink. Finding our lane just at dusk, we stopped at the first house there. Out came Lama Jamie, greeting me beautifully in traditional Tibetan style, touching foreheads. His wife, Sara—lovely! One young woman, Kari, emerged effusing warmth and welcome.

They were gathered for an evening party at the home of one of the center's secular tenants. Sara was charged with leading us up the long, steep gravel lane in their pickup. Cutty negotiated the potholes and bumps, the precipitous edges. We were all captivated by the verdant, wooded gullies, enticing pathways, and somehow, even the derelict refrigerators and car bodies along the way. Diane and Cutty exclaimed breathlessly, "This is a beyul!" Indeed, special energy here.

Then, at the end of the road, a cluster of small buildings, and in the center, a garden headed by a towering, painted statue of Guru Rinpoche. I almost burst into tears. In the center, a pond with carp, and beside it, a treasure vase statue. Well-tended plantings, surrounded by dry-land forest of oak, madrona and evergreens. The little piazza with picnic tables was surrounded by several buildings: lama quarters, kitchen, outdoor shower, and the place where I was to stay—a beautiful, jewel-box cabin, one room, with a cupola on top.

Sara opened the door. My first thought: So small, bed on floor, little furniture, where will I put my things? Then, communal kitchen seemingly in chaos, complete with mice droppings, and no room in the fridge. These things rose up in my exhausted mind after the twelve-hour journey. But simultaneously, the overall sense of place: beautiful. So I just plowed ahead. After helping me unload, Diane and Cutty left because hungry, tired and late in the day, and they swept Sara up with them, causing a sudden vacuum. There I was, alone with a sea of boxes and suitcases. I slowly put my linens on the bed, got water, brushed teeth, visited the outhouse—all the essentials for this night—staying with the idea that all I need do was take care of the present moment, without jumping ahead to the morrow, or at least I tried.

I was *so* tired, thought I'd conk out. Thought, I could read a bit to quiet the mind, but instead chose to go solo, no distraction. And in this state where my mind was both too tired to think and also revved up, anticipating the morrow in a good way, I wasn't anxious. Instead I felt tremendous happiness and literally had a smile on my face. I stayed like this, floating in and out, up and down at the surface of sleep, for perhaps three hours. Staying with happiness, no frustration at non-sleep, but aware of special energy.

Then after midnight, was aware in this unusual state of part-sleep that I was receiving a transmission of energy coming in through the top of my head. It didn't come with a message nor an image. I remembered at that moment that dream yoga was one of Chagdud Tulku's specialties, one that he taught, and that this cabin where I was now lying had been built expressly for him, the first structure to go up decades ago, and he had stayed in it many times. Then I drifted off to sleep.

> *High in the French alps in 1990, at a retreat of a thousand practitioners, I entered our hotel elevator to find within a short Tibetan lama, slight, with long wispy beard, thin white hair tied to the top of his head, and in total possession of himself, the very picture of a wizard. I had been to some of Chagdud Tulku's teachings in Seattle previously, so I knew instantly who he was. We politely spoke a few words. Then, in his nearly unintelligible English he invited me to share a ride in his chauffeured car down to the teaching tent. Of course I accepted.*
>
> *I was to have audiences with him several times over the years, in Seattle and Nepal, and went to his further teachings. He embodied the ancient wisdom of Tibet, of the old school, the Nyingma, which famously includes shamanic practices plaited with those of buddhism. He was renowned for many things, including his chanting voice—iconic, rife with layers of meaning. And so he had been invited to that alpine gathering as the chant leader. All the Tibetan lamas in attendance, along with the thousand Western students, keenly followed his melodies, his intonations and cadences, from old Tibet. There are recordings of his chants, and to hear them is to time travel, and perhaps to stir devotion if one can catch the meaning, beyond the words.*

SEPTEMBER 9 – JOURNAL

Awoke at 4:30 remembering a clear dream about protecting an Irish setter from a pack of wolves at the door of this cabin. After walking down the long trail to the outhouse, I returned for morning practice. Then got back under the covers and drowsed until 9.

Happy day, slowly setting up the altar, rearranging furniture, getting to know the kitchen; then took a shower in the outdoor stall. Lama Jamie and Sara took me on a tour of the shrine room and some of the other cabins. They seemed eager to get to know me, but I felt unusually tongue-tied with little to say. Even though moving slowly without schedule today, still I exhausted myself. Tomorrow I'll make the opening supplication for the buddhas and protectors, restart the daily Riwo Sangchöd, conduct the service for Dad, and do an offering puja for the dakinis. All good.

SEPTEMBER 13 – JOURNAL

Last evening, while reading in bed, a band of four marauding kittens came around, looking for something, probably scraps, trying to get into all the cabins while yowling and scrabbling about. Having been told about them already, I tried to ignore the feral, fuzzy cuties the best I could. Then one of these teenagers jumped onto my window screen with his tiny claws, scratching and squalling, making a huge racket. Closing the window didn't help. It was only by turning off the light that they went away, probably to hit up a nearby cabin occupied by a young mother and her two girls, who, it was said, had been feeding them.

Then many hours later, when in a sound sleep, a small frog landed on my forehead! Startled awake, I put my hand there on its cool, damp, soft body, with suction cup toes, realizing "frog!" and flung him off with, "Oh my gawd!"—as in, what next?! A small part of me realizes the humor, but the larger part wonders if I'm getting more intimate with nature than I'd bargained for.

SEPTEMBER 21 – JOURNAL

That first week I had the great good fortune of overlapping with Nyichang Rinpoche and his attendant Hideaki Inomoto, who were staying in the main lama cabin. I was instructed not to approach the elderly lama, but to wait until invited. But of course, I thought. On my second day we two sat out on our respective porches eating and sipping tea. Inspired by his infusion of utter presence and place, in the way of imprinting, I also sat thus. Imprinting sometimes works, and that day, with frays of imagery and poetry of mountain hermits wafting around the edges of my mind, it seemed so. Just being-sitting, without inner stir of wish or wonder or myriad possibilities. Simple. Still, we hadn't yet spoken.

Later, Inomoto appeared in the small lama kitchen next to my cabin, preparing soup for the two of them. He told me the lama's story. Nyichang Rinpoche had, from an early age in Tibet, been recognized as a reincarnated lama, had studied for years with the famous enlightened female adept of Shugsep Nunnery near Lhasa, and became a scholar of the

Longchen Nyingtik, a major cycle of Nyingma teaching and practice. The latter makes him a rarity, since most serious practitioners of this lineage emphasize practice over study. After he walked out of Tibet into India with the original diaspora in the late 1950s, he was eventually asked by the Dalai Lama to settle and teach in Japan. There was an old tradition of Vajrayana in Japan, and though not a large community, they would benefit from the presence of a tulku and scholar of the Nyingma tradition. So Nyichang Rinpoche went.

After decades, he had become fluent in Japanese, and well-established in Tokyo, teaching at a university there, creating a small center, and attracting students. Inomoto became his right-hand. In recent years Nyichang Rinpoche had purchased land in the eastern Himalayas of India, and had made great gains in constructing a monastery for the furtherance of the Longchen Nyingtik tradition. I later saw photos of the place, on a lush hillside, buildings of modern, Japanese-inspired architecture, beautiful, peaceful, and inspiring.

He and Inomoto had been coming to the States for some years, for teaching. And they always stayed for a retreat holiday on Lama Jamie's land. Their presence absolutely smoothed the way for my acclimation. Inomoto and I, both having served and apprenticed with lamas for years, had much in common, and so we thoroughly enjoyed our exchanges.

One morning well before dawn all hands were on deck for a large-scale Riwo Sangchöd puja. Still exhausted by the move, I had to pry myself out of bed in a morning so early it was yet night. This puja was Nyichang Rinpoche's request and as senior lama, he presided. In a fire pit at the center of the piazza a pile of large cedar boughs had been stacked high, courtesy of Kari and a friend. People ran around locating texts, setting about food offerings, wrapping up against the morning chill, and finally settling onto their outdoor cushions. The puja began.

Lama Jamie, like Chagdud Rinpoche before him, was a renowned chant leader, his knowing, gravelly voice intoning the old melodies for the assembly. This group of Westerners was well-trained with the musical accompaniment of drums and bells. In fact, the young fellow next to me thought my drumming a bit boring, so he ended up with my drum, beating with enthusiastic emphasis. As Kari and friend repeatedly splashed water onto the sometimes-flaming, mostly smoldering, cedar boughs, clouds of smoke billowed and overlapped pure white, up and up in front of the Guru Rinpoche statue, in an auspicious and sublime display. By first light the pile had burned down, in concert with the puja. And all was good.

During that week I had two chats with Nyichang Rinpoche, one in which I gave fundraising advice from the American perspective for their Kalimpong institute, quite different from the way of finding funds in Japan, or in Tibet, for that matter. Perhaps they didn't really need advice so much since the institute was nearly complete. Rinpoche told the story of how he'd saved his meager pennies early on while still in India, by buying Indian government postal certificates. All of those he had saved, and decades later they were worth enough that they were able to buy the Himalayan land and begin construction.

By the time they left I'd become quite attached, and let loose a momentary sob after they drove away. I recovered pretty fast, but still sometimes imagine the lama here, emerging from his cabin, slowly walking, staff in hand, around the *kora* path.

Every Thursday evening the whole sangha came together in the shrine room for a puja led by Lama Jamie. It's actually a requirement of staying on the land, partly an effort to create sangha, and also a way for the lama to check in with retreatants, to see how they're doing from the practical to the spiritual. Others from the outer community would sometimes attend, or buddhist friends passing through.

There would be a brief, entry-level sadhana, open to anyone who might show up. And then Lama Jamie would usually stop at some point to talk extemporaneously, akin to a sermon but more informal. He engaged the group for discussion, or to jostle reflection. Photocopies of poetry of the ancient Zen master Dogen might pop out, or pages of a book he'd been reading, perhaps the biography of enlightened medieval bridge maker, Thangtong Gyalpo. And then we'd find ourselves in choral reading, alternating with discussion. And sharing of news, prayers for people who recently died, that sort of thing.

At first I wondered about it all, if I should even have been there given the seclusion of three-year retreat. But once I got used to it, it became tremendously companionable. And my appreciation of Lama Jamie grew.

Lama Jamie is modest in self-description, saying he's not a real lama, that it was just a convenient title Chagdud Rinpoche gave him because of his commitment to the dharma, and his leadership by buying and transforming this land into a retreat center. But he not only holds the teacher role well, he perhaps has something beyond. He certainly carries the lineage of Chagdud, the transmission and feeling and sense of that great lama—in Lama Jamie's own style. It's nice to see.

Then there was that sadhana translation that Kilung Rinpoche and I had been trying to complete before I'd left Raymond. We still had a ways to go, and so from here in Williams we began again via cell phone, this time with a new deadline: he's about to take off for teaching in South America. Just in time, the translation is now complete.

But not without one drama. We needed to send the file back and forth twice, but there's no internet here in Lama Jamie's pureland. I mentioned my need to Kari and she immediately thought of the house down by the main road, saying that the tenant had wireless and that she would ask him for me. Several days later, I felt some urgency to move ahead on the project, and not knowing how to find Kari, I walked down to the house to inquire. No one home, but I thought surely he wouldn't mind if, from nearby the house, I piggybacked for a moment of sending a file, a choice any city person would make in that situation. I left a grateful note for the resident.

A few days later I mentioned this to Lama Jamie, and was surprised that he appeared not at all happy, although he relaxed when I said it had been Kari's suggestion. I said I needed to go back one final time. He explained he didn't want retreatants invading and asking for things from tenants. But I felt I had had permission through Kari and had a strong need directly related to retreat—without any other recourse. Plus I'd been responsible by leaving a note for the tenant. Finally, Lama Jamie didn't say not to, so I returned two days later for the last file transfer.

Just as I was finishing, Lama Jamie drove past in his pickup, so I popped out from a side yard to say hi. He went ballistic, yelling at me and speeding off up the road. I was in shock. Wondering what I had gotten myself into, I walked the mile back to my cabin with a sense of dread. Later, he left me a note scrawled in red ink, saying that if I didn't write my teacher about what had happened, then he would do so himself. Whoa! Upsetting for both Lama Jamie and for me!

So, what to do? We must have misunderstood each other at our last meeting, I thought. So I put Lojong, mind training, into action—taking all blames into one, that is, accepting all responsibility myself. I did first call my teacher, a sympathetic Kilung Rinpoche, who had many helpful things to say, including that Lama Jamie and I are certainly getting to know each other better—that's for sure! And he also had the strong sense that this would blow over with no problem. I thought, *really*?

Then I set to writing a formal apology letter, explaining further about the need for completing the translation work for my retreat curriculum; that I remembered having told him that I needed to return to the internet source one last time; I apologized profusely for pushing the boundaries with perhaps wishful thinking; and simply, for upsetting him. Then the letter I printed out, signed, and folded into a long envelope.

Crossing fingers, and still terribly upset, I decided to attend the Thursday evening gathering. I laid the envelope on Lama Jamie's puja table and took my seat. When he came in he seemed quite recovered, even ebullient. In spite of the large crocodile tears that silently slid down my cheeks throughout the evening, he elicited comments from me in the discussions, and generally included me. I kept thinking, is he going to dress me down in front of the group? Is this going to turn out to be a cult scene, in which case I'm out of here. But no. Instead, in earnestness and without directing it toward me, he spoke about the damage that can be done by expressing unrestrained anger. I thought, is this his version of an apology? He hadn't even read my letter yet, but here I was. I had come to face the music, and he saw that.

Rinpoche's words about it blowing over were prominent in my mind today. Indeed, kind of miraculous, because it seems true already. I hadn't slept well last night after all that. But this evening there was a gathering of a different kind. I hesitated about going, just wanting to stay quietly by myself, but something made me go: the sense that it would help things along. It was also my way of accepting his "apology" the night before.

The gathering was focused on a special walk that they had created on the land. Meandering along the trails through forest, you find plaques with lines of teachings on emptiness by 3rd-century Indian mahasiddha Nagarjuna. The text includes commentary by present-day Tibetan Khenpo Tsultrim Gyamtso. Each one is *koan*-like, providing inspiration for contemplative meditation, placed in green nooks or glens, in some places with logs to rest on. One could make a weekend retreat just based on this. We did a small part of the walk in an hour and a half.

When I showed up, Sara walked right over and deliberately thanked me for coming. Without saying so, they had apparently read my letter. I was initially subdued. As we walked from one plaque to the next, we meditated and then Lama Jamie would lead a short discussion. He seemed quite fine, and as the tour continued, I slowly got into the swing of it, finding the text and discussion quite interesting, and glad that I'd come.

After all of this, I felt my actions were done well. Even though I'd been upset and had displayed some of that outwardly, I had shown up, demonstrating my basic okayness to Lama Jamie and Sara, and so had done my part in moving things forward. Not only does it seem Lama Jamie has forgiven me, he's also shown his own capacity for quick transformation.

You know what? In just twenty years, if I'm still alive, there's a chance I'll have short-term memory loss, and all this journal writing will be of no interest to anyone. Who am I kidding? For whom am I writing? Maybe Nagarjuna is having some effect.

If there is no "me" in the first place,
How could there be anything that belongs to me?
When "me" and "mine" are found to be peace,
Clinging to "me" and "mine" ceases.
                                    –Nagarjuna

SEPTEMBER 22 – EQUINOX, JOURNAL

I haven't been sleeping well since Dad died one month ago today. While I was in Raymond it was okay, but since moving here two weeks ago, something else has been keeping me awake (besides my mind)—the small creatures.

The bed is on the floor, so small ants have sometimes been crawling into bed with me. The screens covering the cupola windows weren't on properly, allowing in all kinds, including mosquitoes. After a couple days Lama Jamie fixed the screens, but apparently many critters had already entered. There was the frog already mentioned, of course. One early morning a biting fly bit my upper lip in the mustache area—deeply and sharply painful! What a way to wake up. The welt actually increased over a week's time and only now is subsiding. No-see-ums, attracted to the bedside light, bite my hands while holding up a book. And the small ants tickle me awake at any time.

Every night, going to bed, I'd gotten to rather dread it, banishing the lovely sanctuary of bed and sleep. Now jumpy—after all, there are scorpions and poison oak in these woods. And so many exotic-to-me creatures. A magnificent, lime-green praying mantis visited my porch one day, with a penetrating presence. We observed each other for some time. *Many* butterflies. Darling frogs and lizards. I've seen one lizard leap! And watched them race along the ground from my perch on the porch. In my room one day I saw a dark black millipede—with a head that looked up and around—a little creepy, like putting intelligence on a worm. Swarms of gnats at evening, and beautiful moths.

So, in the last week I've tried a few things to stem the visitations. I vacuumed and keep the place spotless. I turn on a lamp across the room, rather than next to the bed so the no-see-ums and moths congregate elsewhere. I've used lots of bug spray on myself and the bed. All this seems to be helping, plus the change of season. Lama Jamie is going to make a platform to raise the bed from the floor. Hope rises, even as samsara is futile. Nothing has intrinsic existence, I tell myself, we're not separate, we're all of light. (There goes a gnat.)

SEPTEMBER 25 – JOURNAL

I'm beginning to love my room. The season has lessened the insects so I've relaxed and am starting to sleep again. It feels like home.

Except last night a young woman came and started using my kitchen because she couldn't figure out the gas range in the large retreat kitchen. After Nyichang Rinpoche and Inomoto left, I moved into the tiny lama kitchen attached to my cabin, while still sharing the fridge in the main kitchen. So today I went to show this person how to use the stove, but she was resistant to every suggestion. Later she came again, looking for offering bowls. And later still she left a storage door open for several hours, with edible things out on the retreat kitchen counter—as critter bait apparently.

I guess this is *it*, isn't it?! Invasion while on retreat. Samsara bumping into one's ego, amplified by retreat. During one practice, I watched the internal turnings as I could hear her footsteps outside my window, probably doing kora. Each time she passed by, I wondered if she was going to invade my space again. At first my mind found it bothersome, then an unusual merging of sublime and awry. Finally footsteps stopped and I easily slid into a deep practice, happy.

She had brought me an interestingly shaped tomato, seemingly a peace offering, from her father's garden. I put it on my altar, as a wry reminder of my habitual patterns.

Working these last few days and weeks by phone with Rinpoche has been so warm and positive. Today we finally completed the text and teaching for the second major phase of retreat, which I shall be starting a few days hence. I'm eager to do this practice, which happens to be centered around my personal deity, my *yidam*.

It must have been twenty years ago that I first connected strongly with this deity, at a retreat center in the south of France. We were encouraged to do the practice on our own. Mala in hand, I went on walks, reciting the mantra and visualizing this enormous wrathful deity. One day a retreat friend joined me for a walk. We happened upon a beautiful Japanese teahouse deep in the woods which we assumed to be a small rest house for the lama. It was closed up and curtains prevented us from peeking inside, but it was beautifully crafted, and perched above a burbling brook. We sat on its porch, meditating, in the tree-filtered sun. I silently recited the mantras.

First, a brilliant blue dragonfly, the color of that wrathful deity, appeared and hovered around us. Then sacred sound emanated from the brook, a guru mantra that I knew well. My friend later said she heard something, too, the mani mantra of compassion. After that, I felt a close connection to the deity, even affection, sometimes as if I was doing his dance myself, shaking the whole heaven and earth to the core! in the service of clarity and kindness.

Then today, while I'm in the middle of a sadhana, Rinpoche texts to see if he can call me, just before he leaves for South America. I say yes. He calls. He is giving me his *phurba*, the one he's been using for years. Giving, not lending. He says he wants me to have any of the objects and images I'm using on this retreat because they're being imbued with three-year retreat energy, my created energy. If I haven't yet "gotten" the esteem and value he places on me, I don't know about my little, small, miniscule mind.

Humility and pride, two sides of a narrow ridge walked by the good and humble princess of fairy tales. She needs to hold both without falling down the mountain on either side. Vajra pride, confidence in one's own buddha nature and embodiment of the deities, as light. Confidence in meditation, in connection with this energy, in one's own wisdom and experience of timeless awareness. Then, humility to see that one is not separate, nor different, nor above. The "good" part is the resulting compassion, and the action, sometimes requiring fearlessness, extends from that. And then is born true nobility.

SEPTEMBER 26 – JOURNAL

These woods, these woods! I feel like Thoreau in a sanctuary. It's all so different from the wet forests of my childhood. The trees are placed sparsely, made more so by the lack of undergrowth. At the same time it seems a confusion of varieties, probably because so many are unfamiliar to me. Madronas—many!—tall and spindly, not like our massive coastal ones. Ponderosa-type pines, maples, oak, and a different type of cedar where the flat needle fingers are more spare and deliberate. Everything seems more spare, in this dry-land way.

Today just before the sun was lowering behind yonder hill, I wandered over the creek and up a ridge where I hadn't been before, on an offshoot of a well-worn path. So magical and quiet up there. The ground everywhere is covered with layers upon layers of dry madrona leaves, familiar from my family's island summer place. But here all kinds of trees add their slippery dry detritus, a beautiful sound as one's feet crunch and slide along.

The air warm. It's fall here, but there's no crisp chill. Because of the spaciousness and little undergrowth, you can look deeply into the woods and see the patterns of tree trunks and limbs. In one place I stood for awhile and rested my eyes out over the crest of a steep hill where the tall trees stood layer after endless layer. They all had the same branch pattern, paralleling each other, the lower branches curving downward, mid-branches straightening out, upper branches curving skyward. I wanted to photograph it in black and white, angles of art and light. Words will have to do.

Close by, a big orb of spider web was pulsing, breathing in the slight breeze. The setting sunlight made every silken thread glisten. Then all the surrounding web strands hanging from the trees caught my eye, too, a slow sunset dance.

All this after a long meditation on the porch, leading to deep appreciation, quiet joy, and deep happiness. No shred of loneliness or wishing for anything else in the world.

I returned to my new tai chi spot: a round platform in the near woods. With every turn, the body faces another depth of forest, or an imposing trunk of tree, or off toward the creek, or, through the tree limbs, glimpses of the Guru Rinpoche statue. Today I took a broom and cleared the center space, like ritual preparation of the offering ground.

So many dzogchen teachings say, "It's not like this, but it's like this... If you're doing that, watch out." I read Mipham Rinpoche today, and then this evening Dudjom Lingpa was read aloud at group practice—both 19th century and both esoteric. I seem to remember, Dudjom said to look at space. I'll have to find the passage to understand more, but it resonates, going right into the heart of it. Join with space—without being spacey.

SEPTEMBER 29, EVE OF FULL MOON – JOURNAL

I started the second major practice today, with my friend, the indomitable blue yidam. Years ago I had asked Rinpoche if this could be my personal deity (it's traditional to verify one's choice with a lama)—his answer, an enthusiastic yes! I was happy: it seemed I had chosen well, and I knew I had this strong connection. So, today embarking on a journey of many months, and in some ways, a continuation of years.

It was a good start. The text we prepared is lovely, poetic and evocative enough. I found images for my puja table, and the mandala, and rearranged the yidam thangka so it's now straight on, streamlined for connection.

I'm feeling a lot of gratefulness for Rinpoche lately. This is a good period.

Yesterday Kari took me on a walk to see her *darling* little house, a hobbit's home. Woods paths, then crossing the meadow, then through more woods. Impossible to find this place without a guide, we eventually turned down an abandoned grassy lane lined by a tall fence of vertical wooden boards, moss-covered. Kari pushed open the gate, revealing a small, handmade cabin, with popped-out alcoves, shake roof, and cedar trees towering all around. We stepped through the curtain of mosquito netting. Inside, bookshelves lined the walls of the kitchen and beyond. An alcove was filled with a big wood-topped bathtub, windows all around. Built-in benches serve as anything you like, sitting, eating, sleeping. Idyllic, to my mind. She's been living there for seven years already, the center of a hermit's existence, yet seemed not so very attached. That is the center of a hermit's existence.

OCTOBER 5 – JOURNAL

Thoughts arising about my adjustment to being here, on this piece of earth. I'm still skittish about the little sentient beings. If a shadow suddenly appears, I'm so quick to think it's an invading insect. Yesterday on a walk to the big meadow, I stood in different places, each one for a long time while practicing, gazing out toward the near hills, or sky, or space in front of tall trees. At one point I thought to leave and return to my cabin. But the way my feet touched the ground, I felt slight sinking into the earth, as if stepping on foam—and intuited this as an internal message, an antidote, that I needed to deliberately sink down in.

So I went walking around, intensifying a sense of connectivity with the ground, instead of squeamishly tip-toeing around, holding myself up, off, and away from the ground. It must come from a feeling of vulnerability combined with my normal airy tendency. Now I really need to remedy this.

Today I went back to the same meadow, taking an outdoor cushion with me. And for the first time in Williams I sat on the ground. I meditated for a long time, in the shade of tall ponderosa pines. No one, large or small, came to bother me. It's said the fall rains are starting soon. This thought sent me back to the cabin a bit prematurely. I wonder what is so up with this.

Two days ago I was sitting in some high woods, on a fallen madrona. A still and deep place. Through the trees two weasel-like creatures, martens, appeared. They were running around, checking out all their little places. After awhile I could see only one. He was coming in my direction so I started to make some quiet noises so he wouldn't get too frightened of me at the last moment... and I didn't want him too close, either! Quite large animals, beautiful, like sea otters of the land, alert, moving fluidly with infinitely flexible spines.

I've seen deer a few times. I recently scared the bejeezus out of three who were feeding right outside the back kitchen door when I swiftly emerged on my way to the outhouse. Their sudden getaway scared me, too! I had to stand there for a moment, and then let out a large whoosh of a sigh.

I counted twenty-five vultures in the sky the other day. Kari said one time she counted sixty. Lots of jays here, too.

Recently while meditating in my chair on the porch, a small squirrel came running into view, checking things out. He suddenly leaped through the blue fence surrounding the carp pond, ran to the pool's edge, flipped himself upside down—apparently going for a drink—while still hanging on with his toenails! After a moment, he ran off.

Last night I heard an otherworldly, weird sound, high pitched. I could only think of a cougar. Or someone else being made into cougar's dinner. Somewhat chilling, as it was in the direction of the patch of ground where I pee at night.

Lately while in the woods, or even in my room, I've had these experiences of deep stillness that go on and on. I realize how quiet it is, and then, half-expecting something to interrupt, it doesn't. Instead, the quiet continues, lengthens, and I go deeper, to a deeper place inside. Then I become aware again of the quiet... and it continues, and I go deeper again... relaxing to a new level of inner quiet, and rapport with this exterior quiet.

It's a kind of listening, and hearing the quiet. It's not totally silent because it's the woods. But so quiet, it's profound. It's almost waiting for something, like the empty matrix—shunyata-emptiness, pregnant with possibility—to open up in front of me. At any moment a tree branch could fall, a corvid could caw, an iridescent beetle could fascinate by, a helicopter could fly overhead. But none of these happen, and that continues to unknot my mind while I sink more and more deeply into a relaxed state, releasing the outer world, too. I think earlier I may not have been ready. But regardless, I'm here and ready now!

Lately I notice increased social sensitivity again, and caring less about news. Still a little interest in the presidential election, but not much.

OCTOBER 6 – POEM

Only Quiet

Only quiet in these solitary woods;
Interruptions there are none.

Two neighborhood weasels do not gambol and cavort over fallen logs and rock outcroppings;
I descend into the silence.

Blond winsome Heather from nearby cabin does not float down the trail, white towel thrown over shoulder on way to shower;
I deepen into the continuity of spacious time.

Twenty-five vultures do not circle far beyond the tops of firs and cedars above my head;
Unfolding further into palpable tranquility.

Cell phone does not beep, boingle, or bwap to nudge me;
This space of stillness rolls out one more beat, and then another.

Earnest Matthew does not lope down the hill, with studied eye-contact avoidance of a serious retreatant on his way to lunch;
I ride this quiet like an ocean wave.

OCTOBER 7 – JOURNAL

Last night after falling asleep I half-woke up, and for hours was in that between state, finally back to sleep around 5. Later in the day during practice I remembered that Guru Rinpoche had been present with me that whole time. He didn't want anything, or want me to do anything; I had the sense that he was just present, that he was watching over me. There wasn't anything to protect *from*, that I was aware of, but he was there in case.

Here's the thing: my (slightly) more conscious-level mind was grumbling about being awake-ish once again. I didn't say, Hey! That's Guru Rinpoche!

and please give me a message or advice, or teaching or transmission. In fact, he was more in the background, perhaps watching my grumbling and obscured habitual mind, but he was patient and didn't give up. Then, today I didn't feel at all sleep-deprived. Was it all a dream?

OCTOBER 9 – JOURNAL

Highly emotional today, beginning with a feeling of sadness and loss, but not so specific, somewhat lonely and easy to burst into tears. But I write because three lions appeared.

The first was a beautiful face in the golden brocade fabric from Varanasi that's part of my altar. It's been right in front of me as I sit on my cushion, in the center of a large woven flower, but I hadn't noticed it until today. Artful, with a look of great kindness.

The next two were in the clouds. The first lion-cloud was nice, but not exactly memorable. The second was amazing, again a beautiful, kind face, with large body, and then there were large angel wings. A winged lion. Seeing three in one day (!), I put it together with my feelings of trepidation—like the cowardly lion who needed to put the power on. And then another literature lion with spiritual overtones, Aslan, representing God, who showed his wrathful side—tremendous! He had sun energy and light. I connected all of this with the yidam deity, of course. The immense purity and sun-like radiance, with the love of the wisdom being at his heart—manifesting the vividness and power of the (compassionate) wrathful.

So I got this crystal clear message today: LION. Sun-radiant, unafraid. I feel so vulnerable and afraid at the moment. And burst into tears many times, grateful for the relief these appearances provided, in the message, and in the practice.

OCTOBER 15, NEW MOON – JOURNAL

We had our weekly chat evening, Barbara and I. We were talking about my recent feelings of trepidation because I mentioned this in relation to the puja for my dad's fiftieth day after death. She was reminded of a book, *The Idea of the Holy* by Rudolf Otto. She said, "It's about the idea of the divine as Other that leads to a feeling of fear—and awe, which can be a kind of fear. We often feel this in the presence of the divine sacred. It's a natural, instinctive reaction, the overwhelm of the glory and power and majesty of this other reality. This he called the *mysterium tremendum.*"

Barbara felt full of dread in relation to her former Chinese Buddhist teacher:

the reality of that much greatness in a human being. It shook her profoundly. This wasn't ultimately a healthy thing for her, she said, but reading this book explained this as a phenomenon. We both said we'd felt this in the presence of some of the great lamas.

"So, it's an archetypal thing, this feeling around the sacred," she said.

We were thinking that because my current practice is wrathful, this could perhaps be feeding this sense in me of late. Definitely it explains the feeling I get while preparing to do any puja or ritual where it's up to me, where it's not totally prescribed, where I become "the lama" equivalent. It's in situations where the words are mine, where I'm directly supplicating the deities and protectors without a script or liturgy. Suddenly I'm out there, naked, in front of the larger-than-life, real deities, feeling tongue-tied. I feel a lot is at stake: to be *genuine*, to be *present* and *clear*, with a sense of timing, not messing around, and not being tongue-tied! It's always exhausting—which is why moving to a new place is doubly exhausting—this vulnerability is built in. And I was exhausted after Dad's fiftieth day puja, which had again required this unadorned activity.

Maybe I should practice this more, using my own words just in a simple way, in prayer. And then maybe because the wrathful practice has this enormous power and majesty, I'm feeling an undercurrent of overwhelm by that—not by exhaustion, but by trepidation. Barbara's advice: Think of the *lion*. And more, manifest the lion within.

Earlier today I felt this again, trepidation and melancholy. But later in the day after more practice, better. I expressed to Barbara that approaching the one-year anniversary may be cause for difficulty. I've felt the past year was long and quite hard, and the phase of mantra recitation tedious. So the prospect of more of that feels... long and hard and tedious. I wish the time felt short, so that I appreciated each moment.

Also, today something helpful. While in the mantras, while continuing to progress from bead to bead on the mala, came this: Just drop everything and go to dzogchen mind, or something as close to dzogchen as possible. Stay with that for awhile. Then slowly bring the visualization back in. Even back and forth. It gets the spacious back in, the light, and renews everything.

OCTOBER 17, ONE YEAR IN RETREAT – REFLECTIONS

I'm not sure how I did it. I could list the ways that I utilized therapy, practice, perspective, patience, and sometimes handholding by Barbara (as confidante), Diane H. (as therapist), and Dechen (as retreat attendant). But considering the tremendous upheaval, the sense of being on the surface of a great stormy ocean, and realizing where I stand now—calmly looking out from a bluff on that ocean, the scene of a dynamic day, with my clothes and hair blowing back in the wind—considering this transformation, an ordinary explanation isn't enough. I can still vividly remember feeling these former stormy onslaughts, can get teary over a sense of injustice, and deeply saddened that my marriage had to end. But the onslaughts, the gales of tears and anger don't come anymore. That is the most miraculous "sign" of my progress. And it's something I can take with me, from this day onward, whenever I leave retreat.

But there's more: I accomplished the first two sections, out of five, of the retreat curriculum, and am now in the third. I worked with Rinpoche to edit and produce a newly translated Longchen Nyingtik text—a condensed, yogic version especially used for long retreat days, a practice I've already begun.

My father, Randy, passed away two months ago, and I weathered his demise and death, then completed end of life practices for him over the fifty days. Two months before he died I began reflecting on what I would write as a eulogy. That process illuminated the importance and influence he had in my early life, even beauty.

I've stayed at four places in the past year, each one with wonderful attributes that supported my retreat and my heart-mind at the various stages. Of course moving from one place to the next was distracting, but each also brought something beneficial and actually needed. I'd like to find one last place where I can finish the rest of the retreat, and so now here, testing the retreat center at Williams. This place, with its scores of acres of forest, has unplumbable depths of quiet, and clearly there is great blessing.

What happened spiritually? I'm not sure. I feel a little bit that if I had been doing solely meditation the whole time I might be enlightened by now—a joke, but doing months and months of mantras often feels off-topic. Isn't that funny? You're supposed to maintain dzogchen view while yes, doing the mantras. But my mind wanders numbly off after awhile, and then mantras seem counterproductive. However, Rinpoche feels confidence in me and my progress, which counts for a lot.

Then, I kept various notebooks: the regular personal journal; a beloved retreat notebook mostly with notes from consultations with Rinpoche; a small art notebook which is filling with childlike images by a non-artist; a small booklet where I'm tracking mantras recited, books read, and days practiced; and a prayer book with a growing list of people needing prayers.

OCTOBER 20 – JOURNAL

Two days ago, the sangha here happened to do tsok—for fun! without a feast day or any special reason. What a concept! So I announced that I had passed my one-year anniversary of retreat. A companionable time was had by all.

About my sleep. It's been two months now, both difficult and special, since Dad died. More and more I'm having some degree of lucidity in sleep—luminous light, brilliant, warm, golden, even yellow hues, sometimes lemony. Everything glowing. Those parts of the night are, of course, great. And *restful*. Nothing needed there.

But then the awareness tends to drift into other phases, let's call this three phases. The second phase will be more busy, dreaming with awareness, but without this quality of light. Still, interesting. And fairly restful.

Then the third phase is awake. Actually this has two parts. The first is drowsy enough that it seems I should be able to return to sleep. Then it eventually shifts into wide awake. Of course this is what I'd like to switch off since it can go on for *hours*, maybe four or more. Rinpoche suggested staying very relaxed, and doing some open meditation.

Last night I actually enjoyed the whole night, including the time I sat up in bed meditating, lying down meditating, in the dark asking, what is the *nature of mind*, et cetera. All this didn't help me sleep though. Maybe it was six or later when I fell asleep, and then the alarm at 7:30. So, because I've had a run of sleeplessness, today was drunken, felt like crying like a baby, even staggering around. Finally had a thirty-minute nap in the afternoon, which made a world of difference.

I'm unsure of this. Should I be embracing night practice, or really trying (without trying too hard) to get on a normal schedule? Is something out of balance? Or does something new want to come forth? Am I practicing too hard, or the opposite, not disciplined enough? Is it lack of exercise, or something of a deep psyche—or psychic—nature?

OCTOBER 22 – JOURNAL

I stumbled upon a magical place. I decided to have a look at this one jumble of things in a cleared area that I pass on my daily walk down the gravel road. Sometimes a car parks there, or two mountain bikes, and some intriguing things, like a half-made basket sitting on the ground by a pile of willow branches. On the way out I noticed an actual path heading into the trees, and decided to explore, thinking there could be a nice walk, free of poison oak.

Walking down a steep incline in some lovely woods I could hear the sound of water. Further on, a creek appeared, with a gigantic fallen tree over it, really huge in girth and length, out of a storybook. When I got closer, a pile of stones at one end had clearly been put there by human effort, as stairs. Closer still and the log had been fashioned into a bridge, the top surface made flat and a hand-rail put up along the expanse. The railing was held up by some growing trees on the far end. It was like something found in the mountains of Nepal. I was enchanted.

Peering around I suddenly caught a glimpse of a wall through the trees on the other side of the gully—a house. I exclaimed, "Oh!" and backed up, not wanting to intrude. The small house looked well-kept and lovely, even though I couldn't really see details. Then I noticed that the whole forest there had been swept and cleared and organized. Piles of twiggy branches surrounded some of the trees at their base. Small fallen trees had been put next to each other in par-allel. Seeing this had the effect on me of inspiration, right to the heart. That this wild place could be tamed and made hospitable, with the potential of home.

I thought later, I need to know more about this place, and I'll ask Kari. Now this evening, I find out it's *her* place. Her darling hobbit-y home, the back entrance, is the one through those trees. My. I guess I can go back.

OCTOBER 24 – JOURNAL

Right now enjoying post-tsok—this one on a feast day with the group, having had a full glass of vino, so a little tipsy. I'm now lying in the heaven of bed, with a snackling fire going. Hard to find fault with samsara in this precise moment. But still can look for *dharmadhatu*-space—even nature of mind—in tipsy. In fact, that's the point!

OCTOBER 30 – CONSULTATION WITH RINPOCHE

I said: I've recently been developing a keener and deeper sense for the pur-pose of deity practice. I think being here with less distraction is helping with that. What does that mean? Not big signs, but a feeling; things are really slowing down; sense of time is slowing down further; there's something happening with the perception of and relationship with the deities that's supplanting ordinary perception. And yet no visions; just a feeling, or a sense.

He said: The goal is not visions, but the first important thing is a sense of no separation between self and the deity. The Buddha said, "Happiness is the key to success; success is not the key to happiness." This stage is meant to develop a oneness quality, oneness between oneself and the deity, and the wisdom of one's own mind; to feel that the deity is a manifestation of one's own mind. When one feels that, then the connection is established.

I said: I've been particularly spacey lately, concerned about a lack of common sense in a few instances.

He said: While not ultimately great, it could be a step into breaking patterns of responsibility, detail-orientation, critical thinking, or being in-charge, and going toward accepting things as they are.

NOVEMBER 4 – JOURNAL

Sleep difficulties still visit on and off, but are improving. At this point the problems center around falling asleep, rather than being awake for hours. Sometimes lucid nights, but sleep overall is leaning toward normal. Let's go with that!

NOVEMBER 5 – JOURNAL

While sitting in the big field I saw a praying mantis. Is that praying or preying?! Beautiful, intriguing, he was camouflaged with the grass, barely moving, or not at all. Sitting in meditation, I was barely moving, or not at all. The first mantis on the porch had come to greet me. This one, we meditated together.

Just finished an evening talk with Barbara. They've been stretching out to three hours most times now. We both look forward to them so much! So helpful, actually indispensable. I feel so often that relating with others is a samsaric time-waster, which I'm not always above by any means, and these conversations with Barbara are rarely so. She reminded me of that Greek term, kenosis, a spiritual emptying out—that difficult but legitimate part of the spiritual journey, with its self-questioning, shaking up of the foundations. I feel it a bit lately again. She said she's been experiencing it herself recently.

Last evening I called Margi, my mother-in-law, for her birthday. A most delightful and deep sharing of life, love, marriage. She talked about her years of living in Peru, and dancing. We were both elated by the end. She kept asking me if I'd found *Peace* on my retreat. I kept answering in different ways. I guess the best answer is I've experienced it some, but maybe the nature of rigpa is so dynamic—even if you get stabilized in it, would you call it "peace"? I'm not sure. Perhaps it is. But there's easily movement, subtle, at the same time.

NOVEMBER 6 – JOURNAL

Election day. My neighbor, Jana, listened on a radio and brought the news. Obama re-elected. We had a small late-night celebration.

NOVEMBER 15 – JOURNAL

Now almost too sleepy to write, but I want to record this. While in forest practice, the sense of dream-time was vivid, beautiful. Then at night during the deity *dissolution*, I realized something that I had neglected nine years ago while in a nature-of-mind meditation. At that time I saw the particles of space open up, and therefrom emerged the actual deity *Tara* floating before me, a true vision; at that time, I experienced that all the universe was made of this space and this light and potential to expand in this same way. However, tonight I was struck with the thought that I had not previously applied this potential to myself.

So that is what I did just now. Suddenly understanding that myself has the same potential of space and light and expansion as every other thing in the universe, including an arising of deity out of space; then actualizing the dissolution vividly, and seeing self in this light energy distinctly—all this resulted in a more profound meditation experience than usual, with some interesting visual phenomena. At that moment I thought, "This is tripping out," and that phenomena then quieted down. But remained with the overall sense of things infused with meaning and depth; profoundly merging self with the mandala while in dissolution; field of focus expanded outward, beyond room; hot hands and feet, and other sensations of body.

NOVEMBER 19 – JOURNAL

Writing by candle and flashlight. Big windstorm today put out the power. I saw some large tree branches fall to the ground as I stood on the porch, looking into the forest of dancing trees. They know how to dance! Riveting entertainment during today's practice, this exhilarating and sometimes frightening dynamism.

Now 10:30 pm, after a wonderful weekly talk with Barbara. No wind but monsoon-proportion rain. Went out for the last pee of night and got soaked, followed by toweling off my wet head. The storm must be from the tropics because here it is November and exceptionally warm out there.

This morning outside for practice, watching fast-scudding clouds over the big field, I saw a wonderful snow lion in the clouds. The head and face were in perfect detail; the body more impressionistic, but in proportion.

Yesterday morning above the same field, the clouds formed a huge arrowhead, symmetrical, which remained for a long time, a high-up cloud, pointing south-southeast.

Then in the afternoon I walked a different direction, up into the forest, and sat beneath one huge ponderosa or sugar pine. I've been visiting it for weeks, sometimes touching it. One day I backed up to it and crouched down, almost a squat, and meditated. That was good, so yesterday I took my outdoor sitting pad and sat there, back grazing against trunk. I didn't feel quite settled, maybe because the wind had begun slightly, and I didn't know if a storm might start up. At one point some big gusts did come, and these tall trees really sway.

But these trees there are special. The trunks are denuded of branches until high up. Their girths are huge, and their height. The texture of their bark is rich, and regular, and in certain lights the variegated colors come out. There's almost a pattern that each has, each unique from the next. The proportion of girth to height, in combination with the patterns, gives the impression of painted columns of ancient temples. These trees are in a meadow-like opening in the forest, a place of light. The largest of them number about six with most of them grouped together, almost in a circle, a holy grove.

When I first came here to Williams, one evening at dusk on the outhouse trail, a dark shape sliced through the forest, a shadow flying downward at a sharp angle, swift and precise, over the creek. Like a raptor or a silent owl, but far too large to be one, it was about ten meters away. I'm not sure what I saw. It didn't feel sacred. Nature spirit? I felt slightly afraid.

Rinpoche later said, "This spirit or whatever, was not necessarily sacred. It's for the reason of being in a sacred state that one is able to see these kinds of things without obstruction."

I was reminded of a story about the enlightened and famed lama Jamyang Khyentse Chokyi Lodro, who when younger, saw spirits like this with some frequency, which he found so frightening that he had someone sleep outside his door every night.

More recently I heard a story from Jana. She saw what seemed to her to have been a Sasquatch, right here at the statue garden. It was two years ago that she was eating dinner at dusk just in front of the statue, when a tall dark form came from the creek and went behind the prayer wheel, making the sound of a gorilla. Her two cats got really frightened. She went into her cabin, the one I'm now in, to get her meditation chimes. When she came out to the porch, the figure was moving back toward the creek. Thinking it may have been a bear, she rang the chimes loudly over and over again, for ten minutes, she thought. She said that one lama also had a Sasquatch story in this place.

Bear stories also abound.

NOVEMBER 21 – JOURNAL

I began packing today, back to San Juan Island for the winter. Partly I'm glad to go—to see my folks, to a lovely house with all the comforts of modern civilization, and its incredible view. In other ways I wish I wasn't making another transition. However, maybe it will help enliven the practice, which has again seemed a bit dull.

Here's the current thing: all day—mantras. During this time I go in and out of connection with the visualization and deities. I enjoy the connection but it seems to lack the vividness and wildness of this major wrathful deity. The best part of the day is taking the show on the road—walks in the forest during mantra recitation, while getting exercise, communing with the space, the setting, the trees, the light, the sense of things. I bring in the visualization while out there, or just do a dzogchen-style meditation—while in the recitations—vividly present, deeply quiet, peaceful, connected to earth and place.

By the time I'm returned to the cushion, it often feels pretty flat. But then, late at night, during the dissolution, the practice again becomes quite strong, with clear energy, and experience.

Tomorrow is Thanksgiving, a nice convergence with the tsok, the food-offering puja, that the group will be conducting. Also, a chance to say goodbye... and thanks.

These months at Williams had been intended as a trial period, so I was slated from the beginning to take my leave at this point. Not only for that cause, but my cabin had already been reserved, along with pretty much the whole retreat center, for a major gathering of the Chagdud lamas. Local sangha members and Lama Jamie had been preparing the place over the previous weeks, scouring, fixing, making pretty all the cabins, the kitchen, shower, garden, and shrine room. So, off I was to go. Still wondering a little about returning, to poison oak, scorpions, all the wildness. But ah, the wildness, the quiet and the blessing.

CHAPTER FIVE

San Juan Island, II

> Obstacles are a natural part of life, just as boulders are a natural
> part of the course of a river. River does not complain or get
> depressed because there are boulders in its path.
>
> *–I Ching*

*Kind and generous Buddhist friends from Oregon, Jim and Dana, came to
Williams in their truck to collect me. On the way out of the mountains, a
thick fog cloaked the roadway, and Jim, figuring he had remembered these
parts from long ago, got lost up an unknown branching road. Then, the engine began to malfunction, and we thought we were going to get waylaid up
in the remote hills. But by holding our figurative toes up off the floor of the
cab, we made it into Grants Pass, where, day after Thanksgiving, we were
grateful to find an open auto shop with all the needed parts. After an hour or
so we were on our way once again, heading back up north. I stayed the night
at their house near Portland, and next morning Bainbridge Island friends,
Diane B. and Keith, picked me up and took me on the second leg—all the
way to San Juan Island. So many good friends were cheering me on, and in
their own ways, participating in this unusual endeavor.*

*This would be the second stint at my folks' place on Cattle Point for the
three months of winter, holding down the fort, greeting the storms, while
my mother and her husband made their snowbird journey south.*

NOVEMBER 28, 2012 – JOURNAL

Full moon—this morning, lunar eclipse. This moment, night. The moon
has risen over Lopez Island. A healthy wind moving, but not whitecapping, the
bright night sea. The sky full of white puffy clouds at full tilt headed north—
white except surrounding the moon, a night rainbow lighting up any clouds
that cross over into this radiant aureole. A dynamic moonbow. Stunning! And

a substantial planet just off the starboard bow of the moon.

All day no wind, but this evening after dark a sudden gust blew open the seaside door, startling me! What's that?! Only air and wind-sound rushing in.

After all the social contact with friends who transported me north, and then a few days with Mom and Tom, who left today on their sojourn, I'm finally alone, and happily so. Perhaps for the first time I didn't feel pangs of loneliness or abandonment. Just normal, in a sweet and matter-of-fact way. I started prepping the altar for full practice tomorrow. And I made the reopening puja, including supplication of the deities, about which, also for the first time, confidence.

DECEMBER 6 – JOURNAL

These last days, I've had some experiences of time slowing down. Not much else to report, except the general calm. And sleeping well, catching up.

DECEMBER 12 – JOURNAL

I saw Jupiter rising in the eastern sky at dusk. Huge with binocs—present, clear, solid. Marveling at stars and this planet.

Last night Thinley Norbu Rinpoche appeared in an extensive, clear, and lovely dream. I can't quite believe that time has moved on to this point that all these great lamas have already passed away. Sad to think of it. Time is moving along. Perhaps now I'm beginning to look older and feel older, just in time to turn sixty. Fifty sounded old when it happened, but I didn't feel it. Now, perhaps if I look old, then maybe I'll begin to believe in the passage of time.

DECEMBER 19 – JOURNAL

We've had some big storms here recently. Two days ago was an extreme high tide with storm, but the winds came from behind us, from the west, so an amazing entertainment played out—watching it while not inundated by it. You look out to the south, to the straits to see huge waves moving in from the ocean ninety miles away, quite a fetch. But here at the house we're under protection of a point, around its corner from the direct hit. However, the water of Cattle Pass right in front of us is stirred up by the tremendous energy from the straits, but not as big waves, more roiling and swelling in. Then, some of the wind leaking from behind us over a low place at Fish Creek whips the minor surf up backwards, like the fringes of a horse's mane getting blown around, or creating large white patches of tiny bubbles that skim around on the surface of swells.

Today though, it hit us straight on. The storm had turned direction in the night and disturbed my sleep. The morning's super-high tide brought swift, gigantic rollers straight at us, the house creaking with the really big gusts, and sustained winds of around fifty. Big waves hit our low bank, shooting spray three stories into the air. Tiny shreds of seaweed stuck to the windows, with salt glazing the glass.

I couldn't concentrate well and felt slightly trembly most of the day. Sometimes I utilized the dzogchen method of looking directly at the fear, finding nothing there. It worked a bit. The same practice had worked beautifully with some arising anger a week ago, really collapsing the whole balloon of hot air. Today a bit different. By early afternoon I was exhausted! I tried napping at lunch break, but no, and then almost fell asleep many times later on. In the afternoon I tried a homeopathic, Rescue Remedy, and the fear really dissolved, but by then I had been holding onto the morning's fear, like gripping bicycle handle bars so tightly that when you let go, the fingers take awhile to loosen up and go straight again. So I was still worn out. Now, the storm continues on the Salish Sea outside this window, but much abated. I should sleep well tonight.

Christmas is coming. I've invited Rinpoche and family for a short stay. They gave me a Kindle as an early Christmas gift. Interesting and certainly lovely. I've made a list of a dozen dharma books that I may want to download, including biographies of lamas and yogis. It will be good for nighttime reading.

DECEMBER 20 – DREAM

A sudden disc came spinning in, like a weapon, and arrived, BAM!— half-Aztec calendar and half-sun god, colorful, radiating with razor-sharp sun rays, with the adamant message: STOP! ... which was written on the face and spoken to me as a sharp directive. I woke up immediately, middle of the night, and asked, "Stop what?!" I could only think that I've been allowing some of my discipline of retreat to weaken. And why Aztec? It's the Mayan calendar that's been spoken of, the famous last day of the aeon, the predicted end of world. That's tomorrow.

DECEMBER 23 – JOURNAL

The visit with Rinpoche and family was great. Rinpoche and I were able to have two consultations, quite wonderful ones. If I had had doubts, now I feel confirmed in my progress and practice, and inspired by his confidence in me, by our talks, and the general blessing of being with him. When they left I felt satisfied, not sad at their leaving and the loss of visitors, but at ease and contented.

DECEMBER 26 – JOURNAL

Christmas was fine alone. I had treats to eat and drink. I listened to sacred music on the radio, sang and danced along with Handel's *Messiah*. I spoke to family on the phone. So I took care of myself and enjoyed things as they were. All of this, the contentment, felt like huge progress.

DECEMBER 28 – EARTHQUAKE

Close by here, a 4.0 earthquake around 10 pm. This is the second quake on retreat, the first one while in Raymond.

JANUARY 13, 2013 – JOURNAL

On a forest walk, sky darkening at end of day, I turned back from a brushy trail near the water's edge, heading the mile or so back to home. I often walked in these woods, avoiding people where I could to maintain retreat boundaries. Risking contact seemed worthwhile to get into the quiet cathedral space of the tall trees, finding mossy embankments, or rounded rocks to perch on for meditation. Very few people roamed around this small mountain during the winter months anyway. Dusk, and the quiet that I'd found on that walk, continued back on the main trail, mantra practice following along.

Suddenly a noise of someone running toward me from behind. I startle, afraid, turn my head to see it's only a jogger, no problem. A tall, lanky, scientist-looking guy approaches, then passes. I let out a big sigh of relief, heart pounding. After a moment, my heart starts to squeeze—in a big way, and feelings of pressure on my left side of chest, back, and shoulder. I don't panic, but think: I have to keep walking to make it through the woods, over half a mile now to the road. If I collapse out there, someone might find me; if in here, I spend the night, in January, lying on the trail. Sensations continue for ten or fifteen minutes and then subside. The fellow jogs toward me, now going the other way. I wonder, should I ask him to walk me to the road? I don't, and keep going with intent. I make it home. I write a note that I put on the floor near the front door. It says: If you find I've died, please don't try to resuscitate.

I wish to complete the afternoon's practice session, but after a short time decide that's stupid. I look online at heart-attack symptoms, then call my brother, a surgical nurse who's had heart surgery. He's emphatic, saying, immediately hang up and call 911, so I do. From that moment I begin feeling afraid, then jittery, swept into a stream called "the medical establishment," beyond my control.

The EMTs come almost immediately, many of them now occupying the sacred retreat space here. One of them announces he's the county sheriff who lives in the neighborhood, and also an EMT. I'm suddenly ultra-conscious of the thangkas hanging on the walls, some wrathful, some naked, wondering if they're wondering. Yes, the EMTs and the deities both. An ambulance has pulled up.

All are wonderful and reassuring, but from that moment I feel like a butterfly caught in a net, and then by the time I'm in the ER with an IV stuck in my arm, the butterfly is now pinned onto the display board.

The hospital is so new for the island, I'm the seventy-fourth patient to receive treatment. They do all the tests, electrocardiogram, and blood test, and the results are perfect. The emergency room doc says it isn't serious at this time, but the combination of symptoms plus family heart history means I should follow up with seriousness. I take a cab home, considering the upcoming disturbance to practice.

JANUARY 17 – JOURNAL

In the clouds several days ago I saw a phurba, a three-sided ritual dagger, and yesterday a three-sided arrowhead. More ritual weapons arriving.

Today I went walking to the high lighthouse bluff. Gazing out to the southeast in meditation, absorbing the intense blue waters and bluish sky, then both became overlaid with a golden, undulating light. I've seen this many times before, but today it was persistent.

Sitting there on a split-rail fence at the cliff's edge, counting mantras on my little modern thumb-counter, a man walks toward me. I get up and with a flourish invite him to pass by on the narrow trail between fence and precipice. But it turns out he was making a beeline for *me*.

He said, "Are you meditating?" I said yes. He said, "Oh! It's such a beautiful place." I nodded. He said, "How do you meditate?" I drew my fingers over my mouth and said, "I don't talk." He said, "Oh, I've disturbed your meditation. But I really want to know how to meditate." I nodded and peered at his name tag. I saw it said Latter Day Saints, and also noticed that he looked kind of goofy, the face of a carnival clown, long and narrow with big lips and an over-eager way of speaking. He continued, "Do you think things when you meditate?" I nodded slowly. He thought and then said, "They say we Mormons don't meditate enough when we do our sacred prayers. So I want to learn how." I continued smiling and nodding.

Then he said, "Is it like you see two burning bushes, and then you feel amazed and get down on your knees to pray and then you go pick blueberries, or something?" I'd been nodding in amusement and then laughed when he said blueberries.

He started to go, giving me his calling card (Elder McIver), saying, "Well, when you're talking again, give me a call and tell me how to meditate." I received his card and bowed slightly. He went back from whence he came. Feeling happy, I returned to my seat on the fence, and the blue sea and sky, and my non-thinking thoughts.

Later I was struck by his mention of burning bushes, for me an inadvertent reference to my wrathful deity practice. But perhaps even more, his melding of the sacred and profane was almost a teaching right out of the Vajrayana playbook: to note mystical experiences, but not to grasp onto them nor get too excited; instead to integrate the sacred into ordinary life with an understated attitude (go pick blueberries). I felt I'd been visited by a *daka*, a male dakini, in the form of a Mormon carny. Life is wondrous.

Tonight a connection came to mind between the sadhana's wrathful Tibetan deity and Worf, the fearless Star Trek warrior. I recalled his battle cry, "It's a good day to die!" As amusing as it sounds to gain inspiration from a tv character, we use what we have at hand. It blew huge energy into the deity visualization, including love and compassion, fearlessness and nobility. The deity came more alive, and it took my breath away, accompanied by some tears.

I also added in an element I'd been recently neglecting: the fire that's ever-present for this deity. Once I put that back in the visualization, the practice ignited!

JANUARY 23 – JOURNAL

Becoming enlightened isn't about staying boxed up in a predefined set of outer and inner behaviors. It's about precisely breaking out of *all* boxes. As a Westerner on this ancient Eastern path, how do I claim my own authority and authenticity—without waiting for the final goal, enlightenment? After all, this is sometimes called the "path of fruition." With that in mind, it's vital to come from where we authentically are, rather than as a prim, goody-two-shoes version of what we imagine is permissible.

I've just spent years somewhat boxed into the role of lama's assistant—and fundraiser, sangha organizer, liaison for Rinpoche, et cetera. Requirements: being diplomatic, politic, and gracious. A year or so before retreat I began reforming my sense of self and how I expressed in the world with a new relaxation of formality, more authenticity, and humor. It was freeing, and people noticed. Now I see another level. It wants to go outside the box. It's looking for one's own authority, permission given by self—to express self, express the dharma, in the Western context, for home—the home of one's own culture and community, and home of one's heart-mind.

This has been brewing for some time. I've wanted to ask a few of my western women friends who are simultaneously Buddhist and self-promoted shamans and healers: How did you gain your authority? This was a topic with Barbara in our talk two days ago, and she was also interested to know their responses. We've both been plagued with the goody-two-shoes thing all our lives, with its inherent prison. Permission. Do you need it? Why, even as older women, do we need to seek it from outside ourselves?

The Tibetan Buddhist translation of "outside the box" is crazy wisdom, shown to the world by the proverbial crazy wisdom master. Traditional Tibetan teaching stories abound, and a handful of well-known lamas who came to teach in the west have taken this route. The model could be male or female, the latter sometimes known as a dakini, sky dancer. But there is a prerequisite for this path: Enlightenment. Without the vast compassion of awakening, a charlatan could do much harm, never able to bring the benefit of awakening to those on the receiving end of some cooked-up crazy wisdom.

What is the point and the benefit? By witnessing something so outside of the box we might have our concepts blown out of the way, clearing our vision—in order to see the inherent nature of things as they are, to expand our consciousness and compassion, and ultimately, to become enlightened ourselves—ultimate freedom.

This search for freedom is not only Eastern. I grew up with a stepfather who kept on the wall of his workshop a humorous watercolor print. It's of a middle-aged man, naked, seen from the back, running along a sandy beach, with arms joyfully upraised, entitled "Free At Last!"

Even though Bill has been long out of this temporal world, the print still hangs on the workshop wall, as a reminder of his joie de vivre, and for me, his life's inner work. After a difficult upbringing in Depression-era Seattle, later serving as a member of the ski troops during WW II, then having a failed marriage, in the early 1960s Bill dove into psychotherapy. He happened upon one of the first human potential movement therapies, embracing zest for life, inherent goodness, aware presence, clarity and insight, loving kindness, and inner freedom.

It was in this community that he and my mother met. Our two families then joined, Bill became a central influence in my life, along with the credo he, and my mother, tried to live by. His energy was filled with exuberance and positivity. He was an encourager of us young ones, inspiring our minds and hearts to fulfill our potential, encouraging us to help the world however possible, and to find our own happiness and inner freedom.

JANUARY 27, ONE YEAR AND THREE MONTHS INTO RETREAT — POEM

What Did I Do on Retreat?

I watched the earth turn.

I watched the cycles of sunrise and sunset,
the pre-dawn lightening of grey to subtle colors, then ungreying,
the gathering dusk bringing quiet anticipation
of pink clouds and achingly saturated hues.

I watched the intensifying midnight blue,
Vajrakilaya's anthem, before the dark black of night.

I watched Jupiter's rise as the Evening Star,
tiny spot of light flanked by suggestions of moons,
every day a little higher in the sky when sun's blaze had faded.

I watched earth's single moon, its broad, brilliant face, virtually
                                        whiz through the sky,
        from one elongated meditation moment to the next.
    Moon—holding its memories of full moons and crescent moons
                                and blue moons of all my life.

I watched Orion's starry points lie down and get up, again and again,
as he traveled through the dark velvet of winter sky.

I watched the clouds move on the wind, going north all day,
                going south the next.
    The clouds, endlessly laying out images, designs, textures, messages,
                                                        signs,
        delighting my mind, or surprising, or mystifying, sometimes knowing.

I watched the tide rise and fall, covering, revealing.
                Coming in, the sea a river relentlessly filling up.
Where is it all going?

Then going out, emptying into the unfathomable ocean,
cycling on the moon.
I watched the seagulls, eagles, geese, ducks, oyster catchers,
                              great blue herons, cormorants—
live their lives as sky dancers, lovers, fighters, hunters.
           Coming, going. Going, coming.
The seagulls with seagull habits. Eagles with eagle habits.
I watched the grass say, "Green!" so loudly,
           I stopped to stare, replying, "Oh! *Green*, I get it!"

FEBRUARY 2 – JOURNAL

Orca sighting again. How glorious. I'd been turning over images of Queen Elizabeth and Prince Charles—unlikely, but like in a dream, who knows what will arise—wondering what the wisdom of the queen would look like now that she's at the end of her long reign—this in the middle of morning practice (!). And that's when the orcas showed themselves. Naturally I was struck by their majesty, which normally hits me anytime they appear. The ease with which they glide through the water, their great mass on this glide—the combination pointing to their power and the perfection of their design. For my human mind this is Beauty and Awe. And this morning I was also intrigued by the synchronicity of my musings on royalty and the orcas' appearance.

There seemed to have been four. One leading, plus a male with two females at his side, looking like a classic formation. They were going south through the pass into the Straits of Juan de Fuca. I heard that the local orcas have made a truce with the seals and leave them be. It's thought it's because there's enough salmon, but who knows? Seals nowhere to be seen this morning.

FEBRUARY 8 – JOURNAL

I was overcome today with a deep gratitude for everything that went into making my outer life what it is, and all the people responsible; not only my life, but for everyone similarly affected. Completely commonplace aspects of life came to mind. This was not in the realm of inspiring teachers, or kind neighbors, or philosophers. I found I wanted to write thank-you letters—to the departments of electricity, and clean water, and highways; to plumbers, washing machine makers, telephone workmen, and farmers; to all the inventors and engineers, down to the maintenance crews—for the last couple hundred years. It was just a fantasy, because who would you write to? It would be like writing to Santa Claus.

FEBRUARY 15 – JOURNAL

Losar, Tibetan New Year, passed four days ago. The world is still in one piece, and I'm happy to see it. That's what I told Rinpoche the next day, following up on a prophecy among Tibetans and others of a world cataclysm around this time. He laughed and said, "Yes, but it's really out of balance." My reply, "But it's always been out of balance." Now I have to follow through with my recent pledge to myself which is this: If the world survives to this Losar, then I am never again going to get sidetracked by earth-ending rumors or prognostications of civilization collapsing. Of course, it could and will happen one day, perhaps eons from now, but live with it!

My feeling-tone report is that I've felt quite stable and happy most of the time.

Rinpoche and I started working on a translation of a second buddhist text over Skype. As always, satisfying work.

I'm soon to be moving back to Oregon, and will be going into a different cabin, further into the woods. The cabin needs a kitchen, so friends Brent and Bruce, highly skilled in building, said yes to putting that together. They've been procuring items: propane cook-top, fridge, sink, counter, cupboard, and on-demand hot-water heater—some used, some new. They'll show up in Williams for the installation the day after I arrive, and I'm planning to cook for everyone. A big adventure coming for all of us.

FEBRUARY 22 – JOURNAL

That "upcoming disturbance to practice" originating from the heart incident happened yesterday—all the way to Seattle to see a cardiologist. It was a good trip, very full. Friends drove me both ways; there were visits with family, and, as long as I was there, a dentist appointment.

The cardiologist said that what I had experienced had, indeed, come from my heart, but not serious, more of a spasm. It may have been a variation of Takotsubo cardiomyopathy, or "broken-heart syndrome," mostly experienced by older women. If short-lived, no damage. There are many triggers, including a sudden surprise, like the jogger. I thought, wow, I'm still holding onto "stuff," with more work to be done. Or, my body is lagging behind my emotional recovery.

FEBRUARY 26 – JOURNAL

Last night, after a long phone conversation with SH, I was mid-practice. It was the full moon. I had turned off all the house lights, feeling the effects of the moonlight streaming in, the reflection on water, the lights of the altar which were beautiful and plentiful because it was a buddhist festival day. Then thoughts started creeping in of how fortunate I was that I hadn't taken my own life (although I never actually considered it), starting two years before retreat when our marriage had begun to dissolve. I felt very sad, sitting there in the moonlight, about how much I had suffered. Then it was as if the clarity of the moon was telling me that what had opened this sadness up was a long phone conversation, hearing SH's happy family distinctly in the background for the length of the call—and that I wasn't ready for this. How unwise to have let that go on and on, a kind of ignorance. Now my wisdom was telling me.

Then today, I thought, I need to share this with SH, so it doesn't get repeated. But how to tell him without upsetting him? I sent an email, written kindly, without blame or emotion. However, he did take it personally, and so when we got on the phone again, his reaction triggered my tears. We spoke for an hour, sometimes both of us heated, him lecturing, me yelling. But somehow, in the end, it was good.

By the time we hung up, my dam of tears had broken, and there was no shoring it up. So I took the heavy catharsis onto my cushion in front of the altar with its array of allies. And suddenly I realized I needed to begin the process of finally forgiving SH for having chosen someone else. I got out my Ngöndro text, turning to the offering practice, and there I was again, offering all my forgiveness, as I had done several years before. And going further, offering all my love without attachment. It was a big step to come to. When I was finished, I opened my email to find that he had written me a kind and beautiful, heartfelt letter.

FEBRUARY 27 – DREAM

I dreamed I found an abandoned bike on the street in a neighborhood of Seattle. I was with my family of long ago, my mom and stepdad, first husband Skip, and our kids. The bike, which was unworkable because of gunk in the chains and spokes and brakes, just needed a thorough cleaning, so I decided to do that right then and there. When I finished, one could see it was sturdy and basic, a three-speed, one you could take anywhere. It was moss-green, old-fashioned, not a racing or mountain bike—almost antique. However, it was way too big for me, the seat coming up to my chest. Funny that not I nor any of us had noticed this before!

I decided to take it to a place a few blocks away where it could be sold. But then I realized it still needed more repairs of a technical nature, so I decided to give it away. We all walked over to a coffee stand nearby where you could leave free stuff. When we arrived to find there wasn't anything else there of value, we knew the bike would be a real treasure for someone. I put a sign on it, "Free," and left it there with the coffee-stand guys.

The dream seems to reflect the work I've been doing on the stuff of the psyche: With one's family (allies) as support, doing one's best, cleaning it up, seeing it as sturdy and ancient, but finding it doesn't actually fit anymore, and besides, still needing more deep adjustments. Then easily and happily giving it all away, giving it up. Ah, freedom!

CHAPTER SIX
Williams, Oregon, II

> The map is not the territory.
> *–Alan Watts*

These transitions came with flurries of activity, arrangements, social inter-actions, and travel—stimulation of all sorts. I am by nature happily social, and normally had unlimited capacity for all the above. But now having taken the hermit training of retreat, it was a different "me" out in the world—ultra-sensitive and heart-open, absorbing it all as wondrous and welcome, and also as onslaught.

For example, while zipping past a person walking by the side of the road, from inside the car window I would look deeply for an instant into their face, and maybe exclaim aloud, "There goes a human!" sending loving energy as if they were my long-lost cousin—which ultimately they were... are. I knew how it would seem, the amusement caused, for whoever was driving me. They must at times have felt they were caretakers for someone on a psychedelic trip. My driver and I might then laugh. But my experience was always genuine, not made for entertainment.

The aftermath of shifting places was exhaustion.

MARCH 15, 2013 – JOURNAL

Oh my gosh, three weeks have passed since I wrote last. While still at Cattle Point, Rinpoche and I finished the text translation via Skype; over three days I packed up and cleaned up; and my folks returned home from their winter travels. My Bainbridge friend, Diane B., drove up to get me for the 550-mile trek from that northern Washington island to these southern Oregon mountains. On the way we picked up her husband, Keith, for the remainder of the trip south. After the long drive down I-5, we spent the night in Grants Pass. The next morning included a provisioning stop, and soon we were making our way, once again, up the gravel road of Lama Jamie's retreat land. Diane and Keith stayed to help for more than an hour. While Keith chopped wood for my cabin—a lot of it!—Diane and I arranged furniture. On their way out, Keith, like a brother to me, said in a serious tone while talking to Lama Jamie, "Now take good care of Diane." Such generous friends, they still had a long journey back to Bainbridge.

The next day Bruce and Brent drove down from Raymond with a kitchen. I had been prepping an empty neighboring cabin—the rooms where they would lay their heads at night, and the kitchen where we would be eating and I cooking for their stay. By the time they arrived I was deeply exhausted, but more to come.

Brent's specialty was carpentry, and Bruce's, electricity, plumbing and appliances. They had an easy way with each other, problem solving everything beautifully, including spontaneously deciding to shift the project's location from front porch to indoors—a welcome modification! They worked for two solid days while I cooked in the other cabin, and puttered around setting up my altar. We thoroughly enjoyed our talks over lunch and dinner. By the end, I was totally wasted, energy sucked out.

They left early morning yesterday, and from then until midday today, I was not only exhausted, but depressed, feeling abandoned (I know, irrational), and so far away.

It took two things to rebalance. The first was re-entering the practice, the familiarity with which provided grounding. And more than familiarity, it was returning to the home of my core self and my purpose. The second was taking a long walk during afternoon practice. It was a sunny day and I was headed through forest that surrounds this cabin to a now-familiar place, the large meadow with its all-important view for meditation.

But here is what's been coming lately—a sense of having lost track of the thread of "Who am I?" Suddenly in a moment of quiet, the question came again—with no answer—in the midst of exhaustion and the whirlwind of ten days (essentially out of retreat, traveling, shopping, hosting, being hosted, socializing). When I think about "life before onslaught" it feels like two months ago, not two weeks—and in all that activity, which is simultaneously familiar, I lost myself. Coming back into practice, even though not in top form at this point, is coming home to myself. And it seems it is the loss of that which causes this total exhaustion.

I wonder if this depletion is also, on some level of psyche, because my current purpose, three-year retreat, comes with a *samaya*, a kind of Buddhist oath.

And so, breaking retreat to shift places (with all the inevitable activity) might be a breakage of this samaya, causing a loss of impetus. And further, because of the involvement of "the unconscious elements or forces... 'the spiritual agencies' " (Carl Jung's term) in such an oath, this breakage seems to cause a breakdown of energy. It feels it could cause real illness if continued. But here I am, again refueled and feeling fine.

Another thought: The physical activities of being out in the world are so different—sitting for long spells in a normal chair with legs hanging down, facial muscles smiling and interacting—even these turn out to be tiring.

Now onward. I'm about to finish the wrathful yidam practice in a few days.

MARCH 17 – JOURNAL

Rinpoche and I made a detailed completion plan for the yidam practice, and all going well.

Recently one morning while bringing forth the visualization, I was inspired to connect with the scorpions who I assume are living beneath this cabin. While invoking their energy and protection, I thought of their connection with Guru Rinpoche in subduing negativities. Instantly Guru Rinpoche rose up from beneath, not as a vision, but as a clear, spontaneous visualization, however in this case not of my own making.

He appeared as transparent, without color, as energy, but with all his features. As he was rising up, this merged with myself so that I experienced the upward movement, and also expansion into a huge space. I was also of clear space. As Guru Rinpoche/I rose up, it morphed into the wrathful yidam deity and self, with similar light and expansiveness. It was quite beautiful, and tears came. Then practice was very good.

> *A vision: a spontaneous appearance through the sense perceptor of the eyes, appearing as "real" within our three dimensions of the world and physical "reality." At the same time, the perceiver is not under a delusion that what one is beholding actually exists on the material plane. In this sense it's not the same as a hallucination or an apparition.*
>
> *A visualization, in the imaginal department, can be willfully constructed, and is perceived in the mind's eye. Through practice, it may be extremely detailed, accurate, and clear—like recalling in detail a favorite painting, and then learning to hold it in the mind, to merge with and manipulate it, and to fill it with light. This type is developed in normal deity practice.*

Another kind of visualization, such as the one that arose on this day, happens spontaneously, not constructed or directed. In these ways it is like a vision, but the quality is imaginal, "seeing" it in the mind's eye. It could be three-dimensional, but more like a light-filled animation. Different from a vision since an actual vision is appearing as if outside one's mind, in physical space. One might wish for more terms to distinguish these appearances.

There's this sense when in the middle of—and after—a spontaneous appearance, whether visionary or visualized, since consciousness is embedded in all the particles of space, that it makes supreme sense, that the object of appearance has an undeniable veracity. For those holding the scientific materialist viewpoint, "consciousness embedded in all the particles of space" is still debatable, although I hear the quantum physicists are looking into it.

MARCH 20 – JOURNAL

I woke up this morning with a toothache. It's been worsening through the day, now to the point that feels beyond a temporary affliction. Darn.

Today is momentous because I reached a million yidam mantras.

Also, I've been experiencing a lot of anxiety. The toothache isn't helping, but isn't the cause either. So I spoke to Rinpoche this evening who had good advice, only half of which I retained. He said to do Ngöndro as a home base. That was when I started crying, because of the word "home." I feel again so far from home, vulnerable. So, he said to try doing Ngöndro exactly *because* it's so familiar, a kind of practice home. Also, to read dzogchen texts—to bring my mind around to the ultimate.

MARCH 23 – JOURNAL

Much happened in three days. Two days ago Lama Jamie drove me to his dentist in Grants Pass. He was kind about the inconvenience and we had a pleasant time. The upshot: an abscess above a tooth with an already-existing root canal. Good news: tooth is in good shape so they can save it. Bad news: expense way beyond my budget or savings to redo the root canal. Good news: the dentist seems great and he has confidence in the root-canal specialist. Bad news: have to wait for weeks to have the work done. Good news: antibiotics against the infection.

So, the tooth was extremely painful—a cartoon classic—and interfered with sleep. The meds and painkillers made me woozy for a couple of days.

All this was the setting for the yidam completion rituals, which had to begin on a specified day, and the time: nauseatingly early in the morning. My alarm went off at 3:30 am, my tooth hurting so much it seemed better to just get up immediately. A triad to surmount: Toothache, in combination with feeling sickly from the infection, and the pervasive anxiety that tightened my stomach. But I went ahead and accomplished the rituals, afterwards wandering back into bed by 8, and gratefully sleeping until 10. Then got up and did Riwo Sangchöd practice.

Still the anxiety remained, this unreasonable paradigm sense in search of a lightning strike of grace. It did finally come today. Mostly sleepless last night, waking every so often for a variety of reasons—the extreme cold in the cabin, or so it seemed, and for awhile because I thought I was going to throw up.

Woke at 9. So cold, the pipes froze and there wasn't any water. I thought, oh wow, then, I need to eat something so I can take my medicine. Looked in the fridge and the door fell off! Again, throughout, anxiety is plying its way around my psyche. I then have diarrhea in the twenty-five-degree outhouse, but feel better. I look around to see if Lama Jamie is working on the water pipes. Nope, so I call him and by phone he walks me through checking different spigots. We figure out which pipes froze and which not. Then my morning finally gets going. More anxiety. For three post-completion days my practice is supposed to be extra-relaxed, so that's good.

I open some packages that Lama Jamie had dropped off for me earlier at the outhouse. First is from Mom. A beautiful heartfelt letter in the old-fashioned way of writing. She sent new leggings and wonderful copies of her art.

Later still, I opened a huge box from Diane and Keith. So many thoughtful household gifts, including a clothes drying rack. Also, a wonderful card in which she writes magic words: "If you need anything let us know. We are right there!" I cried. Then later decided to use that as a starting point for a formal, self-therapy session for twenty minutes. It was great.

After, I did Ngöndro in a long, thorough, loving way, for two hours. Showered. After all of the above, anxiety gone. Gone! Hope it lasts, but I think so. Some grace of transformation came through.

Nearing the end of this hand-written journal, it now feels physically heavy, as if each word has added something tangible. So significant the phases—if not the writing. It's been with me through so much change, to many different homes, from secular life into (mostly) renunciate life, and conversion from extroversion to introversion.

A different, larger notebook became the retreat advice container. That is a precious book. This also is precious, in a different way, as soul's path; as a continuation of journaling throughout my life; of value to none, but a conversation with self along the way; this feminine need to converse and to share, to explore via words and expression. I don't know why. Maybe no one knows why, but there it is.

Oh, after the anxiety lifted, a wonderful, well-connected, after-dinner practice. At 9 pm, remembering the international day of switching off lights had already begun, I did so too, leaving on just the altar's xmas lights and one candle. Then, beautiful, deep practice. Happy.

MARCH 29 – JOURNAL

Just a few more pages, perhaps I should have left the journal ended with the word "Happy."

Here I am, lying in bed with covers off, because the cabin is warm—by a truly beautiful fire, seen through the glass window—soft, undulating, licking, dancing flames. The whole box is full of fire, in a slow way, because damped down.

Today was warm in the sun. So many gnats in the woods, impossible to sit still there. I took a cushion to the big meadow and meditated for an hour. Lovely. A few meadow gnats, too, but okay. Gnat season must be right when it warms up.

A robin became obsessed with pecking at the windows all day, on three sides of the cabin. All day until dusk.

I'm feeling better. Still sometimes a little anxiety, but basically quite fine.

Tomorrow I'll meet with the other three-year retreater, Josh, and his Nepali wife, Susmita, about helping me split firewood.

Right now life seems simple. That's good.

APRIL 3 – ESSAY

Tree of Life

Starting a new journal leads one to reflect on time, the passing of stories, the present moment, and the mystery of what is to come.

At the moment, holding this book in my hands, a treasure even empty, because the symbol on its cover is a Tree of Life. This one, while detailed, is actually quite simple. Like the trees outside my cabin windows, it's natural without added ornamentation. Branches on a trunk, with many leaves, radiant with flowers. Healthy, proclaiming existence, drawing energy down from the heavens to the earth, standing guard, witnessing.

I find myself in a place called Williams, a corner in the Siskiyou Mountains, at 1800 feet. This cabin is on the edge of three hundred acres of private land devoted to Buddhist practice. Not many of us here at the moment, so it's quiet, as retreat is meant to be.

Sometimes, though, such solitude is the thing you wish you hadn't wished for. But the trees here are a resolute presence filling in the empty gaps. In the deep quietude of meditation, somehow they embody the pregnancy of the moment. Without movement, and yet, pure presence—the magnificent big ones, the young saplings, and the spaces between them—this energy, whether it's imputed or actual, not sure. But it's reassuring; it's company. Or, part company and part context.

When I get very quiet here in the trees, it's as if the trees' breath supports my own breath, and the connection supports a deeper level of meditation. Even at this moment while writing, I'm sitting indoors in a comfortable chair, looking out the long door window, and observing how it is. So, it works even from this vantage point.

What is the pregnancy of the moment? It's the potential for something. A sense, subtle, that things could be otherwise. At the Salish Sea the environment there is always in motion. Even on days when the wind isn't blowing the trees and inspiring the gulls and eagles to sail, to kite around in the sky, the sea is always moving. The current going one way or the other in a gigantic mass of exodus or invasion. That movement inspires a certain kind of meditation, where one finds stillness while riding this motion, riding on the top of it, within it, sometimes in spite of it.

But here, the environment itself is usually still. The trees in position, maintaining their stances. And in that I can somehow sense movement, or the potential for movement. This supports a different kind of experience, experimenting and exploring various depths of my own stillness. Perhaps it's my own pregnancy—which is emptiness after all, and the potential for anything to arise.

APRIL 3 – JOURNAL

Sometimes it seems that the anxiety from being remote and on my own, in solitude, doesn't come from the present circumstance. Everything is fine. The cabin is lovely; there's enough to eat; there are people I can call. Instead, it seems to be the feeling that I'm in so far, into the middle of this ocean. I look back in time and it's been a year and a half since I began retreat. It sounds like a short time, but it feels like several years have passed—in slow, painstaking periods. There's no way I can return to that shore from which I embarked, nor would I want to. In any case it's not an option.

Then I look ahead. Only ocean, unfathomably vast in every direction. I seem to know "the" direction, the same course that I set out on. I know there's a shore there, somewhere. And now I know how it feels to be on my way. Long, slow, ups and downs, changing weather, with little changes of scenery. At this point I'm in the middle section. If I were to take zero days off, there would be another two years ahead of me. The prospect of solitude for such a stretch, or sometimes even for another day, sets off this anxiety. And yet, when the present moment is revealed to my mind-heart, then there is no problem.

Ani Seltong, friend and ordained nun highly experienced in retreat, suggested "one day at a time." Or one week. Can I do the next week? Yes, I can. It seems by playing tricks with my mind, I can persevere. One hundred and four more weeks. This is not the optimal attitude! But at the moment needing tricks to pass through this queasy, bumpy spot. No blame.

APRIL 7 – CONSULTATION WITH RINPOCHE

Without my having mentioned anything about the ocean imagery, Rinpoche surprised me by saying this:

> This particular period with feelings of anxiety could be like being in the middle of the ocean. You've been crossing to the other side without being aware of your progress. The ocean is so big, and unconsciously you've been forgetting where you are, and it's in this boat. Just now you've woken up to being in the middle of this huge ocean, and suddenly you're wondering, am I moving? Am I getting anywhere? But yes, you are moving ahead, in the right direction. You don't have to be scared of any storms and big waves. They're all just passing by, passing by.

He also had this advice:

> The great yogis say, if no problems come up, then practitioners won't develop the *skillful means*. Otherwise it's just reading in a book. You think you know all about it, like a person who has just gotten a degree in something like architecture. They think they know, but until they start applying it in the real world, they don't have the real knowledge. This is the same. You now get to apply the teachings. That is how to accomplish this great exercise.

When the feelings build up, let it go. The idea is not to hold onto them. But do it without hitting your head against the wall. Don't investigate, obsessing and thinking too much, which is a kind of fabrication.

There's a gap that I've noticed is strong for Westerners, between spiritual life and daily life. Westerners easily feel one or the other completely. They can give themselves over to one or the other, for example, having a really profound spiritual experience. And then when in daily life, throw themselves into that without any spiritual perspective. But there's no unification. So, even when one is in a spiritual state, remember this is a part of samsara.

In Tibet we have an idiom that's based on the idea that whatever you're missing isn't necessarily good or bad. The idiom goes like this: Even the hell beings, when they're liberated they'll long for the old times, they'll miss their hell experience. If you long for samsaric life, it might be like that.

On the other hand, Westerners have some good attributes. For example, they're quite independent. This is special and makes one's actions and decisions genuine personal choices. There's no one else to blame if one has conflicting feelings about it. Whereas in Tibet people often do things simply because their lama suggests it, without hesitation.

APRIL 11 – JOURNAL

Rinpoche did a *mo* (divination) for me. This I requested because I've been feeling weak and poorly, my health and psyche. The mo showed that my health will be fine. A second mo for the retreat showed the results will keep getting better and better. This put my mind at ease, in a certain way.

Rinpoche said that he had done a mo before retreat that showed some difficulties in the beginning, but really good results. I don't remember this mo, a lifetime ago.

APRIL 14 – JOURNAL

I began the third sadhana today, the feminine of the triad. It's the elaborate liturgy, an old friend for years. My hope is that embarking on this phase with its more structured day will help my frame of mind. I've still been unsettled by external things, like appearances of large spiders running through the cabin, or the firewood stockpile dwindling. But I'm doing specific things to redirect my mind, and I can see it's improving.

At the same time, I'm happy to put on the skin of the Great Bliss Queen, the skin and her universe. Wonderful to put my head into the text, at my own pace, considering it deeply. In the old days of doing it as a group once a month, so many aspects slipped quickly by me, even some rather essential pieces. That was then, this is now. All good.

APRIL 17 – JOURNAL

What a rocky crossing. Yesterday I was so "me"—strong inner core, happy in a stable way. I truly felt I had myself back and there would be absolutely no problem with two more years of retreat. Then today came in, a big inner storm, huge seas—and I literally felt seasick, or call it morning sick, nauseated with that feeling on the top of your head where you think you really might toss it.

As soon as I finished the morning session it disappeared, although energy at noon break was low. With the afternoon session I was so exhausted, I sobbed deeply for a bit, then continued mantras while lying down on the bed, taking a short snooze. After that I moved practice outside in the sun and found improvement from both nap and nature. Wonderful evening practice. Clearly, the storm has passed... for now.

I remembered this same feeling of nauseating fear when I first went to junior high school at age twelve. Such a young innocent, among these big kids, many from different cultures who for me were intimidating, entering a world I didn't feel ready for. Every morning I felt ill, and sometimes threw up. My mother recognized it as fear, not illness, and kindly drove me to school every day, knowing I'd adjust. It was hard, but she was right, I did. She did a good thing for her daughter: In the face of fear, be resolute.

Through the treetops in the clouds today, I saw an upside down sun and moon, a tiglei, like at the top of the Tibetan letter *Hung*. It went zooming by in an otherwise clear blue sky.

I love this dakini, "a light body of brilliant radiance." While prepping the text for this, I had some feeling that the sadhana and its wording was too constricting for this vast and wild entity, too constrictive an approach to the Great She! Now that I'm doing the practice, there are truly beautiful sections which inspire.

Then by coincidence, Rinpoche said not to be too restrictive with visualizing her, but to think of her whole universe! I thanked him for saying that, recognizing it as an answer to my unasked, secret question. So, I can see my previous reaction to the text was my mind, the way my mind can be too small, a view with too much *self*-constraint.

It's the mantra accumulations, hours in the day, where my mind often shuts down. What to do? to stay focused on She, better yet, *embodying* she, during all the mantras? That's the conundrum. I want to stay with dancing, expressive, bliss queen, wild. Partly that requires raising my *chi*, expansiveness, at least into the normal range.

APRIL 19 – JOURNAL

Another rough patch today. So terribly depressed, I cried and cried, sobbing, all afternoon. Nothing really triggered it. Just that I felt incapable of continuing retreat, not at all, not anywhere. The futility of the situation had extended itself to any other life possibility in any place. The futility of samsara, I thought. I didn't feel quite anxious, just heavy and depressed. Even on a walk, I seemed to "see" every literal step I took as an echo—of both past and future—of my time in retreat, which felt endless. I did feel in prison (in spite of Rinpoche's previous admonition not to see it so), as if I couldn't leave because... to what life could I go? There's nothing for me without finishing retreat, but it's a torture to stay in.

So, after two or three hours of crying I contacted Rinpoche, who called back soon after, and we spoke for an hour. It was amazing, because he didn't say much that was new, but it helped very much. Three things stuck in my mind:

1) When I asked him, how much afflictive visitation is too much? his answer: To have such intensity come up in three-year retreat—this is normal. [*Normal?!*]

2) Don't be a victim of these feelings. Staying stuck there is allowing myself to be that. That's not who I am.

3) If it's actually better to leave retreat, it can't be decided while in the midst of intense feelings. Because it's a big decision, wisdom is needed. If, while wisdom is active and talking, the answer is to leave retreat, then it should be considered.

I really needed Rinpoche's help. Thank goodness for it.

APRIL 21 – JOURNAL

Spring came out with a big gush! It happened a few days ago. Suddenly on a slightly sunny and barely warmish afternoon, a whole field of crickets was chirping loudly, not your usual midsummer evening chorus, but an urgent rush of sound cracking through the air. Bees humming in the grasses and circling me on my walk. Songbirds showing up in the trees. Smells of springtime forest and meadow, opening up faint memory alleys of who knows when or where.

That was the meadow. The forest is slower, more of a walk to the warm season. Slower, or maybe just more reserved. Earlier the woods have had sheltered delicate wildflowers, two species of purple doodads, sprinkled anywhere you look. One is a star, the other, teeny closed umbrellas pointing down, ready for fairies. Also, a fuzzy-topped maroon thing with silky petals spiking out sideways and down halfway—reportedly an herb for relaxation. People scour the woods for them to sell.

Today, warm! Walking toward the meadow while still in the woods, I began hearing a low thrum, which intensified as I approached. The only thing I could think of was bees. At the meadow's edge, the sound was so loud, I thought, bee convention. I stopped, curious, but a little frightened to investigate. Maybe they wouldn't want an intruder. So I turned around and walked a different path to the bottom of the meadow. There was a wonderful patch of grass to sit upon, warm, even though in shade. I was there for a couple of hours in practice, and didn't want to leave when time to leave. Some deep inner space had thawed immeasurably, relaxed, exhaled.

APRIL 22 – JOURNAL

Today was the holding of tension—in the Jungian sense. Barbara and I spoke about it in our weekly talk. She said, it's not necessarily a negative, not at all. She experiences this as part of the creative process. Sometimes it's uncomfortable, or even as intense as a trapped animal trying in vain to get away from something. In my situation, I'm going deeply, processing new changes and levels, perhaps with something about to emerge, so of course, like birthing pains (ah, the morning sickness).

This sense of futility keeps surfacing. I've never wanted to embrace futility (or even renunciation), the buddhist idea that samsara is futile. Some say that we need to get to a point of accepting futility in order to move ahead on the path, but as a lifelong optimist, there seemed something inherently *wrong* with this tack. Lately though, futility seems increasingly true. For example, I feel detached in the few conversations that come up, which have lost their former meaning. This seems like the emergence of futility in samsara—or the emergence of *depression!* But maybe it is a sign of deeper change of another kind. And for this I can see the need for the experience of solitude.

Barbara brought up imagery of the ancient alchemists. There's one where the alchemist is sitting in a boiling caldron, with his assistant who, by his instruction, is adding more fuel to the fire. There's a white dove emerging from or landing on his head. She said, a holy spirit of God dove. I said, that sounds good—a dakini symbol, dancing, flying, light. I feel I've been in the stew pot and am ready for grace of dove.

She told me of an experience of depression she had once—which she recognized as creative tension—because life had interfered and there was no time to create art. So, she bought for herself a beautiful box to work on later when her creative life returned to normal. The promise of an art project, sitting there in the form of this box, helped her get through this period. Maybe something is in her idea for my situation, not a box, but what? Or, just be satisfied in the caldron.

APRIL 23 – JOURNAL

Last night, a bald eagle appeared in a dream, flying, visible through forest treetops.

Had a good day. The days usually, though not always, follow this pattern: Morning has some degree of anxiety which shows up in my torso. Then, working on it, and by sitting outside in practice, it dissolves. Afternoon and evening practices are good.

Today at end of practice, while sitting in the meadow, I finished mantras, dissolved the visualization and went right to meditation—a samadhi. Gazing up above the treetops into blue sky, I saw everywhere the tiny sparks of light. When I brought the gaze down, in the periphery of vision, the sparks were still happening in the blue sky. Then this morphed into golden pulsing light. The mind was serene and open, peaceful. Then I walked back to finish with daily tsok offering.

I read tonight Jigme Lingpa's advice for solitary retreat with Khyentse Rinpoche's commentary. Seems all beyond me, the level of renunciation required, for one thing. Ah well, here I am.

APRIL 24 – JOURNAL

Yesterday Rinpoche called to see how I was coming along. We talked about this sense of futility I've been experiencing and reflecting on. He said, even though one does see it in the texts, not everyone needs it. It's sutrayana, outer preliminaries, which has its place and purpose. To get stuck there though, in combination with a pervasive sadness or depression, is a kind of lost experience, a wandering. He said what we want is to find nature of mind. This is what will help the self, and particularly, others—through the heart of compassion, the whole point. Of course I agreed and have always agreed. What I forgot to say to him is that I'm not *trying* to cultivate this renunciation-futility of samsara thing, only thinking maybe it's a necessary phase since it's been coming up so much. At any rate, he basically urged me away from it. He also said maybe I'm getting clearer, so this "stuff" is more visible. He also reminded me of Guru Rinpoche's words about obstacles coming up when real progress is happening.

This evening, reading Longchenpa reminded me of something I'd said to Barbara in our last conversation: The way these feelings arose, stayed around, subsided, and arose again, felt capricious. That stopped her for a moment, and I said, yes, really it's like that, as if it's almost external to my sense of self, and yet, of course it is coming from "me." I had to look up the meaning to be sure: "Capricious: Sudden and unaccountable changes in mood." Yes, that was it.

Then here this evening, in Longchenpa's *Chöying Dzod*, saw this: "Within *awakened mind*... the way in which everything arises as dynamic energy and display is unpredictable." Yes, there it is. Maybe that's part of this, showing me how this works—it is like the weather; things arise in some kind of natural flow, on this great ocean. I saw that early on in retreat—the inner weather patterns. Certain displays you have to ride out. One hasn't control in the arisings themselves, it seems to be saying in this quote. But of course how you ride it out, release it, liberate it—or not—*that* you do have control over. I've been tested, and not sure I did well at all. But today was a really lovely, great day. That's all to say on that.

I've seen only one person all week—Josh, the other three-year retreater—when he came to split my wood. For about fifteen minutes we spoke about dharma books. A sweet and lovely person.

It feels actually good at this point, the solitude. Weird, huh!? But I've spoken with family via phone, so not completely away.

APRIL 26 – JOURNAL

> *Sometimes I go about pitying myself, and all the time I am being carried on great winds across the sky.*
> –Ojibwe saying, *Essential Crazy Wisdom* by Wes Nisker

Reading this, immediate sobbing came, for its familiarity, company, reassurance somehow.

Holding such opposites. Who can understand this? Well, someone did—when they thought of, said, and eventually wrote down that saying. On the one hand, a humble, wretched, contracted mess. On the other, arrived, liberated, fearless, expansive, connected, supported. In some ways simultaneous, or nearly so.

APRIL 27 – JOURNAL

I was first introduced to the existence of "lung problems" years before retreat through reading an article in the buddhist Snow Lion *newspaper. An interview with a western nun described it as a problem of too much wind (lung) in the subtle body system, according to Tibetan medicine, something that could be brought about by too much meditation. She went further, saying that while it famously sometimes afflicted buddhist practitioners of Tibet, it was a particular problem for modern-day Westerners. We tend to try too hard, with severe levels of expectation, pushing the meditation and mantras as if our lives depended on it, focusing on perfection and achieving the goal.*

The outcome of a lung *problem could range from temporary physical discomfort to serious psychological problems. I later heard that some people had to stop meditating for many years, or even permanently. I tucked the cautions into the back of my mind.*

What am I trying so hard to do? What is this little *lung* problem about? I want so dearly for this great effort, of myself and the many others who are helping me, to have been worthwhile. I want to follow the prescription as closely as I can. I want to be a good little camper, a little goody two-shoes. I want to express in signs and development, to get somewhere, to be happy and to have others be happy. The two little shoes are dancing and dancing. But not the dance of joy, like Shugsep Jetsun Chönyi Zangmo, but the dance of the demon, like the tale of the red shoes, in which the girl collapses from exhaustion.

Today began with a new ailment: dizziness, a kind of global dizziness, hard to define, but different from a visual dizzy spell, with ringing in the ear, an intermittent affliction of long ago. Once I went to a Tibetan doctor in Boudha, outside Kathmandu, for these spells. He said, "Too much meditation," even though I wasn't meditating much at that time. Maybe even then my pulses told of a tendency of too much *lung*.

This morning I first told myself to relax everything about how I was approaching the morning sadhana. That helped. Then walking the path on the way to the outhouse I watched my feet contact the earth and thought, oh good it is that the earth, this planet, is solid, or that our human minds perceive it as such, so we can be supported by this solidity. Because at that moment things didn't seem that solid to me, and I felt as if my feet could just as easily push through the surface of the earth, and keep on going.

Then I sat on the ground outside. When I looked upward, too dizzy. So I looked down, at the earth, the brown things, the leaves, twigs, dirt, forest detritus. I felt better. I gazed at this one enormous tree stump of revered, old-growth size, and I felt better. That said it all about solidity and stability, even if not permanence.

Toward the end of practice I felt much better. Clarity happened, a sudden focusing of an ordinary level of clarity. And no more dizziness.

Sometime in lunch break came a shaky, slightly anxious state, tremulous like a toy poodle. So I contacted Rinpoche. We talked for an hour. He gave advice for a practice especially for *lung* problems, something that could help over time. But he said, the problem really emanates from the mind, so I should work with that, the key. The exercise did help the shakiness dissolve quickly, but not the knot around my heart. What helped that was lying down reading after dinner for quite awhile. It's all gone now and all's well.

A wonderful scene unfolded this evening. My rest was interrupted by Lama Jamie, Sara, their young daughter and a friend, who suddenly appeared to clear some things off my porch. They were in wonderful, high spirits. I joined them outside, a lovely warm evening, and helped carry things to the truck. The kids were covered in mud from playing in the garden. It was so spontaneous, warm, caring, and happy. Sara lifted each kid back into the back of the pickup, and jumped in herself. They all called out to me as they drove away, "Bye Rigdzin!" like it was a hayride, like it had been the best day of their lives. A happy moment for me, too, able to connect at heart level, no futility anywhere to be seen. Nor poignancy either, just simple.

APRIL 28 – JOURNAL

I had a pretty good day today, smooth and even. I walked for an hour and a half before finally sitting in the meadow. I got hot and felt fatigued. But it was good, all echoes of kinks worked out.

I see that in the morning when I'm chanting the sadhana, I go too fast and don't really breathe well. Then I get tight around the heart chakra. So, this morning I tried slowing everything down. I wouldn't have discovered this but for Rinpoche's instructions yesterday.

Dzogchen reading is wonderful in evenings, along with meditation, with good effect.

MAY 8 – JOURNAL

Spirit came as planned to join in my retreat. She stayed two nights so we had one full day together. It was a tonic. I had her into my retreat space for all meals and we talked into the night. She looked and seemed wonderful, a great person to visit me on retreat, with all her years of retreat and practice experience, her positivity about life and Buddhadharma, and her supportiveness.

On our full day, we did Riwo Sangchöd in the morning. As we were just ended, she plunked down right where we'd been standing, and started to meditate, gazing out into the forest over the downhill slope, sky through trees. After putting away a few things, I joined her. It was potently expansive, peace, riding a wave of calm. Present, aware, stable. It seemed we both had a similar, beautiful experience.

Then we packed a lunch, things she had brought, and hiked up to the high point with small meadow and the really huge ponderosas, the temple of columns. From there I led her on a loop, over the stream and back to the Guru Rinpoche statue.

The weather started to change, a storm brewing, but I really wanted her to see the big meadow where I meditate most days. She loved it. We could hear the towering inferno of bees (I still don't know where they are), saw the wild yellow irises, the snow-covered small mountain behind, and the big sky. Again, meditation.

After awhile the storm increased—more wind and some rain, so we headed off to see the shrine room, and meditated there, too. Then hurried back home through the forest, now dancing with wind.

Once back, we settled into my "shrine room" area to talk. The sky turned dark, more from storm than from dusk, blusters of wind whipped up the foothills, and lightning flashed with its latent rumbles. We turned off the lights except for the colored lights on the altar and one flickering flame, and now hush, we enjoyed the show outside, the stormy twilight.

Spirit surprised me with many gifts, including a comfortable, outdoor chair that I'm sitting on at the moment. She brought lots of food, including salmon, already cooked, and lent me a Lakshmi statue.

She had brought to her previous retreat a two-foot-tall statue of Lakshmi, the Hindu goddess of abundance and increase, on the instruction of the Buddhist lama conducting that retreat. So she was temporarily known to everyone there as Lakshmi. When she got here, she set the statue up in her room along with other altar items. That's how I ended up with Spirit's other, smaller Lakshmi statue—she was suddenly inspired to give it to me. I hesitated to accept it many times, but finally suggested borrowing her, so that was the happy solution. Odd to have a Hindu goddess here, but maybe good to break out, if slightly.

Spirit left yesterday and I felt sad to be alone again. But today back on course. The stormy (outer) weather continues. Tomorrow solar eclipse.

MAY 14 – JOURNAL

A week since Spirit was here, and I'm doing so well, feel back to my old self, in my own skin, on the earth, arrived here. Several things worked up to this state of okay-ness. Definitely Spirit's visit set it into place. But before she came things were already improving. For one thing, the exercises Rinpoche gave me were working.

Then, there was a wonderful visit with someone named Vern who I met during the weekly practice in Lama Jamie's shrine room. He was here for a few days visiting a friend of his, Ani Nyima. The two of them invited me to join them for dinner one evening, and then he and I talked until quite late on a relaxed, warm evening in front of the Guru Rinpoche statue. He's been in semi-retreat for *nine* years, acting as retreat manager for a well-known lama's retreat center in Colorado.

Hearing the number nine – 9! – had a big impact on me. Here I was, struggling with the prospect of completing three and a half, and he was happy after nine... although working much of the time within that retreat container. He said his aspiration was actually to go into permanent retreat, in seclusion. Even though I don't share the same wish for permanent retreat, I was awe-struck with his wholeheartedness to go further in, and his apparent confidence about it. It stuck with me for months really, every time my internal seas got rough or bumpy, like a salve or a blessing.

We had so much to share about our common experience working with lamas for many years. We got down to some details about texts, too, because we're of the same lineage. Then, even though a bit late by that time, I said I had some specific retreat questions, and he encouraged me to go ahead. So we talked a long time further, way past dark.

Vern was definitely encouraging about my being able to complete retreat, in spite of the arisings. He said, Don't investigate or view your various states as a barometer of how it's going. That means whether it's depression, negativity, or discouragement, or on the other hand, feelings of connection with the practice, the deities... or successes, experiences, etc.... Just keep going. There was something about how he said this that I found particularly helpful. It's common to do this, he said, but his point was that it's not relevant. He noticed that people who can push through the hard periods are the ones who can finish and who will benefit, and said that I pretty clearly was one of these.

He was such a "real" person, not full of himself, easy to talk to. I wish he was coming again, but soon he'll be back in his Colorado retreat for another year.

MAY 14 – POEM

Prostration Pilgrimage

Laying my body out on the ground,
hands slide, knees kneel, arms stretch, forehead rests,
five points touching earth as witness,
headed ever east, soul's forward direction,
Buddha Dharma Sangha, finding safety under this three-jewel tree,
breathing in: dust motes of blue carpet,
breathing out: until all realize the nature of their mind.

Laying down a track from here to Dorje Den,
once in the present moment of retreat,
twice on a sweltering day near the Bodhi tree,
surrounded by sweaty prostrating monks and one pristine lady
meditating coolly in her tiny tent of screen,
five points saluting the sacred banyan, a shelter
anchored to the center of the earth.

Three times, within a nunnery on Samye Chimphu,
their celestial morning puja complete,
the temple, left empty, invited.
i hung back, finding a small corridor,
in spite of altitude, body flying the repeated homage,
buoyed by meeting the enlightenment of place,
discovered by perplexed Chinese tourists.

Sitting before the great Jokhang
among a quartet of old women, pilgrims with shaven heads,
raggedy but beaming, of buddhist warrior stock from east,
with few words but knowing smiles one offered me her board.
basking in self-arisen devotion and clear joy of onlookers,
and the glare of surveillance cameras,
i laid my body down, and down, and down.

Five bows, before the great Khyentse lama,
one thousand in a French tent, on a French mountain,
together in awe bowed down,
said, with bodies touching earth,
You are our witness,
O Same As Buddha, Enlightened One,
we honor you, offering body, speech, and mind.

Six joys, a vision, three men, laying their bodies down,
itinerant yogis in dark scarlet heading west to Lhasa,
in the road of a broad valley, jagged mountains encircling,
one *chak*, three long steps, and repeat.
witnessing from our fast passing jeep i
burst into tears of happiness,
first time in Tibet.

Seven surrenders, first session, a new Buddhist,
steeping deeply for weeks upon this gesture,
body and mind aching to begin but listening for proof,
never Catholic but an inexplicable longing to kneel.
here finally outer truth meeting inner truth,
this yoga of the three doors,
home.

MAY 18 – JOURNAL

I had heard scorpions were prolific in the mountains around Williams, and yes darn it, including Lama Jamie's land. I didn't want to see one, and yet I also did. One day recently Lama Jamie had advised me not to stack up the half-circles of fir bark that pop off during splitting as I'd been doing, calling the short towers "condos for scorpions." So, wearing leather gloves, I gingerly tossed each one into the woods.

Then yesterday it occurred to me that there were a few discarded boards lying near the porch, and perhaps I should move those to a better place, too. I turned one of the long 2x6's over. Indeed, two small scorpions were already under there, and they weren't too happy with this disturbance. One was brown and translucent. The other was black, the one I was closest to. Fascinated, I crouched down and watched. The brown one sidled away, under the cover of the forward one, who was guarding his turf, perhaps his very existence, in defensive posture. His pincers were up, and so was his famous poisonous tail. He stayed thus for quite awhile until I moved away, and then slowly he also sidled off.

Their way of moving seemed preposterous. They have these strong but tiny, needle-like spider's legs that they perch on, like toe shoes of ballerinas. Then they have to carry their equipment, the pincers and tail, which all three bob up and down. If there wasn't something so primordially creepy about scorpions, the whole thing would be hilarious.

Remembering that one retreatant had said he'd had at least one scorpion visit inside the cabin where I was staying, seeing them in the "flesh" made me a little jumpy.

The washing machine got fixed and hooked up, so I did laundry yesterday. I changed bedding to new flannel sheets, just washed, that Diane B. sent last month. Also, I changed futons, and the new combination was quite luxurious. Too much for retreat? No, only the attachment.

Attachment—aversion. New flannel sheets—scorpions. There we have it.

I called Ani Seltong for her birthday, she also in three-year retreat, or mostly. She, like Vern, continues to manage a retreat center in Colorado, although only a few hours a week.

She mentioned something beautiful: Indra's net which describes an aspect of our universe. The image is in some Tibetan Buddhist sadhanas, but I hadn't known the meaning till now. Indra is a Hindu god. His net is vast as the universe, in three dimensions, at least. At every intersection is a jewel with a thousand facets, and each of them reflects every other jewel in the net. Each jewel represents consciousness, or, a conscious being. So, this interdependence expands the possibilities for prayer, for positive motivation, for clear awareness and enlightenment. Interdependence leads eventually to nonduality, so the imagery is potent.

MAY 20 – JOURNAL

"The Cloistered Laundress." This is what came up, with much hilarity, at the end of my weekly talk with Barbara.

I'd been talking about all the recent laundry, and hanging up too many undies in full view of anyone who might pass by—not exactly a public place, but still, a humorous sight. I'd bought extra panties just before retreat since I didn't want to have to ask someone else to buy them for me later. With a backup of washing due to the machine having been on the fritz, and now fixed, well, there was an extra-long line of them, one after the other, like a cartoon. And add to that the absurdity of a hermitess with so many pairs! Then Barbara and I got going, and "The Cloistered Laundress" became the imagined title of a memoir about this retreat. We belly laughed until we both became quite congested and couldn't go on. Good therapy!

More seriously, Barbara and I talked over the advantages of monastics having an identity and vocation, and how that could be inspiring in retreat—even though perhaps too much concept. This came up after something Ani Seltong had said. She had all her life wanted to be a monastic in retreat, whether Catholic or Buddhist, spending her life in prayer and spiritual practice, with the outer structure of the ordained. And here she is. I found this inspiring in my practice, unearthing strands of my pre-Buddhist life when I had occasionally felt a similar pull. And yes, I'm doing it now, too, the hermit life. But without the outer identity. No interest in robes here.

MAY 22 – JOURNAL, THE PULL

Something was triggered while reading a passage today, from Dzigar Kongtrul's book, *It's Up to You*. He wrote, "Most of us enter the path of practice because we can see the unreliability of samsara. We can see that instead of the lasting happiness and well-being we all hope for, samsara produces pain. The teachings resonate with us because they speak directly to this question of happiness and pain... and we long to cultivate the causes of happiness."

My instant thought: this was not me then, and isn't me now. I wonder if it's an east-west difference, or a personal difference.

So, what *did* pull me into the Buddhadharma? That is a long story, but two things come. First, there's been this spiritual calling all throughout my life, an inner sense that has continually crested and plateaued and then swelled again. Clear spiritual dreams in early childhood led to investigations and ah-ha's in teenage years, then ardent searching beginning in my late twenties. I sensed there was something I was aiming to find which resided in my heart and my body as a deep longing. When finally I found it, I knew I'd found my way home.

The second pull was also central—the feeling that I wanted to give of myself to the world somehow, to alleviate the problems of the world in the most effective way that one single person could. What emerged was what seemed the ultimate path, the spiritual, and I took it.

Now I'm wondering if this motivation is more cultural or generational than personal. If so, if this pull toward Buddhism is beyond the wish to lift oneself out of suffering, then awareness of this has the potential to be important—in the understanding of the Asian teachers as they approach our western heart-mind, in the way the Dharma is presented, and in the teachings that we need. It would certainly make an interesting survey.

MAY 24 – JOURNAL, INCREASE

A rather large *hare* just ran by, a few yards from the back door. Large ears, large body, loping along.

A few days ago a beautiful monarch-type butterfly flew toward me, flew around clockwise, and then away. So beautiful, the first of the season and haven't seen another yet. Many other types though, mostly all white, or a few periwinkle. So many varieties of wildflowers. I heard this year has been *much* more prolific than normal, with all kinds of life. Lama Jamie said that these prolific years, while at first seeming to be advantageous, can come at a cost. He didn't say how.

MAY 27 – JOURNAL

Good morning! A fire going in the stove, strawberries in my granola, and raindrops sounding on the stovepipe. All good.

Someone made a comment at group practice the other night. He had asserted that if one saw beautiful flowers, it was best to make an instant, mental offering of them to the deities, rather than being swept away by them. I wrote this in response:

> The wildflowers, the wildflowers!
> Drop the purposefulness, the proper propriety
> of seeing them as the ground of the mandala
> and offering them to the Buddhas—
> Let them wash over you,
> in Awe, in Love,
> Wonder at them, spellbound, as a little child,
> And offer *that*.

MAY 30 – JOURNAL

A few days before, I had spotted some bear scat next to a nearby trail, and wondered. I'd never seen bear scat before, surprisingly large and black, but had heard bears could be around. As a girl raised for four years on the Olympic Peninsula, and then hiking and camping in the region over decades, I had always wanted to see the large mammals, the bears and mountain lions, but never had.

Recently, too, my son had told me of a Tlingit artist, Norman Jackson, he had met up in Ketchikan, of their companionable conversation over their shared enthusiasm for the Seattle Sonics, and of his wonderful art. I was inspired to look him up, and then meditated with images of his indigenous paintings and carvings in Northwest Coast Indian tradition—of orca and raven and bear.

I had grown up with this imagery in our Seattle home where it had sunk in as part of my own landscape. Later during college I spent a summer on an archeology dig on Makah land. I'd made friends with some young Makahs, and felt connected to their culture. I never lost sight, no matter where I am in America, of being on indigenous land. So now this path emerged as another way to go deep into this place, the natural world here, through shared human and my early connections. I stepped in, sinking deeply, tears came, and it inspired my meditative sense of the present moment for many months.

After seeing the scat, Josh had been over for wood splitting. We talked about bears, because he'd been hearing them messing about in the woods between his cabin and the creek. I said that I'd always wanted to see a bear in the wild, and pointed directly over to the forest "gate," saying, there is where I want to see one. Then it began.

Evening. The bear that I'd been wishing to see from the window I'd imagined seeing him from, I saw. Just now! Huge! He walked slowly to the edge of the dense forest, about thirty yards away, emerged, and stood there calmly looking around, as if presenting himself. I stood there for a moment, inwardly welcoming him, then ran around the cabin searching for my camera. When I came back to the window, too late, he'd wheeled around, disappearing back into the forest.

His back must have been four feet and his head higher. He was medium-brown, the tawny shade of a lion. His coat was full and healthy. Beautiful! What a privilege. Thank you.

JUNE 2 – JOURNAL

Morning. Second bear sighting. I'd been out for a little stroll to stretch my legs during practice, and with thoughts of the bear running around in my mind. I'd been hearing some rustling around in the brush, thought it was deer, but unusual because usually deer move along as they graze and you see them at some point. So I was on alert. Almost back to the porch, I saw him/her lumbering along through some woods below the cabin, quite near. He was on the large side and healthy, black with a brown nose. He didn't notice me. I quietly went inside to get my glasses, camera and a bell. At first he seemed to be heading into the woods, but then turned toward the shrine room. So I went back onto the porch and loudly rang the bell, attempting to head him off. He stopped in his tracks, quite close to the road, then hurried off, but the wrong way—toward civilization, so I gave up. Ah well.

Darn, one bear was one thing, but two (different ones) in two days? Definitely I'm now more nervous about being in the woods than before! However, these human sounds do have an effect.

Night. A something-else sighting. Almost dark, intense twilight outside. While meditating I heard a sound out the north windows, the sound of a large animal stepping on dry madrona leaves. Stealthily, I tiptoed over to the open, screened window and peered out into the near-darkness. Directly below me a large animal was moving parallel to the cabin, toward the porch.

The early night afterglow of summer fairly lit up its light-color coat, giving it a spectral quality as she almost floated, rather than walked. Her torso moved slowly straight ahead as if on wheels, while each of her shoulders rotated in a perfection of coordination, with such precision—part-mammal, part-machine, something from another world system. No bear, this one, but a finely tuned feline predator, careful and deliberate. I was awestruck. And curious as heck!

I went swiftly to the porch-side door, switched on the porch light so I could perhaps see her more clearly as she rounded the corner of the cabin... and quickly opened the door. In that instant she skedaddled, and I just as instantly slammed the door shut! But I didn't see her. I was quite sure it must have been a cougar, far too large for a bobcat. But when it fled it didn't have the sound of a heavy animal. Only the sound of one quick footfall on dry leaves, and gone.

JUNE 3 – JOURNAL

What seemed to be a grey fox trotted along this morning, along the divide between the deep woods and my sparse woods. He was a little far away, but I recognized the size, trot, and behavior, going along in a beeline at a consistent pace.

Otherwise no big sightings so far today, and glad of it! I took a walk this afternoon, but stayed on the road.

Dream

In a dream this morning I was pregnant, walking around a hospital. The baby was born—not in a hospital room—effortlessly. And yet I was still pregnant... with the placenta. The baby was a girl, and fully lucid, intelligent, and walking. We communicated telepathically and she already understood everything. The placenta would be born later, when the time was right.

This afternoon while doing practice, I was struck with the sadhana's wording in two places, "the womb of the Dharmadhatu," thinking the dream is showing me that the womb of my dream—the womb of the dharmadhatu, via my practice and retreat—is nourishing me; while nature of mind is here, available anytime, having been born already. All this symbolism and messaging in the language of the feminine—while in the dakini phase of retreat.

Barbara had some thoughts about the meaning of the bears. Animals in general are associated with instinct—which can be troublesome, but also wise; and of course natural. The Bear = the mother, even "the great mother." We humans have an ancient connection with this animal, and this association.

Steeping further... I'm daily in the feminine aspect of my practice curriculum. And, "the great mother" is one of the names for Prajnaparamita, who symbolizes the empty, womb-like aspect of space, of the dharmadhatu. Musing on connections here, circling back to the dream.

JUNE 5 – JOURNAL

A young skink with electric blue tail slithered by today. Fabulous! It really surprised me and I didn't know what creature it was at first, although the word "skink" scuttled through my mind. It looked at first like a bright metallic object in the brambles. It moved like a snake, but was too short to be a snake. And then there was that tail that flashed blue among the dried leaves! wow. I continued watching it twist and "run"—more like slither-run—among the leaves and sticks. Then gone.

Two more bears, tawny twins! First, this yearling came out of the woods at the forest gate, and looked around. He headed for the large, crumbling stump and was engaged there for awhile. There were many trees between us, so it was difficult to see what he was up to, but easy to guess—seeking insect snacks. Suddenly he ran, dashing north and down into the ravine. He was so fast, bounding and away. I had heard bears were fast and now I see.

I thought, okay, now what? I sat back down on my cushion, back to practice. Five minutes later, another bear just inside the thick woods was visible, seeming to look around. Pretty soon she was at the same entrance, and made her way to the same stump. She was perhaps a bit larger than the other, but both were considerably smaller than the full-sized bears I'd seen already.

Then this sibling gradually walks toward the cabin, as if curious about the house. I'm standing at the closed back door, which has a long window in it, running the length of the door, so I'm in her line of sight. I have my camera ready and take some photos. She now comes close to the laundry that I hung to dry a few hours before, just a few yards away. I'm not moving, but the sun is shining directly on me and I imagine she's seen me. Suddenly she takes off—BAM! Same direction as her brother and just as fast.

I'd been trying to decide at what point do I start making noise, to discourage them away from the cabin. So as she's making her getaway I slam the door repeatedly, the only thing at hand. They were about the cutest things I'd ever seen, curious, with that innocence of a young being around the eyes.

This makes, in one week, four bears, one cougar, one fox, and one skink.

I was becoming known as the retreat center's nature ranger. Lama Jamie said he'd seen only one bear in his forty years on that land, even being outdoors there so much of the time, and I think he said he'd seen no cougars. Hardly anyone ever sees cougars. Bears are slightly more common. I heard stories about them getting into the large communal kitchen on occasion. One time Lama Jamie, to dissuade a bear who'd been coming around and raiding the refrigerator, had secured an invincible metal strap around the fridge. The bear got in again, and bent the fridge door around the strap so he could reach his paw in and get a snack. It was stories like this one that was feeding my worry.

It didn't help much to hear from one resident who said, Oh, they don't want to hurt you. They're wonderful animals. No need to worry. *I could see they were wonderful, beautiful animals, but there I was, alone in the woods. No one could hear me if I yelled. I began thinking, I'd rather not end my life as a meal for an animal. But my sense of humor was still alive.*

JUNE 8 – JOURNAL

Two nights ago I heard a frog jumping around, landing on things. I fell slightly asleep, then awoke around midnight, and switched the light on. He was on the windowsill. I came back with a glass to capture him and saw that this teeny frog was in a stand-off with an equally sized spider, meaning large. This was a little hard to take in the middle of the night.

What to do? Which one do I capture first, or at all? I thought, if I catch the frog first, the spider will run away to a good hiding place. If the frog hops away I can probably catch him later. So I chose the spider. He was the fast-runner type, but they were in a life and death match, and so the motion of the descending prison didn't even register, and the spider didn't budge. Then the frog, eyes still glued to the now-caged spider, didn't budge either, and so with a second glass he was easily captured. I released both outside.

I couldn't fall asleep then for a long time, with images of their face-off still in mind. I wondered, which one's life had I saved? What *karma*?

I also seemed to continue hearing frog sounds. And indeed, next day captured another, while on the phone to Bruce about the holes they had made for pipes incoming to the kitchen. The holes I thought could be little doorways for the amphibian relatives. He advised having a look under the cabin. That had to be a kind of nightmare job for me—imagined spider and scorpion territory—so I made a plan, preparing large sheets of cardboard as ground cover, and rags to stuff into gaps with a screwdriver... and called Kari to come for moral support.

She came straightaway and actually ended up getting under there herself, with no problem, just head and shoulders. She didn't mind at all, brave one, and it all worked out. However, frog noises still heard. Hmmm...

Last night I did something, though. I set up my bug screen tent—indoors—on top of my bed, and slept in that. Completely relaxed, no worries about small cousins plopping onto head in middle of night. All good.

There is a bird, or more than one, at dusk, close by and clear, singing the most beautiful songs I've ever heard.

JUNE 10 – JOURNAL

Challenge du jour: Water pump broken as of nine this morning, and Lama Jamie out of town. Oh well, brings community together in a nice way. Still ongoing midafternoon. Seems we may be without for another day.

It's my job to water the garden. Fortunately water is available right there in the pond which is fed naturally by the nearby creek, so I'm able to scoop water out manually with a bucket and take it around to the many plants, vulnerable in the summer heat. I've become quite happy to have this responsibility, keeping the central garden in front of the statue green and beautiful, an offering.

JUNE 13 – JOURNAL

Two spotted fawns came by today with their mother, grazing along, infused with cuteness.

The water did go back on the next day. But now hot water for the shower is broken. So today I washed hair outside with the handheld shower that Bruce had installed next to the front porch. Cold! I'd forgotten how frozen the head gets when inundated by cold water.

JUNE 15 – JOURNAL

Yesterday I took an unusual break after getting tired with the practice. Rather than relaxing, it became a study day. First I meditated, then began creating a long list of questions for Rinpoche about the dakini sadhana. This was based on combing over the text in detail. Then a long lunch break with laundry, watering the garden, and helping clean up after last night's tsok.

Back to investigation of the text. This sadhana has one section that's like taking a graduate course on Buddhism, placing all the major concepts in parts of the dakini's (one's own) body, then assigning deities' names to each! It's lengthy and difficult to visualize or hold all in one's head simultaneously. Lalapalooza! So I created a chart with drawings of the deity, labeling it with all the mentioned aspects, something I'd been thinking of doing for some time. Today I tried it out, using the diagram to contemplate visually in meditation. It did not help in the least, which wasn't really a surprise. The day had been an enjoyable break, though, and I was reenergized today in a calm way.

JUNE 19 – JOURNAL

Yesterday I turned 60. It feels like the threshold of venerability. I had a lovely day with greetings from family and Rinpoche. Riwo Sangchöd in the morning. It was also a Guru Rinpoche day, so I did a long tsok in the afternoon. Some packages showed up in the evening, including the text of a major *tantra* with Longchenpa commentary. Wow, a huge tome, and precious. I can feel it humming from the other side of the room.

Around 8:30 this morning I saw another bear! It was next to the house, black with a slightly brown nose, full size. I'd heard him or her near the front porch at first, and by the time I leapt up from my cushion, he was near the back door. No food at the front of the cabin, he knocked over a small solar light that was stuck into the ground, snapping it in two, leaving its plastic spike stuck in the ground.

Around the back door he was nosing around alarmingly close to the cabin near the large fallen tree, probably six feet away. I peered out from behind the door curtain, and started banging the door, opening it slightly, to make noise.

He looked up and actually started *toward* the door! I quickly got my bell and started ringing it. He stalled, took a step toward the door. So I started banging the door again, but louder. He thought better of it, turned and loped away. After he'd gone off quite aways downhill, he slowed down and started grazing again, heading off away from the cabin.

I hadn't felt like showing myself to him, and had kept the door curtain mostly down the whole time. I hadn't used my voice, either. Perhaps I should have. So, now I'm again feeling nervous as heck, and wondering about staying on here. It seems it would be silly to leave, but maybe not silly to at least think. I'm glad of my walking stick, one I made out of a straight and sturdy madrona branch.

Trying to work with my mind-heart-body. Challenging.

JUNE 22 – JOURNAL

A three-bear day! I got to experiment with pot lids and yelling—advice from Ani Nyima, who is much more experienced with bears than I, from her years in the Colorado mountains—and it did work.

The first bear was another yearling, next to the side of the house, and black. The side window was already open, so with pot lids clanging up a storm, the cacophony was enough, and he ran off.

Second sighting, I was on a walk down the road toward the big vegetable garden. Undeniable rustling in the undergrowth drew my attention, then, looking back, I was alarmed to see patches of black fur through the greenery. I froze to consider the situation—should I go back home, passing the animal by again? or go on to the garden, a temporary reprieve? I walked on, fear feeding nausea, and arrived safely at the big garden. No other retreatants there, but the tall deer fence gave me a sense of comfort—the logical mind realizing it couldn't possibly keep out an insistent bear. I picked some lettuce, cherry tomatoes, and greens for supper, knowing I'd have to soon retrace my steps past the bear point.

Conjuring up my courage, I stepped gingerly down the dirt road. No rustling, no black fur patches. Getting safely back into my cabin, I started sending a message to Rinpoche, to tell him about the bear (and cougar) situation, when suddenly, out the back door window, there appeared the largest bear imaginable, the size of a bear in a folk tale, yes, one of those. Black and fluffy and healthy, he was coming from the direction of the previous sighting, on a parallel path with the one I'd just been on. Oh my!

More courage needed. I found the pot lids and started clanging them together—loudly! Undeterred, the animal turned toward the closed door, toward me, and took a step in my direction. Did I mention, he was just a few steps from the door, with the door curtain pushed aside, so I was visible? This is not going to work, I thought, what to do? In a split second I opened the door, thrust my hands out and clanged the lids together like a nutcase, yelling at the top of my human lungs. Now with no wall to obscure it, the sharp cascade of sound waves hit his sensitive eardrums directly. He turned and made a hasty and impressive retreat. Impressive because of his size, such a huge animal in flight. It wasn't until three hours later, after I'd recovered, that I realized what a magnificent and beautiful animal he was. I was awestruck, and felt honored and quite fortunate to be in his presence. And of course, alive.

I was seriously unsettled by all this. Josh texted that they had seen a huge, black bear this morning, too. His wife was too scared to go to the garden alone, so she and I may walk over together after a few days.

From well-meaning friends and family I received one canister of pepper spray, two bear jingle bells, and one emergency whistle. The pepper spray, with its depiction of an enraged grizzly and red, bold, large lettering screaming "Bear Spray!", came with interesting warnings. One was to practice with it in advance to get the hang of it, but once used, must be discarded. Then, it had to be used within close range. Confidence instilling. And one should use it only upwind of the target, because the spray could permanently blind the user. The Alaskan joke about what bears do with pepper spray canisters suddenly came alive in my mind.

However, I did wrap a jingle bell around my walking stick, and carried the whistle with me on walks. The bear spray I hid from my own sight, and managed later to give away to another retreatant.

JUNE 25 – JOURNAL

How is it that one can have one of the flattest, most discouraging days of practice, I mean with visualization and recitation, for hours, with no concentration whatsoever, and then one of the loveliest, developed dissolution sessions at the end? Today this happened, while with wild mind, and worry about one family member. But the dissolution: expanding the womb-space of the dakini, the three-sectioned, blood-red, dimensionless space of dharmadhatu—expanding this warm bliss into space, sharing with everywhere and everyone. And then further, clear, spontaneous related physical sensations and perceptions.

A recent consultation with Rinpoche opened this up, confirming the three-dimensionality of the mandala, for example, and suddenly I could see that it is exactly a uterus. Remarkable. Completely expandable, warm, full of bliss and love, alive, familiar, feminine in actuality, not just symbolically. One can ride in it, become it, anything.

JUNE 26 – JOURNAL

This morning I woke up early, around 3:30, and couldn't return to sleep, so got up to practice. Then fell back asleep. Nice. It was raining outside, and dark all morning. I felt simultaneously happy in one facet, and tremendously vulnerable, jumpy, in another. Even though it's been four days since bears, they're still present in my mind.

However, the practice was amazing in the morning, easily staying with clear aspects of the complex visualization I had earlier tried, without success, in getting a handle on through creating that diagram. When I got to the recitations and gazed at the syllables—in English script—it was so beautiful I burst into tears. Then, afternoon practice was completely off again, wild conversation with self, and sometimes the opposite—sleepy. But the final dissolution again great.

JUNE 27 – JOURNAL

It's not just the large creatures. I'd just come into the shower room, and taken up the broom to sweep the small bits of grass and dead ants out the open door, when wow, a formidable black scorpion, almost six inches long, came walking out from behind the door. He was probably making a getaway, but on the way, he was definitely walking toward me. Slightly panicked (can one be *slightly* panicked?), I swept him out the door with the broom, hearing his needle-pointed toes scraping along the wood floor like miniature fingernails on a blackboard. I let out a gasp while uttering "f--k!!", feeling I'd dodged a bullet. Even though I still had my clothes on when it happened, they were soon to come off for bathing, and about to get into the shower was a little too close to scenes from *Psycho* for comfort. Second thought: did I hurt the creature? I looked out the door, and he was nowhere to be found. I figured he must have hurried off under the house, and I hoped only his dignity was bruised.

Another recent experience was seeing a large black scorpion in a discarded, small-necked glass bottle in the meadow one day. Fear overcame fascination, and I didn't investigate to see if he was still alive. Mulling over the possibility that he was stuck inside, and how that had happened, I found it disquieting that scorpions were hanging out in "my" meadow, where I'd been sitting and meditating every day for months.

I heard from Josh that a few small scorpions had occasionally found entry into their cabin. One time he was stung by one while putting his hand into a blind corner of the kitchen counter while cleaning up. What he found was that the sting was so relatively mild, about like a bee sting, that in comparison to the fear that the iconic scorpion evoked, it seemed quite a small thing. And that experience substantially lessened his fear of the little creatures. I suppose I could have tried petting one to cure myself of my own fear, but I have my limits.

JUNE 29 – JOURNAL

I feel I should find a new place. Am I running away from an opportunity, or being reasonable? The opportunity is to crack the fear open, or to accept where I am right now—the place, the fear, the unknown.

I feel afraid anytime of the day, and frightened to go outside, to pee, to take compost into the woods, to take a walk or sit and meditate on the earth. Afraid to walk over for a shower, or go to the garden for vegetables. Afraid to go do my job watering the statue garden. I take my walking stick everywhere I go, and talk loudly, or sing. When going out to pee I bang on the propane tanks a few times on the way.

At night I don't go out for a pee anymore, and have had thoughts of a bear coming into the cabin while I'm sleeping—because they can do that. So even indoors doesn't seem a complete oasis. Some days there's only a little of this, but today was high anxiety.

I've spoken to Lama Jamie and Sara several times about the bears, suggesting some different solutions for compost since currently everyone scatters their food scraps around. I'd been burning mine, but now the weather is so hot a fire is out of the question. But Lama Jamie's response is, "I've been here forty years and only saw one bear... We went up in the woods to try and see one, but couldn't find one... You're lucky." It feels like they're not hearing me.

Yes, I feel lucky to see them, beautiful creatures all. But they're too close, right up to the cabin. They're big, I'm small. And I can't predict them. I was just becoming adjusted to being here in this beautiful place, and now...

JULY 2 – JOURNAL

So much turmoil. One family member has been in a crisis. I was sad in afternoon practice. Then in a phone call with Rinpoche, he had a redirect for me on this person's issue, pointing out that their problem at root is the same one I have—a need for approval. After the call, while sitting back and taking in his apt advice, part-disgruntled and part-relaxed, I started seeing many little pops of light around the altar, especially around an image of one wrathful deity. When I sat up for formal practice, it went away.

It's been HOT. Today outdoors was 90 and indoors maybe 85. In my present state of "Miss Vulnerable," the heat feels like a crisis. What a case I am. I need to be more positive, less negative. I don't need people's sympathy. If I'm not used to the heat because I'm from Seattle, I don't have to say that! If I need something I can say *that*, but otherwise, let's be positive.

JULY 7 – JOURNAL

Another blue-tailed skink appeared yesterday. This one must have been more mature, because the blue was like paint, whereas the previous one was electric. Sara said don't touch them because they're poisonous. I said, Jeez, I can't imagine trying to touch a blue-colored lizard!

Quite wonderful, last week's group practice—many people came, including a young translator who got his training at Rangjung Yeshe in Nepal. Also, Kari's friend, Sergio. And a lovely woman staying for a week or so. Everyone happy and friendly.

Sergio served everyone an ice cream concoction as an offering. He had taken a couple of muffin tins, filling each with layers of coconut ice cream, creamy chocolate, nuts, and raspberries. I realized I was a little over-the-top delighted with it, not at all anything-disciplined or equanimous, instead a child or a fool... or a scrawny hermit who's been on a desert isle for years, suddenly presented with an alluring dessert delight from the Arabian Nights. I was both inside the experience of delight and observing with dismay and humor my location on the continuum of inner development.

People have been giving me advice about the bears. It's of course intended to be helpful, but often feeds my fear. The advice is usually the same, comes in the form of: black bears rarely hurt people; carry a stick, a whistle, bear spray; talk to them with kindness (!); and don't worry.

But there's something else I seem to be searching for, some solution or assistance that this isn't fulfilling. What has been helpful lately is that the community here is doing a bit more, like offering to walk people to their cabins. It's a margin of support and is making a difference.

Wild turkey, tall, with two chicks walked past the cabin, around 6:30 pm.

JULY 8 – JOURNAL
The weather is starting to get hot again. My interior is also heating up. A few days ago I noticed my breathing was hot, my nostrils felt it while exhaling. This was similar to a time more than twenty years ago, just after entering the dharma, a potent spiritual period, when I was running a lot of energy, including sexual energy. Don't feel the latter at this time though. heh... At that time so much fire energy, the top of my head started getting small soft spots in the scalp, and I often breathed visible steam, even in a warm room, sometimes visible to others. It lasted for a year or more, then dissipated. After that, the heat transferred to hands and feet, which is, of course, more common.

In this sadhana practice I'm enjoying so much getting to know the retinue, hundreds of thousands of dakinis. What could be better? I imagine them in each their own tiglei, which isn't mentioned in the text, but seems obvious. Each the queen of her own universe.

JULY 14 – JOURNAL
Karen, my friend and doctor, drove the long way from Whidbey Island for a visit, for a little retreat, and as a birthday present to herself. We've had such a great time—a little practice together, Riwo Sangchöd, meditation, Ngöndro. Plus I gave two instruction sessions, on altars and Ngöndro. We took one long walk, visited the big vegetable garden, watered the statue garden twice, and put together one of the Adirondack chairs that Spirit sent—a beauty, wood painted red. It's been so wonderful to have Karen here, I'll miss her when she's gone—leaving early tomorrow morning. But it's been a good break. Maybe it will feed extra practice energy.

I've been in the woods so long now and so continually, if I see the wide open sky, or the moon through the branches of crisscrossing tree branches, it's startling. What is that!? It's the moon! I miss the celestial bodies.

JULY 15 – JOURNAL
We're skipping our Monday chat, Barbara and I. I've had enough social and she's been deeply exhausted with a new museum opening featuring her work.

I checked my email and found that Mom broke her ankle, was flown to Seattle late last night for surgery. She had a roomful of family there with her, but even so, I fretted, wishing I could be there. But I had a beautiful, rich, effective practice this morning before her surgery... for her surgery.

JULY 19 – JOURNAL

I can still hear the planes doing passing rounds. There's been a fire nearby. Sara said five miles away, forest and house and outbuildings. Earlier this afternoon I had noticed hazy space among the trees and wondered if it was my imagination. Later I went out for a pee and the smell of smoke was strong! Thought to call Lama Jamie's house, to let someone know in case it was emanating from close by and no one knew about it yet. Sara picked up the phone and said she was monitoring it, that she'd let me know if we needed to leave. She said Jamie had been in town and she didn't know if he'd be able to get back through the fire zone, the only route home. This means the fire zone is blocking any exit from this retreat land!

I returned to practice which alternated between two things. One was sending energy and prayer to the situation. I imagined sending with great strength the essence of the Guru Rinpoche statue on this land to balance the elements, as well as the energy of Tara and Vajrayogini. And also sending prayers to all the countless impacted creatures and the family who lost their home. The second focus was making a list of things to grab in case of sudden exit.

Now 6 pm, writing outdoors in eighty-degree-plus weather. The smell of smoke has gone. The haze in the distance has pretty much cleared. But the fire planes are still making their sweeps. Fortunately, little wind today.

When I was seven my family moved from the very dry side of the mountains to the very wet, close to the rain forest, the latter of which got laid down in my cells. My eastern Washington uncles would tease that we had grown webs between our toes, but I didn't mind. The wet side felt an Eden to me, green everywhere.

Now here in a different world, surrounded by the ongoing drought, the tinder-dry trees, many young ones losing leaves or needles, then not making it. The forest floor covered with layers of dry madrona leaves, like discarded pages of whole libraries—crunch, crunch, as you walk along. The dry heat, sometimes with wind—all the elements a set-up. The danger of making any fire, even in our cabins' woodstoves, a single spark being enough to set off a whole hillside. It made me nervous, and there was a small place in my mind where my fingers were constantly crossed. It went like this for months.

JULY 20 – JOURNAL

Late last night the smoke came back. Just as I was resolved to go to sleep, the possibilities unsettled me and I stayed awake for a long time. I checked the bare-bones internet on my non-smart phone and found some news indicating things were safe for people, though the close-by fire continued. This put me at ease and I fell asleep. I had packed some things in case I had to go in the night. Was this too grasping for retreat-mind? Or sensible? Yes, to both, I think.

This morning woke up tired at 8. I was struck with the depth of weariness, something about being here. In spite of its beauty and quiet and natural state and blessing, this place continues to feel foreign to me. I still feel vulnerable. The three weeks with bears and the cougar continues to affect my relationship to the land—how I use it, or don't. I feel confined by my perception of this place as inhospitable. I've confined myself mostly to the cabin and the land right around it. Most of those sightings were right around the cabin, so going outside at all is always accompanied by looking around carefully.

This confinement means no sky view, which feels like a gap in my meditation. I knew this could potentially be a drawback here in the forest, but I could always walk to sky view places. No more. Then there are the scorpions, ticks, mosquitoes. So now a forest fire.

Last night I sensed a tiny part of me was hoping for an evacuation. But I wanted to leave *with* my things. I then thought strongly, I wish for a vacation— to *rest!* And why rest, when here there is so little demand on me. The answer was that I feel under a strain of the raw nature here. But is it in my mind only?

So today, worn out, I took an hour and a half nap, and felt better. I went into practice feeling dull and deadened. Suddenly I snapped out of that with an urge to spin the mantras and beads at top speed. It came out like a long rolled R in a booming loud voice. I yelled and then screamed. Once, twice! Started crying and then screamed again. It was this feeling that I'm wasting my time, not making any headway at all; that the practice isn't working for me. I felt absolutely in prison, angry—but at whom?! I cried more. Confinement. Imprisonment. Doing time. What am I being punished for? Why am I so determined to complete this? Commitment is the answer.

I wanted to escape—Now! Not waiting for this sadhana's completion— which is another fifty days at the earliest, probably the end of September. The current idea is to wait it out here to complete the sadhana and then move elsewhere, but today I felt this urgent need to move right away.

I'm longing for fresh air, cool breezes, sky views. I'm longing to relax. I'm longing to see the night sky, the moon, and all the stars of the heavens. I'm longing to watch the clouds pass first one way, and then the other. I'm longing for rain, and for home. Now I'm crying. I've been gone long... Not really. But I've been on retreat by myself long. And yet it's only about halfway. I'm longing for this to be over. There have been too few times or days when I've deeply felt, "I'm so grateful for this opportunity." Certainly none lately that I can even remember. I just feel I'm doing time. Like a prisoner. *Gak.* Then it does feel wasted. I should not be in this!

This cabin is lovely. I keep repeating that. It has everything needed. I have many beautiful objects on my shrine. I have books to read. I can draw. I can take breaks. But whenever I think of taking a break here, there's nothing I wish to do. It's as though I don't see this as my life, not as a life that belongs to me. I'm here, holding my breath, waiting to leave. I'm a foreigner in an exotic and strange country, with no real friends—only people who have been kind.

So, why can't Guru Rinpoche, Tara, the dakinis, be my friends? Why haven't I yet come to embrace them as my true refuge and family? Why can I not see my own intrinsic nature as my true home? Is it lack of sky? Trepidation of animals? Distancing my body from this place in a kind of fearful protectionism? Anxiety and vulnerability? Are all of these actually affecting my ability to relax into the practice? Or will I forever be searching for the perfect externals, never coming to my own inner home?

I feel caught in a moment of H – E – E – L – L – P ! ... ! But all my usual help people need help themselves right now. And what am I looking for anyway? I'm hoping so much for a next landing place. (I have a lead on something, but no answer there yet.) Wishing for someone to tell me to leave retreat? Should I end retreat? Someone to tell me to just take a break? I wish for a break. I wish to complete retreat in a different way. I wish for no more mantra accumulations— ever in my life, unless I'm in a state of rigpa awareness.

To people who ask if they should do this kind of retreat, what could I ever say? No, I don't recommend it...? This seems worse than never having done it myself.

JULY 23 – JOURNAL

Two days ago I had a good conversation with Rinpoche that helped—a lot. Yesterday was slow, but improved in a way, and today was going along beautifully, with relaxed, good practice. It wasn't too hot, either. I thought: effortless. Things feel effortless today, and I'd just as soon stay here even. Well, maybe.

Then, after watering the garden around the statue, and hanging laundry at my lunch break, I came back to find this message from Sophia: "My teacher has died." Oh my! A shock. Lama Tharchin Rinpoche passed away yesterday. I cried a little. Sophia and her daughter were with Kilung Rinpoche when she texted me that she'd been sobbing.

When I started up my practice again, I went back to the statue with three butterlamps and a stick of incense, and did many koras. Thought: He just released into the universe a huge amount of *love*... and *bliss*—his specialties.

I felt sad thinking of all his countless students who must be distraught. He himself had reportedly been deeply bereft by the passing of his own teacher, Thinley Norbu, carrying that for the last year and a half.

Reincarnations are so tenuous. You never really know how the child will turn out. It could be twenty years before it's known, or until they begin teaching themselves. So, in that uncertainty there is cause for sadness when a lama dies. Plus in these times of diaspora, the transition is extra bumpy. And when older lamas go, there goes the connection with old Tibet, with layers and layers of knowledge embedded in original culture, irretrievable.

This afternoon then, I was further spurred on to the whole point of this retreat, realizing that I'm doing this for more than myself and sangha and the nebulous sense of being a better human to benefit the world and therefore all sentient beings. I felt this upgraded sense of mission that's been a bit sleepy of late—to do what I can for the dharma in our world, in this western world and beyond.

Sometimes my mind is so blasted small, limited to what I'm looking at in the present moment and circumstance. I'm allegedly patient, with a reputation for that—but really?

Lama Tharchin. One evening in 1989 I heard he was to teach in Seattle, at the Quaker Meeting House where I had spent many a Sunday morning with my father, and attended youth group evenings. Now the room was full of earnestness, locals listening to this beautiful human being from Tibet, speaking softly, with his heart to our hearts. I was deeply touched, and thought of Barbara. She had twenty years before followed a Chinese Buddhist teacher, but had gone back to her Christian roots. We had spoken heart-to-heart about spiritual issues for a decade or more, and she had become a spiritual mentor for me. I had recently found my spiritual home in Tibetan Buddhism, and a teacher in Sogyal Rinpoche. But Barbara was at that time at a way station, a spiritual in-between place. I called her and said, you should go see this teacher. I think you will love to meet him. So she did. Soon after she became his student, and found the Vajrayana to be the rich ground needed, the next destination on her own spiritual journey.

Barbara took my daughter Sophia to meet Lama Tharchin when she was seven. He took her up on his lap when he was on the lama seat, and I think Sophia pretty well melted at that point. They both adored him and he them. Funny I didn't myself choose him for my teacher, although I always loved being in his presence at a number of teachings over the years. His love and compassion were so strong and palpable and continuous. Anyone, Buddhist or not, could experience it.

Another big American center loses its lama. What happens next? Where do the people go? Too soon to know. A sad day.

JULY 30 – JOURNAL

A break came, in the form of a trip to Seattle. A sudden need for some dental work coincided with Sophia and her daughter making the trip south for Lama Tharchin's cremation and pujas, to the Santa Cruz area. On the way back home, they had to drive only twenty miles from the freeway to pick me up. They arrived late yesterday, at sunset, to an elaborate dinner I'd prepared—elaborate by retreat standards. I led them along the trails to my cabin, yet in spite of our threesome-ness, my granddaughter felt frightened by visions of bears and cougars dancing in her head. But they were amazed and inspired to be in this beautiful retreat place. They had planned to spend the night in my cabin, but the forest fire smoke was too much for Sophia's asthmatic lungs. So we headed out in the dark and spent the night in a motel along I-5. Then we got in late tonight to Seattle. I'll be staying here in a condo in the heart of the city, a place where I lived for many years. It's nice to be back home.

AUGUST 11 – JOURNAL

In spite of being back in samsara, this morning I had a potent meditation experience during morning practice in the city condo. I'll write only little about it, that it was inspired by some reading yesterday, of a book by Sam van Schaik on dzogchen philosophy, *Approaching the Great Perfection*. He was describing the connection between heart and perception of the eyes. The recollection of this brief piece of information triggered some direct experience. You never know in which moment flowers will bloom.

Here I am in the city, having come for dental work. But it seems the "true" reason for this trip is to help Sophia during a time of crisis. Rinpoche had advised me to limit my family contact to greetings, and guard against actual involvement. But how can I turn my back on my daughter in a time of great need? She has just left her husband, and he hasn't been taking it well, acting in ways that frighten her. At least I've kept my involvement within the confines of the condo—listening to Sophia, counseling, advising, and helping her draw up plans. It seems my presence at this particular moment happened by blessing, and I don't regret it in any measure.

Once upon a time there was a yogi, wandering over the plains and mountains of Tibet. This man, named Shabkar, stayed sometimes in monasteries and in caves, sometimes alone and sometimes visiting enclaves of practitioners like himself, all of them seeking the great enlightenment. Occasionally Shabkar would receive a message from his mother, pleading with him to come home for a visit. But he would send a message back to his mum that his journey, inward and outward, was taking him places all too important to return back into samsaric life, even for a visit. And indeed, he was making progress. Then one day he received the message that his mother was dying and it was her last dear wish for him to return to say goodbye. But still, his commitment to the Buddhadharma was so strong, he could not do this. His mother died without seeing Shabkar in all these years, and when he received the final message, he cried and cried.

In the first year of my retreat I read Shabkar's captivating autobiography, unusual for a Tibetan life story in that he openly revealed many almost confessional and human stories about himself. When I got to the part where he received the last wish from his mother, I felt like crying out beyond the room, back across time and space, "Go home, Shabkar! Go home and see your mother, you idiot!" To me, if his karma and diligence and devotion, everything, was great enough that he achieved enlightenment, which he did achieve, then one visit to his mother would not have interfered with that. And his fulfilling his mother's happiness, though temporal, would only have increased positive energy for his ultimate goals. I never regretted having reentered samsara to help my daughter in her hour of great need, a small sacrifice of that moment.

All of being back in samsaric life has been instructive, and I think and hope I'll be relieved to return to retreat. For one thing, it's NOISY out here—

outdoors, indoors, human noises, and human interior noise, even the latter of which I now sense acutely.

I see the frenetic pace of life as just an outer reflection of the frenetic habit of avoidance of the self, of feelings, etc. I see it in myself, too, what I've struggled with since beginning retreat, and have overcome to a large degree, but continue struggling with. So, besides a renewed appreciation for retreat, I also anticipate some layer of social dependency to deal with when I return.

However, there's also a second thing out here, a sense of missing my purpose, which is being in retreat, with the underlying "What am I doing here?!" There's a small alarm that goes off, and it's not always conscious—so this gives rise to an edginess, not quite grumpy, but grasping, perhaps a frenetic-ness of my own—looking with a little anxiety for my purpose, but in the wrong places. Yesterday was quiet, reading a difficult philosophical text. And then I realized that coming together again with this retreat purpose had given rise to a big internal relaxation, above the samsara around me, back to spacious... and then more outwardly helpful, too.

AUGUST 13 – JOURNAL

I've made my way back to my cabin home in the Siskiyous. The cabin is as I left it two weeks ago. It smelled closed up, like cardboard, and was cooler inside than out, not unpleasant. I quickly unpacked and put away groceries. Then sat in front of the altar, not practicing, just being. I ate dinner, after putting away the clean dishes Sophia had washed and dried two weeks ago. I felt happy to remember the two of them here. So few have been to this place, and it was wonderful they got to experience it, even for that brief stopover. Then I took a short evening stroll to look around, found one tree down that Lama Jamie cut up. Did it come down in a storm, or did he fell it?

I may be moving to Bainbridge in six weeks or so. But for now, here I am. A quiet place, without drama—nor story lines, personae, grapplings. No noise but the fan... or the wind in the trees. Still smoky outside from fires, about fifty miles to the north and the west, not quite as thick as two weeks ago.

A deer and her fawn walked by tonight. Seems like few mosquitoes, maybe discouraged by the smoke.

How to ease back into practice again? I feel that even though I continued Ngöndro in Seattle, I'm very far away from the deities and other practices. I wish I had some engaging book to read right now, with the sense that that would help. I'll dig around and see what might work.

AUGUST 14 – JOURNAL

A lovely, relaxed reentry day today. However, I also noticed visual phenomena, actual ones, tell-tale signs of retina problems—dark floaters, more like
streamers, and later in the day, arcing flashes of bright light. My mother had this
many years ago and schooled me in the symptoms, saying if this ever appeared
I should get to an eye doctor immediately—to prevent blindness. So I arranged
with Lama Jamie to take me tomorrow to an eye specialist. Medical adventure
in Medford coming. Darn!

AUGUST 16 – JOURNAL

They found a tiny tear in the retina. The doctor I had hoped to see was on
vacation, so his colleague saw me, a Dr. B. Young, blond, and pretty, she had
the air of Yale meets Valley Girl. Outwardly she reminded me of the young
female doctors I'd met once at a Chengdu hospital. I had thought they were
assistants, they appeared so young, and when I expressed surprise that they were
full doctors, they giggled prettily. This doctor didn't seem like she would have
giggled if presented with that mistake. In spite of her Valley Girl impatience and
disdain, I decided to have confidence in her technique.

The doctor prodded and pulled at the eyeball, trying to locate the tear.
Painful! It took such a long time to find, she said, because it was so small. Then
taking a wand, she froze the outer eyeball in such a way that the cold penetrated
through, back to the retina, causing the tear to scar over, sealing it from further tearing. The sensation of frozen pressure was a bit difficult, and mercifully
short, a matter of ten or fifteen seconds. There were streaks of colored lights, like
many-branched blood vessels, or lightning. Fascinating. During the whole thing
I reminded myself to exhale, and after, let out a long kind of shudder. She said I'd
done a good job. I replied, yes, one tends to hold still when someone has ahold
of your eyeball. She didn't crack a smile.

During all this my long hair had gotten hooked into the lower workings of
the prone exam chair. When Dr. B. went to bring the chair back up to a sitting
position, my hair was caught and was getting painfully pulled. I called out,
letting her know. "Oh, it's not," she responded, and kept trying to bring it up,
while I kept saying, "Ow-ow-ow!" Finally she saw the problem and stopped long
enough to get the hair untangled. She didn't apologize, and left the room quickly.
I thought, wow, no sense that the patient is also a human being? And neither
she nor anyone gave me any post-op instructions. In my current drained state,
I didn't have the awareness to wonder if there was anything I needed to know.

Afterwards, totally spent. Then a one-hour drive in 90-degree Medford weather in Jamie's not-air-conditioned pickup, with no headrest. I dozed anyway. Then collapsed in bed and slept for more than an hour.

Today, exhausted. Eye sore, lots of floaters, scratchy, eye draining. Spent more time in bed than out. I practiced this morning anyway and glad of that. And took a walk to the vegetable garden. On the way there I felt like an escapee from an asylum, not sure where I was going, or why.

But there was a reason, it turned out. I had just received news that I would be able to shift retreat to Bainbridge, back to Margi's house. So when I got to the garden, Lama Jamie and Sara were there, and I was able to tell them my plan to leave. They were kindly understanding and I said I'd miss the people there. I had dreamed last night of this conversation as a sweet one, and it was.

Dream

My son in a kayak was escaping lightning that was hitting his boat, and our family was hiding from the storm in a boathouse. Small strikes of lightning all around outside, and then one flash of lightning burst into the structure by coming up through the water next to the interior dock. I wonder if the lightning imagery came from my eye surgery or from the lightning that caused the forest fires around here. It was strongly elemental and unusual imagery in my dreams. Electric, visual phenomena, power, beauty, light, energy, water, danger, crisis, family... hmmm...

AUGUST 21 – JOURNAL

I returned to Medford for the post-surgical check. All is well and no more procedure needed. I had been feeling some hesitation about returning to Dr. B. Instead I decided to greet her with great warmth and love, which I did, utterly. And our interaction was immediately extremely positive. The first thing she did when entering the room was to apologize for catching my hair in the chair, and I forgave her. She was quite delightful. Still so young, but I had already gotten beyond that. All good.

Earlier in the week I'd been working with a memory from twenty-five years ago, in pre-Buddhist life, when I'd felt I'd healed Gus from an injury. He was a toddler and fell from his high chair onto a sensitive part of his body. Where normally I would have felt concern and fear, I dropped all fear and brought in total love, joy, and white light. Gus immediately stopped crying and never exhibited signs of any injury. This week, I've been working with this around the fear about my eye—or anything. Dropping fear and going straight to love. This combined with light at the heart. I did that with Dr. B.

AUGUST 22 – JOURNAL

No sleep last night. Zero. Yesterday after the eye check, we stopped for groceries and I drank an extra-strong tea too late in the afternoon. This was followed by an evening tsok, eating late, joyfulness afterwards—and full moon—all leading to Awake! all night long.

I had the most wonderful time, though. Lying in bed thinking: philosophy, deep thoughts, which I cannot now remember... like dropping acid, having profound experience, and later not being able to quite access it. I did reflect on current book reading—and integrating that western construct with Vajrayana. Fulfilling, all this musing, whatever it was, and probably informing future understanding.

The night experience of being wakeful and joyful at the same time seems a breakthrough. I got up at one point to appreciate the full moonlight streaming through the tall forest trees, making a mystical world out of night, dappling the forest with ethereality. So still, quiet, soft... I tiptoed back to bed.

Today, sleep deprived, so a little difficult. The eye, still tired, but overall getting better.

Then, an amazing storm. All day dark and ominous, and still. We had two lightning storms. With the second one came big rain, the first in a long time. It soaked the ground, and maybe will prevent fire. Even so, there was one that got started close by. I could hear and see the planes and helicopters. I heard there have been six times the normal fires in southwest Oregon this year. But since I've been back from my trip, very little smoke here, and grateful for that.

AUGUST 25 – JOURNAL

A memory came during the dissolution of this evening's dakini practice: the elation I felt as a young girl that I had been born a girl. From the beginning I had always been happy to be female, but there was a period, perhaps at the age of eight or nine, when I profoundly understood it in that way—that it could have been different—and felt immense joy at having hit the jackpot! In my sudden awareness of it, there felt a freedom in the world of girl, to be able to express all things feminine, which included creativity, and color... but more, of emotion, dance, changeability, lightness, warmth. I never felt else.

I sometimes wish to make a vow to achieve enlightenment in the body of a woman, as I've heard others have done, as if there's more risk involved, or more of a mountain to climb to achieve it. I don't see this as a political statement, or to help a cause, but a statement of delight, or even, of the obvious: and why not?!

So wonderful to touch that early embrace of my gender and inner core, and bring it into the dakini practice, which is what it's about, I think… the spiral, the wheel of joy, at the heart of things. I connected so deeply with the girlhood memory, I cried a little, tears of, what else? joy.

Rained a lot again this morning.

AUGUST 27 – JOURNAL

This evening's practice started out ordinary enough. But at one point I went to a deep level. My mind saw a mandorla at my heart. It's the intersection of two partially overlaid circles, the shape formed by overlapping the circles halfway, cutting off the outer parts of the circles, with only the overlap remaining. Nature is awash with mandorlas, as a pinecone, a lotus bud, two hands brought together in prayer. Today, at my heart, it was 3D, of light.

Its coming was inspired by Barbara's art. She is a fine art painter, creating mystical imagery on canvas, drawing often from medieval and Renaissance imagery and symbolism, as much as from her personal spiritual experience. The mandorla sometimes figures in her paintings, and decades ago she had explained to me its meaning as she understood it in Western tradition:

Formed by two overlapping circles, the mandorla shape is naturally a uniting symbol, two opposites in harmony rather than conflict. The shape is also vaginal and sometimes appears as a womb. Thus it is full of potential. But the shape also appears as a transforming wound, which one sometimes sees in medieval depictions of the wounds of Christ.

One time, Barbara asked Kilung Rinpoche if there was any reference to the mandorla in Tibetan Buddhist sacred geometry, and he said there was.

This intersection of two wholes in symbology brings together the exterior and interior worlds, literally and how they're reflected in our perception, or the shadow and the bright. In this way the mandorla is thought to represent the healing and potential of the human soul. And meditating upon it then becomes a soul-healing tool. The appearance of the mandorla on that day, though, came more spontaneously, as the shape itself, inspired by recalling my sister-in-law's paintings.

So, this mandorla of light was palpable and exuded warmth, vibrancy, love.

I played with it, infusing it with the red color of the dakini practice, and from it sent this energy out to all beings, particularly those who need healing.

Then, as I played, the dakini's triangle became present. At the extraordinary center is an infinite focus, like a womb from which red energy constantly streams out in all dimensions. But like a good paradox is beyond dimension. This is partly because of its pyramidal shape. It has no exterior boundary, nor fixed origination point.

So, this evening this sea of red energy was flowing, which I felt vividly, almost as tiny warm particles. This continued stably for a long time, with increasing bliss—not astonishingly, but as a mellow, distinct, heart-centered bliss. This was all combined with the mandorla at the heart, sending to others. And all aspects of the sadhana mandala were absolutely present.

AUGUST 28 – JOURNAL

During dissolution in evening practice, with eyes closed, I brought to mind again Barbara's mandorla images. This time I recalled her painting of the ovalesque shape as red blood cells, packed in together like an Escher tessellation. Then I imagined them going out into space—on a web, linked, like Indra's net, infinite mandorlas of red light going out in all directions, each one a being's heart center, all interconnected, in relationship, reflecting, communicating.

From this visualization came further meditation experiences, spontaneous, which informed and amplified the dakini practice, and then which reverberated for months.

SEPTEMBER 1 – JOURNAL

For weeks I've had only mundane dreams with an edge of tension. It's like the frenetic quality of Seattle got into me on a sleep level, while I seem relaxed in my practice and waking life. There's a message in there.

Last night there were long periods of wakefulness. One dream remembered: A cougar was outside, lying peacefully out the back door, looking at the door, waiting. In a half-wakeful state I felt I should go look to see if she was really there. Then I thought, oh I'm dreaming, just relax. She was beautiful, self-possessed, alert, calm, large, strong, healthy. Maybe she was just witnessing, or reminding.

The following, like a dream, really happened. During lunch break while watering the statue garden, there was a large trout lying near the pond, flopping and flipping, gasping for life. Of course I grabbed onto it. He'd flopped his way outside the metal fence for which there is no gate; one has to step over to get next to the pond, and at my height it's a slight challenge, needing two hands to assist myself up and over the sharp vertical spears. So from outside the fence, about three feet away from the pond, I gently tossed the fish back into the water. But alas, the poor fish was stunned and quickly went belly up! I felt terrible that I hadn't attempted to somehow step over the fence with him, nor anticipated his fragility in a fish toss.

Then, later in the day, a large spider ran across the carpet. In trapping him with an upside-down glass, the rim caught him. He was dying when I whispered *om mani peme hung* into his ear, before releasing him outdoors. Uff da, the risk of life.

SEPTEMBER 4 – JOURNAL

There's a bird around here, maybe a jay, with a distinctive call. It sounds like it says "suh-phere." Whenever I hear it, I think "sphere." Oh my, we're getting to that level now, the shipwrecked storybook character.

Yesterday I felt angry, so much so that I broke a small dish. I realized that though on the surface it seemed an accident, the anger in my body had traveled down my arm, causing the plates to almost jump out of my hand, dropping not far to the carpet, clinking together in such a way as to break. I thought then: I have to work on this, delve into myself, and discover about this anger.

Recently I had overheard one retreatant by herself in her kitchen banging pots and pans around, clearly angry as can be, and she didn't hold back. Here it was my turn. What did I do? I looked at it, kept it in mind throughout the practices and meals. I looked at self-no-self, anger-no-anger. I looked at the subject. And it did dissipate.

SEPTEMBER 17 – JOURNAL

Practice has been wonderful lately, sometimes transformative. This morning's practice especially clear, and started reflecting: The map is not the territory. This gave rise to a sense of divine presence, not personified, but sacredness of all, and of the experience—the present moment.

There were many sensations in the body. An image came, at the heart, of a continuously blossoming rose... at first yellow, which arose naturally. Then I worked with red rose. The sadhana specifies a blossoming lotus, but suddenly there was this rose at my heart in a constant state of blossoming. I likened it to the constant outpouring of the red dakini essence from the pyramid. The rose, the West's flower of compassion, was so beautiful, the sense of love welling up without end, I felt a kind of bliss. The visualization was so clear, like the whole morning's practice, and so the image of an endlessly blossoming rose—why not? If the red essence pours out endlessly, why not endless blossoming? It was beautiful that the mind could create and sustain that. Completely natural.

I love this idea of "the map is not the territory," from the book I'm currently reading. I've been using it a lot, reflecting on how literal I'm apt to be with the Vajrayana. Literal-ness is a dead end—you just get stuck on the map.

Rinpoche has said things recently that resonate with this: that I have to trust myself more in my own process. See what arises naturally, not fabricated, he said. That *is* the territory. And especially if there's sacred outlook.

At lunch break I went with Susmita to the vegetable garden for harvesting. Brought back a beautiful small rose for the altar, pale peach color with lovely perfume.

SEPTEMBER 21, EQUINOX – JOURNAL

Nyichang Rinpoche and Inomoto arrived yesterday. I was so happy to see them, their arrival coinciding with my near-departure, like the matching bookend to our meeting when I first came to this place a year ago.

I think the elderly Nyichang Rinpoche didn't remember me, but he was happy to see me anyway, maybe reflecting my happiness at seeing him. Inomoto, though, was genuinely happy to see me, and I him. Today at lunch break we had a wonderful talk—picking up where we left off—of the Longchen Nyingtik, Tibet, India, their project in Kalimpong, politics there, of Kilung Monastery in Tibet, etc. Nyichang Rinpoche is now 81. He'll be in silence for five or six days, so I'll wait to speak to him and to give him a photo booklet of photos of Dzachuka.

I'm about to finish the dakini practice, which means the completion of the three main sadhanas of the lineage, altogether a significant body, like completing Ngöndro, but much bigger. Inexplicably, I've had anxiety about finishing, as if something untoward might happen in the closing days to throw me off or stall me. I vacillate between stalwart and anxious, particularly concerned about small health problems that have been arising, like *maras* testing me—aching teeth or eye symptoms. Also, overactive dreams. But actually everything is fine. So my mind has been wild and stirred up like this. Yet everything is going so well, so just enjoy the practice and the accomplishment! I've even had some lovely practice sessions with clear visualization and experiences. I feel like a goofball!

SEPTEMBER 22 – JOURNAL

Tomorrow it's happening, completing this body of practice, rising before dawn to conduct the rituals. This evening I saw the retinue of dakinis in exultation. Not a clear vision, more of a thought and feeling, but with that, then I too had something of that joy. It's something to look back, to when I began this phase of the retreat, a year and a half of full-time endeavor. I didn't think I'd make it a few times. Truly mind-numbing, but accomplished by diligence. Whew!

This afternoon I thought of all the humans who have lived on our earth, and their suffering, so many cultures where suffering has been institutionalized, or built into the fabric of life as an automatic. In bringing that together with the *tantric* vow "not to abandon love for sentient beings," I wept. That so simple way of stating the commitment to bodhicitta is for me most beautiful and compelling, nothing more needed. And tears often come. I want to tattoo it on the inside of my eyelids.

I brought it out again later in the day after an unusual incident—seeing a mushroom hunter in the woods, quite close to my cabin. Just as I came out the door during my practice, to walk around a bit, there he was, through the trees. Then I noticed he was carrying a large, hand-woven basket, was looking around and climbing on the enormous fallen tree nearby. I felt a little afraid—I didn't want to speak because I was in the middle of practice, and wondered if he was going to come talk to me… or what? I think he finally saw me and left. Was he someone on retreat, in which case he should know to stay apart from someone else's retreat territory. Or if he was a forest wanderer, what's he doing here, and why isn't he afraid of being seen? A little unsettling.

Was this a disruptive occurrence coming together with the accomplishment that was about to happen? Well, tomorrow a new pace and sense of things begin. Relaxation, for one thing.

SEPTEMBER 24 – JOURNAL

Yes, momentous two days. Yesterday I had a relaxed number of mantras to meet the goal, so I went through the day taking my time. Finished in the afternoon and did a short tsok, as usual. Around 5, saw the mushroom guy again. It felt a little creepy; he clearly saw me but didn't go away.

I spent a long time after dinner getting everything prepared for the dawn completion rituals, and went to bed, tired. But after reading and an earlier conversation with Rinpoche, I couldn't get to sleep—too much going on in my mind, which included the mushroom man. I didn't sleep a wink, and got up before the 3:30 alarm.

The puja went smoothly. Even without sleep, no missteps. And the suggested timing of one ritual with the moment of dawn turned out to be marvelously precise. However, my mind was sometimes visited by thoughts of a crazy mushroom man! I repeatedly reminded myself of fabricating, which helped a bit; but what helped most was the practice, and wrathful aspects which engendered courage.

It was a challenging situation of one's own mind—no sleep and up basically in the middle of night, always the hardest time for fear or other dark emotions. I also thought: Here is a mara—what are you going to do with it? Believe it? or see it as my own mind, even nature of mind. That helped, too, remembering Shakyamuni and his maras.

Finally complete, sometime after 7, I went back to bed and slept until 9:30. If I hadn't had to pee, I would have stayed in bed longer.

As part of making this completion, I had planned to make a large tsok to share with the resident sangha and visitors. I enjoyed so much preparing treats for them, thinking of their various dietary needs and preferences. I had bought beautiful cheeses, peaches, a pomegranate, cookies, candies, crackers, sliced meat, and wine. I made up a mock bento box out of the peaches box for Nyichang Rinpoche and Inomoto. And little packages for Ani Nyima, and one for Josh and Susmita. I delivered the two packages for the statue cabin folks, leaving them with notes, and tomorrow Josh and Susmita will receive theirs. Then this afternoon (after a second nap), Lama Jamie showed up to cut wood, so I first helped him, then came in and prepared packages for him and his family, too—plus the bottle of nice wine.

I didn't tell people that it was for anything special, just sharing a tsok. Lama Jamie knew I was finishing something though. He's been quite sweet lately. I also told him I was writing a speech for the community tsok day after tomorrow, my last group appearance before departing north. He was delighted, saying that Chagdud Rinpoche would have been pleased.

I know well the Tibetan tradition for giving speeches. Most of the formal speeches I've given have been in Tibet, translated. I've also listened to many

speeches in Tibet, untranslated, which can go on and on, always to attentive
audiences... wonderful, this ancient tradition. It was only later in life that I
found I love writing and giving speeches—because of this experience in Tibet
when it was suddenly obvious I had to do it. I was the lone foreign emissary
of the Kilung Foundation, and Kilung Rinpoche's American sponsor. Most
of my speeches were scribbled hurriedly on the back of a napkin while sitting
at a banquet table listening to the cadence of someone else's speech. I often
found myself expressing sincere gratitude for allowing him to spend time
away, on his frequent trips to the west. Speechmaking always felt a beautiful
way to offer my heart and mind to these people whom Rinpoche loves, and
who I also came to love.

A wonderful day, lazing about. Barbara is too tired to talk this evening, her
museum show having just come down yesterday. I thought, yes, better for me,
too, to be quiet tonight. We both had monumental conclusions with reasons to
be drained, body and mind. All good.

SEPTEMBER 25 – JOURNAL

Oh boy, the mind is funny. The mushroom man turned out to be R, the
older guy on retreat practically next door! I didn't think it was him because
from a distance mushroom hunter looked like a young man, and I didn't really
remember R clearly, having seen him only briefly a few months ago. Now I can
see the goofy fabrications and spinnings my mind did, coming as the final obstacle in the practice, although it didn't decrease my resolve. But why did he hang
around my place? For mushrooms, break rules?

Working on the speech today, here's one part:

The land. How can words adequately honor the natural world
here? Even the smells—is it sassafras, or sarsaparilla—that occasionally come through. The heady sweet fragrance of dropped fir needles, melting back into sun-warmed earth. The stones, trees, stream,
backbones and ribcages of earth, countless relationships. Creatures
of day and of night, of sky and of land, reflections of light in raindrop
spheres. All in movement. All for the meditator to reflect in, join in,
rejoice in.

The quiet among the trees—a depth of quiet to be found, beckon-
ing one to take further and further steps into one's own quiet well.
This is quintessential retreat territory, up to the practitioner to find
her own way.

With bear and cougar sightings receded into memory, and a new level of settled-ness having taken over, and practice development, I was beginning to regret leaving this place with all its blessing energy. I mentioned this to Lama Jamie, who looked quizzical. I said, "But it's too late now, things have been put into motion, I have a place to go, someone to take me there. It's just a feeling, and I'll be very sorry to go, wanted you to know."

OCTOBER 2 – JOURNAL

Now deep in packing house for moving in two days. Last week in group practice I sponsored most of the tsok as a thank you, and delivered my farewell speech, along with one piece of retreat writing. It was so warmly received, one person teary, accolades from everyone, particularly Lama Jamie. I meant every word of the appreciation I wrote about him, Sara and everyone, and the place. They wanted to know where were the bears in the writing, and were satisfied when, in answer, I pulled out photos of their *ursus* neighbors. Then there was a wonderful party atmosphere after. Everyone so positive and warm.

Two days ago, I rose at 5 to join the group for the annual big fire puja with Nyichang Rinpoche, Lama Jamie, et al. Beautiful, bright white billowing clouds of smoke. Nyichang Rinpoche said that it was auspicious the way the smoke lofted out so perfectly and so pure. It was gratifying to work together with everyone to get it organized, even in that sleep-deprived state.

I also had a two-hour talk with Nyichang Rinpoche, both of us thoroughly enjoying it. He told me about the progress at the new institute in Kalimpong, and we spoke at length about our shared lineage. I gave lots of advice about fundraising in America, while knowing his memory is fading. In a follow-up conversation fortunately Inomoto was there, so I repeated some of the main points. It was well-received, with interesting discussion.

I knew they would be leaving sometime this morning, but not precisely when. With relaxed confidence, I wandered down from my cabin after breakfast to say goodbye. Perfect timing. They were just loading their car, and we had a heartfelt farewell.

My friend Andy is coming early Friday morning with his truck. We're going up Highway 101 along the ocean. A long break, it was his idea. Rinpoche said fine, and I think good. Certainly am looking forward to it. We'll be on Bainbridge by Monday.

OCTOBER 3 – JOURNAL

Hefty packing day after I'd spent the morning in pujas. Two retreat friends kindly stopped by later for goodbye visits. Andy expected tomorrow.

At dusk, coming back from a pee, a very large, very silent white owl with big fluffy head flew overhead, quite close. I whispered, "Thank you." Beautiful salute for send-off. Barn owl.

CHAPTER SEVEN
Bainbridge Island, II

> When I remain in this state
> Which is like a transparent, empty sky,
> I experience joy beyond words, thoughts or expression.
> When I dissolve into that vast expanse–
> Empty and clear, without end, without limits–
> There is no difference between mind and sky.
> —*Shabkar*

OCTOBER 12, 2013 – JOURNAL

Beginning a new chapter back at Margi's house. The transition, now complete, began on October 1. It included three days of packing up, four of traveling, four of settling in.

The trip with Andy was wonderful. He had brought a tent which was rated for two people. Yes, for people in a close relationship or an emergency, but... Yikes! I told him this would be too tight, I don't want this much close proximity with anyone.

I think people don't understand what being in retreat entails. I don't want to really even *touch* things belonging to others, much less share a squishy tent! I didn't want to explain all that—about the ultra-sensitivity that develops, which one is actually supposed to encourage and protect. From the point of view of a secular, Western mind, it probably would come off as OCD or something. But aided by the incredulous look on my face, he got that I simply needed space, and he offered to go into the nearby town to find a second small tent.

But not needed: Bug net tent to the rescue! I had no idea I'd be camping in it. Because I'd been sleeping in it for months (on top of my bed), it was like continuing in my own retreat hut, but in public campgrounds. Beyond perfect.

Andy rigged up a tarp for me as the tent fly, since otherwise it was, of course, see-through.

Andy was so generous on the trip, good humored, and completely fun to be with. We watched the stars at a small beach one night, ate at fun seaside cafes, watched the ocean waves go by. He wanted to hear more about Buddhism, so we talked nearly the whole time about that and philosophy. He was cheered up to hear about the compassion component of Buddhism. I taught him the mantra of compassion, *om mani peme hung*, and we sang it up the coast.

> *"Friendship is so tightly linked to the definition of philosophy that it can be said that without it, philosophy would not really be possible. The intimacy between friendship and philosophy is so profound that philosophy contains the* philos, *the friend, in its very name."*
> – Giorgio Agamben, contemporary Italian philosopher

Something I had noticed months ago back in Williams, a sudden sense of wanting to simplify my altar by taking down the array of lama photos. So I did. It felt like a big relief. And when I got here to Bainbridge I had all these images in frames, and again, same thing. I even tried setting them up in different rooms, but no, too crowded. It was as if there was too much conversation all going at once.

Without them the altar is certainly not stark. The main altar is full of small objects surrounding the large photo of Khyentse Rinpoche. There's a small side table with the hundred deities, Vajrasattva, Refuge tree, Dudjom Rinpoche, and mandalas. And on the other side another table, utterly simple, a photo of Kilung Rinpoche and Dodrupchen Rinpoche, a ritual vase and teapot... with space for small tsok plates. All the many lama and other Buddha images I put away.

I feel this simplification signifies some inner change that's positive, strong, mature. Before, I felt a need for them, their support. Now so much presence feels too noisy. Ha.

How is it to be here? A little early to say. I've made a daily schedule which I'll begin tomorrow, and I think good. Rather, I think I'm good.

OCTOBER 15 – JOURNAL

Here I am, in Margi's space, Margi's writing space, writing. I got her pencil sharpener working again. And sharpened my own number 2 pencils, a fistful of them, in true Margi-the-poet tradition. The smooth, worn wood of her sturdy table supports my two elbows, reassuring my borrowed presence here. On it is ample space for my little traveling office, including the large fairy box containing office supplies, Margi's fetish, an enjoyment we always shared. I grew up here, in a way, on frequent visits to my first-husband's parents, beginning in my early 20s as Skip's girlfriend and then wife, then mother of our children. So, daughter-in-law to Margi.

We never would have thought all those years ago that I'd be here now as a hermitess, on Buddhist retreat, keeping Margi's empty house warm, watching over her garden and pond, the wild birds, and her writing table.

OCTOBER 16 – JOURNAL

In some ways I miss the remoteness of the Siskiyous, and the beauty, the quiet. But here much of that is found, too, the mind being the thing that needs to quiet down anyway. I go for a walk every day to the beach, about a block away. My altar is set up looking out a sliding glass door to the east where I can see sky and a small view of Puget Sound. It's fairly quiet—suburban quiet—just enough to remind of the world of humans, but not intrusive. It's pretty idyllic.

OCTOBER 17, SECOND ANNIVERSARY OF RETREAT – REFLECTIONS

Where am I now? In the middle of retreat. On the one hand, I look at the pages detailing experiences of the sacred, and I should feel accomplished. Rinpoche has said he's pleased. I'm pleased.

On the other hand, I feel very ordinary. Pre-retreat years held periods of rigpa and visions resulting from dzogchen openings; of a shunyata that lasted nearly a year; and a vibration, a hum of many months from the experience of retreat at Samye Chimphu. These experiences did change me at a fundamental level, and gave rise to all the expected qualities: compassion, equanimity, love, joy, with positive interactions in the world. Then over time, they faded. At least I know from these experiences where I'm headed now. I also see that I've not yet arrived. It still feels that the location is just in the neighboring valley, and like in a dream, I can't quite get there.

On a daily basis when in formal practice, I continue to have experiences. These not all the time, but frequently. And when they do not occur, I'm also fine. I've come to a new level of acceptance with the ebb and flow of that.

But it's in between sessions where my thoughts say I "should" be showing more progress. I'm still given to talking too much when around others; there's yet a wish for approval; the problem-solver impulse remains; when I have a health problem, I tend to fret. The eight samsaric dharmas still play.

However, there is also progress of a mundane kind: When I go for a day without talk, I'm quite fine. I enjoy each part of the day in solitude, including meals, evenings and nighttime. I enjoy practice, sadhanas, fire pujas, tsok, meditation. When with others I'm present and engaged. With the exception of the difficult periods, I feel well-adjusted and happy. I've been in that state continuously four months now, with other stretches earlier, too.

This second year I've continued to make wonderful progress to heal the split between SH and me. I truly have good feelings toward his wife. The miracle of the first year was healing the pain and anger of the split. The second year I actually forgave him, accepted his wife, and normalized.

I've completed major sadhanas, and millions of mantras, and had meditation experiences, understandings, and connections. Now what? Rinpoche has been busy conducting retreats while I was completing the dakini practice, and still off in yonder lands. This has actually been a little gift, giving me the space and time to be with myself and the practices, and now to mull over what it is that I think I want and need to do next. Of course Rinpoche will have something in mind, but good for me to do this steeping just now, listening.

What do I hear? Not sure. I've barely arrived here on Bainbridge, just settled in. I began making a list of practices that appeal, and a schedule. Besides the usual components, it also includes tai chi (which I've neglected for almost a year), walking, a little writing, reading. It's quite "responsible." And further? More meditation, more dzogchen.

Something to develop—spaciousness. How to hold spaciousness along with discipline—discipline along with integrity and true connection and love for the practices. With too much discipline, I often lose connection. Without enough discipline, I also lose connection. It's tricky, and one must hold this awareness continually.

I certainly don't want to end retreat where I am now. I feel half-baked, but in a good sense of halfway there. I want to better understand the esoteric texts on tantra that I've been reading. And of course to expand the practice experiences into ordinary life, while seeing with the eyes of the heart-mind. I want to complete retreat in such a way that I can be useful to others, to walk with wisdom into all the interactions of life. There is a rumor about long retreat, that one may not be aware of how profound the changes in oneself really are. I hope this may be true of me at the moment. And too much checking on the progress of the carrots while they're still growing, by pulling them out of the ground, will stunt their growth, or so I've been told.

Joy. Profound joy. I think that says it all. It's always been my *modus operandi*, all my life. If you truly have that, at a profound level, then I think you have all the rest.

OCTOBER 26 – JOURNAL

This morning I slept in. Sun on the deck beckoned, so I sat outdoors, still in nightgown and bathrobe, warm after prostrations plus sun. Beautiful.

After some time the garden began to fill with birds. Small grey ones, then robins in the crab apple, then the jays, and finally flickers. They were flitting this way and that, from the pond to the weeping birch. All over, chirping and singing and squawking. The flickers even made a whistle similar to eagles, but quieter. A murder of crows flew past some trees, too. This group of diverse birds wasn't fighting or competing, just showed up all at once. It contributed to a lovely practice.

All my practice sessions lately have been lovely. Lots of physical sensations—bliss, movement, samadhi—most of it not striking, but definite. However, I'm also struggling a bit with a meandering quality. Easy to be late for sessions; distracted by activities at the house, such as a visit from the furnace servicemen; doctor and dentist appointments to schedule and health insurance to take care of. Much of this should calm down when the adjustments and novelty of being here are past.

In the meantime I feel a bit as if I'm straddling the two worlds of retreat and ordinary. And my self-discipline needs strengthening, but somehow through joy. I'm not unhappy. However, when I see myself in the mirror I look pale, washed out, and too neutral, without twinkle or rosiness. Dull. That doesn't seem good, does it? But here's what's good—I feel at ease, no anxiety, no *lung* problems, and often experience bliss or pleasure in practice—engagement, connection, equanimity, and yes, pure pleasure.

OCTOBER 27 – JOURNAL

Clouds scudding from north to south on storm winds formed the body of a dakini dancing. At the level of her head, instead of a head, there was this: "3 + e." Curious. e = energy? 3 + energy. 3 *kayas* plus energy, the dakini's essence?

OCTOBER 29 – JOURNAL

Hummingbird visitations while practicing this morning in the sun on the deck. Also other tiny birds. One hummingbird was flying back and forth from a big bush next to me. Then his green feathers picked up the sun's rays so they brightened suddenly, crystalline brilliance, green sequins, like a glamorous mermaid whose scales hugged her form perfectly—in this case, a slender perfect bird with whizzing wings. As I watched him in the leaves, suddenly brilliant fuchsia appeared. It was so sudden, his whole head, a gift, that I burst into tears. Then just as suddenly—for that is how they come and go—he was right at me, hovering in air, a hand's width from my eyes. I jerked my head back a little, then held his gaze, almost too close to focus, but I did. He hovered there for a minute, not looking at my red jacket, but at my face, his long beak pointing at my human beak. It was indeed a gift. A single frog was croaking nearby.

Soon after, an eagle. Then a little later, that mix of jays and flickers came by.

OCTOBER 30 – JOURNAL

This morning I fell off a perch and got a big scratch and bruise on my leg. When it happened I didn't feel angry or frustrated or victimized—it just happened, although I was surprised. There was no pain. None. Still, an hour later, no pain.

OCTOBER 31 – CONSULTATION WITH RINPOCHE

After hearing how things have been going, Rinpoche said:

"You're doing great, stability and experiences coming together. Some people in long retreat could be getting less stable, even though they should be getting better. So this is very good."

NOVEMBER 6 – JOURNAL

This bliss. It arose in dakini practice this evening. So sweet, heart-centered. I felt in love! Love. *In* love. Suddenly arose the thought: Where is my mate to share this with? Then, wow! Where did *that* come from? Why needed? Is that the typical impulse that leads us humans into coupled relationships?

Then, I began saying out loud, almost like poetry: "Free, freedom. This bliss is free. Not placed, not bestowed, not grasped, not labeled, not defined, not limited. This bliss is freely bestowed, without grasping. Freely streaming, without tracking…" and many more not now recalled. Tears came.

Then, a beautiful sadhana practice, full of bliss. And physical sensations, and other experience.

I had an eye check the day before yesterday, wonderful time with the doc and the tech, and with Diane B., who drove me. Then yesterday enjoyed a trek into Seattle with Tracy to the dentist. After two days, much stimulation, so I let it flow through.

I'm not even sure it's bliss, more like love. A generalized love, spontaneous, heart-centered. Kind of extraordinary because it's not attached to anything, not even to an experience, nor an Ah-ha moment, nor satori. It's just arising, filling, flowing, informing. It's not manic, nor does it have a depressive opposite. In a way, simple. But also filling me with a buoyancy, and simple happiness. It's been around most days for the last ten, definitely today. All the practice sessions beautiful, many sensations, active. Days full of enjoyment and happiness.

Lucille, my dear friend who is now managing our sangha, came for a few days to do retreat along with me, and left yesterday. It was a lovely time, doing practice together, and she brought wonderful food and cooked, a real treat! She conveyed how the sangha has been coming along, that they have moved beyond the awkward transition phase, and now working together beautifully. I needed to hear this, I told her, so I can also move along in my mind, not stay stuck in the past—which could be like waking up from a long nap while the world has moved on, à la Rip van Winkle. At the same time, hearing about samsaric concerns, my mind was whirring in the mundane world. But the moment she left, I re-entered my retreat world, and it all fell back into place, like a wizard had snapped her fingers.

Cloud images during morning practice: A sky-spanning angel with huge wings unfolded up around a chubby cherubic head, Italian style... topped by an ushnisha—the expanded summit of a buddha's head.

Then a huge mistiness coalesced, with mystical potentiality in the center to which I felt connected, as if my mind had some affect. And suddenly a dragon appeared there. It had at first the head of a lioness, then eventually a traditional head of an Asian dragon.

Above that then descended more clouds in the form of an immense Kwakiutl thunderbird, facing south, a typical, elongated side view. Thunderbird—the Northwest coast indigenous dragon. So here they were, appearing together, three winged spirit beings from three continents. This unfolded over an hour's time.

NOVEMBER 28, THANKSGIVING – JOURNAL

Today a thick fog muffling the expanse above the sea, muffling even the sea itself. No wind, no little ripples upon the water. The sea, like a slumbering giant, inhaling, exhaling, soft and slow, the breathing of a deep dreamless state, barely perceptible. The body of the behemoth swelled as the sea edge receded. Then the inevitable exhalation, and the gentle surf came forth to my feet, so quietly, not even a snoring sound of pebbles washing back and forth.

Dream

Dreamed that Andy drove me back to Williams, just as a visit. When we arrived I found I'd left many things in my old cabin. I was surprised and embarrassed. Still in sleep, but with lucidity, I checked with my non-sleep awareness and realized I actually *had* left the cabin empty and clean, so I continued with the dream. Everyone from Williams was surprised and happy to see me.

DECEMBER 2, NEW MOON – JOURNAL

So much going on these days with vivid body sensations in all the sadhanas, energy going up, going down, happening. I have to talk soon to Rinpoche, because I know not what to do with this.

DECEMBER 3 – JOURNAL

Rinpoche and family coming in a few days to Bainbridge, staying with Tracy and her husband, with two visits planned for here. One for dinner with his family, one for a retreat consultation. I have some prepping to do—notes, questions, etc!

DECEMBER 6 – JOURNAL

Lovely dinner with Rinpoche, Chöying and their little girl, Padmasalle. We exchanged some early Christmas gifts. When Padmasalle did three prostrations toward me, Rinpoche commented that she had only done that toward him or the shrine before. I'll take it as honoring three-year retreat rather than any attainment on my part. Later I tried kissing her on the forehead a couple of times, and finally, she came for a kiss, with gooey, runny nose, which I narrowly avoided by planting one on her forehead. The evening felt sweet, natural, and relaxed.

DECEMBER 7 – CONSULTATION WITH RINPOCHE

We reviewed experiences of the last two months related to my practice, about details of the subtle body system, especially in light of recent experiences, and we looked at what's next. Rinpoche said much and taught extensively. Here are a few shareable notes:

I told him that most of my practice sessions have these qualities: bliss, movement, samadhi, pleasure, engagement, active, often beautiful. He said:

"These are blessing support for practice and experience. You don't necessarily need to hold onto or know words for it. Just do the practice... with non-conceptuality. They are a subtle key that all things, anything, can happen. Don't be too eager to hold on. If you connect with it, that's beautiful, but you don't have to get lost or leave the base of practice environment. Discovering that, in that way, is the most powerful.

"Bliss, clarity, non-conceptual mind. These are really big for serious practitioners—not to be attached. When it happens, it happens."

Then I said that on or off the cushion, I feel at ease, no anxiety or *lung* problems, enjoying solitude at all times of day, and happy. He said, "This is so amazing. That is the retreat, the quality. Not only having experiences like visions, etc. This is more of the essential human nature, of ease in the mind, of living qualities. *That* is the result."

When I shared about the sense of an expanded love, he said, "Really bodhicitta quality of love. No object. Objectless."

As well as specific other practices and instructions, Rinpoche also suggested I begin sleep yoga in earnest.

DECEMBER 21, SOLSTICE – JOURNAL

Saw an interesting animal a few days ago. At first I didn't know what kind of animal as it was obscured by bushes—deer? raccoon? fox? super-sized cat? Then he appeared, a small dog with grey-brown coat. He was nosing around on the other side of the hedge and fence just in front of the deck. Coyote! Beautiful and healthy! The first I'd ever seen.

I wrote this for Sophia, who suffers from lack of sun in the Northwest winters:

Star light, Star bright
Sinking into winter's night,
Hidden wisdom for to find
A solstice quest for the Great Mind.

This morning outside for practice early morning. I heard a large group of people congregating somewhere down below in the direction of the nearby beach park. Their voices conveyed happiness and delight. After some time, there was drumming and singing. It was so beautiful! I thought, I want badly to go join them, or at least to see—who are they? what are they doing? It seems something appropriate to my practice, but not appropriate for me to leave my spot, here on the deck, on my cushion, within the confines of retreat. So I incorporated their beautiful, spiritual presence throughout my own practice. After some time, maybe an hour or so, the sounds disappeared. But never the sound of cars leaving. Where did they go back to, and how?

I heard them again, around the time of the summer solstice about sunrise. Again, mysterious appearance, my wish to join their ceremony and song, and, then, disappearance without a sound. Much later after retreat, someone with years of experience in American Indian spiritual tradition shared something that indicated these may have been appearances from the spirit world. So, my decision to stay with my cushion was correct. But my inner vision wasn't great enough to know on my own who they were, or if they had a message for me. Perhaps just spiritual companionship and joy, for it was that.

DECEMBER 24, CHRISTMAS EVE – JOURNAL

A sacred night. I switched on classical music radio with its Christmas program. What beauty—all. Early evening Rinpoche called to warmly wish me Merry Christmas. In the conversation he told me that a friend's father had died. He's been on my prayer list since the beginning of retreat, so he slipped away at 94.

The early dark had fallen, sacred Christmas music was playing, and my cushion beckoned—not in the usual way for practice, but this time as natural expression. Sacred essence pulsing, I wrapped my prayer shawl around me, and sat down. No prayers came, just a vivid awareness of the profound and evocative music, the poignancy of this man's passing, the truth of the vajra lineage, which intermingled with the other truth of our ancient Western mysticism, and the sense of the holy night. I stayed for awhile, through several songs. Reflected on the ancient past, the music easily taking me there, the purity of voices evoking celestial beings, celestial realms. Powerful. Joy was shining, love and a deep happiness. I got up to prepare a Christmas Eve feast.

Then came a beautiful performance of "Silent Night." I stopped and came back out to the shrine room, singing along the words of the three verses, words which have always inspired, overwhelmed me, expanded me at my core. The first verse, so simple, a lullaby, the last two verses transcendent. I used to sing all three to my children as a lullaby, any time of year... and by the last verse my eyes would be streaming tears—as they were this evening, and again now.

The words speak of experience of the divine—in the William Blake sense, luminosity—the mystical aspect of Christianity which still holds truth for me, and which I find aligned with the Vajra path. The richness of the western mystical tradition is strong on a night like this, a richness which infuses and informs my experience in Vajrayana truth. The two together, a multifaceted crystal within. I want to share this with my granddaughter, but know not how.

Then I returned to the kitchen, continuing on in this way, my heart overflowing with joy, light. After eating I set out all the gifts I received on the round table, covered with a deep fuchsia-colored silk shawl, poinsettia in the center, and opened more presents. Happy, realizing that this could be one of the most fulfilling Christmases in my life—alone! Oh my!

I've been quite happy for days. I'm going into seclusion in a week—no check-ins with anyone, even Barbara, communicating by note with my retreat attendants, etc.—hoping the transition goes alright, and really looking forward to it.

On a walk on the beach today two huge shaggy mastiffs suddenly appeared, with no owner, coming my way. I decided to find a stick, so I sauntered up to the driftwood area, and just in time found a large one, much taller than me and quite heavy to lift. As I walked back to the water's edge I slowly righted it vertically, as the dogs approached.

They apparently didn't like the cut of my jib, and started barking in an aggressive way. I spoke sweetly to them while backing up. One of them tried to get around behind me, but I didn't let him, backing up toward the water's edge. Then together they stood there, looking at me. So I said sharply, "Go on now!" while motioning with the stick. They didn't like *that!* and started barking again. So I went back to sweetly, "It's okay, it's okay," all the while slowly backing up.

They turned and trotted away along the water's edge, looking back at me suspiciously. I carried the stick-cum-log with me for quite awhile, checking over my shoulder, thinking, whew, that felt like a close call, on Christmas Eve.

No owner. Wow. Saint Bernard Beach Patrol. What are people thinking? What are they doing with their dogs? (These were not Saint Bernards by the way, but similar in size and fluff, sans friendliness.)

Silent Night, Holy Night
Son of God, Love's pure light
Radiance streaming from thy holy face
In the dawn of redeeming grace,
Jesus, lord at thy birth, Jesus, lord at thy birth.

DECEMBER 26 – DREAM

I was going to be having an audience with Thinley Norbu Rinpoche. There was his seat and places to sit around. With me were sangha friends, honoring my retreat experience. Then appeared my grandfather, Jake! I thought, if he's here the interview won't be able to proceed freely, and maybe Thinley Norbu won't even come. I knew Jake was there as a special happening, come from the dead, so I didn't want to give him the bum's rush. He didn't seem to understand the present circumstance, and at one point was lounging in the lama seat. I thought, oh wow, now I'm going to have to explain *that* to him! I gently went over to tell him it was a special seat for someone coming, and he got off.

He surprised me by asking the group, "How's your meditation going?" One of them didn't understand how out of place he was there, equating his venerable age to venerable wisdom and involvement in the Vajrayana. She started answering him, so I interrupted before it got very far, explaining that my grandfather isn't a meditator or a Buddhist. She realized her naïveté and melted back into her seat.

Some monks entered, passing out dana envelopes. Just as I was trying to figure out how to kindly ask Jake to leave, he asked what the envelopes were for. When I explained they were for making donations, right away he decided to leave. I thought, wow, that was lucky. Then, the way was cleared for Thinley Norbu to come.

The dream seems to reflect the melding through this Yule, of East and West, new and old, the deeply mystical and the mundane. My grandfather, a wheat rancher who passed away so long ago, it's hard to think of anyone more removed from even the Western mystical tradition, much less the esotericism of the Vajrayana. But who in some way represents my Western roots. The West—now so utterly secular, even Christmas has become so. In the dream I was banishing all that, including its shadow.

The dream also seems to be saying, steer away from mundane, secular family concerns as that will obstruct progress on the path. Don't be naïve and communicate too much and inappropriately about my retreat experience. Stay with the program.

And today I did just that—Yule behind me, I reconnected full-on with the Vajrayana program.

DECEMBER 30 – DREAM

Rinpoche and I were working on sangha business, organizing events. Others showed up to help. One of them had been giving interviews and orientations to students, but now there were so many and she requested help. Of course I offered to help and showed the list of interviews to Rinpoche. He said, in a kind way, "Well okay, but do you want to be on retreat, or not? This seems like you're not on retreat." I thought, oh wow, you're right! I drew a line through my name on the paper and wrote beside it, "ON RETREAT."

JANUARY 3, 2014 – JOURNAL

Silence began today. I sent last emails, including a grocery list to Diane B. Then unhooked the wireless router and put it in the closet.

January – Schedule

6:30	Wake up; Ngöndro
8:30	Dress and breakfast
9:30	Open altar; prostrations; Riwo Sangchöd weekly
10:00	Meditation
12:00	Lunch
1:00	Walk with meditation mind
1:30	Sadhana practices
5:00	Meditation
6:00	Dinner
7:00	Meditation
8:00	Reading and study
9:00	Ready for night; further reading
10:30	Sleep

The schedule shifted several more times during the retreat, sometimes more intense, and at the end, more relaxed. After this I kept three more schedules through to the end of retreat.

JANUARY 4 – CONSULTATION WITH RINPOCHE

Among other topics, Rinpoche gave simple instructions for dream yoga. After outlining how to proceed, he said this:

"Don't go into it at this point as a whole big thing, by reading books, as an extravaganza—the Westerner way of being overly enthusiastic and grasping. Go with simplicity first. Then see how it goes."

JANUARY II – JOURNAL

A humdinger of a storm. It started last night, gales of wind and rain from the south. Still cold, below forty, but didn't freeze. Since late last night till now, continuing. There were two sunny and peaceful lulls, but it's back again—dark, windy, raining.

Morning practice also stirred up, with aggressive thoughts up from the depths, like the seas out in front—big swells hurrying, headed north. The sound of rain, cherished rain, coming as a monsoon, filling up the little pond almost to the top. Overflow will happen if this keeps up.

I keep waiting for the power to go out—knock on wood, not yet. We already had that in the fall so maybe the tenuous branches have already fallen. But the little five-colored lights on the altar have blinked a few times in warning. I knew I was risking when I took a shower this morning in the windowless bathroom.

Others might turn extra lights on during this, as antidote, to crowd out the onslaught and the dark. But my impulse is to experience it more acutely, and so few lights are shining. The brilliance of the sunny period, contrasted with the dim of the midday storm, grey, evoking depth, being churned by the storm, wind and rain, air and water. What does it churn up? That is unpredictable— new beach logs, new patterns in sand and pebbles, new messages, arrived as gifts.

At noon break I noticed a large branch in the steep, narrow lane just beside the house, and I wanted to clear it for the neighbors who live down the hill. The elements were tremendous, wind and torrential rain making a loud roar. I suited up and emerged. A storm usually seems worse from indoors—unless it's really bad. This one was medium.

After clearing the branch I thought to check drains. Suddenly a long, *basso profundo* of thunder. And soon after, the skies cleared—blue. Wind and rain stopped. I cleared leaves and moss chunks out of the shop roof gutters since streaming overflow had created big puddles at the shop door.

While sunny and brilliant, washed land and sky, I walked down the lane to the beach. Rainbow off to the north, faint but full. Big waves crashing into bows of two large, laden barges, going nearly in tandem, those stalwart tugs, pulling south, right into the wind, waves, and tide. I returned home, and shortly after, the raindrops resumed falling. And now, as I write, full-on storm, again wondering if lights will out.

From the window with binoculars I watched as one mammoth beach log—perhaps eight feet in diameter, the kind that's been there so long, now a landmark, inscribed with initials and names of teenagers—was being pushed and pulled by the lashing waves at high tide, mighty enough for this big work.

By 5 the storm had passed, or dissolved. Now peaceful. In evening practice of 21 Taras, I looked up and there was Moon—three-quarters waxing, shining brightly in dark sky, attending—a sign of Lady Wisdom, stamping a seal onto this practice, which I did while thinking of a dear friend who has been ailing.

Then, at just-dark, directly in front of where I sit for practice, two deer passed slowly, pausing right in front. A mother and fawn. I could tell their size and movements only by their silhouettes against the still space of the garden.

JANUARY 12 – JOURNAL

It's time to begin letting the deities lead, to take their advice, to allow them to teach me, to listen, to ask. In the midst of practice, perhaps rather than directing the visualizations from one stage to the next, now time to find out from them what is needed next. This means not becoming lazy or free-form, but to become more astute, discerning, awake, aware—watchful for signals arising from my intuition. And then dancing with it.

I began intention for dream yoga the night after Rinpoche's suggestion and instructions. That night I woke up all night with every dream. I remembered a year ago in the fall, I was having lucid dreaming but got little sleep for weeks and became debilitated by sleep deprivation. Then the wakefulness itself seemed to crowd out the lucid dreaming. Difficult!

So, the next night, this time around, I asked the deities to let me sleep and keep the lucidity within the dreams without actual wakefulness. Since then my nights have been heavy slumber, with few remembered dreams, just a few here and there. So funny, so extreme. Rinpoche said, Don't give up, be simple. So I will follow that.

JANUARY 16 – JOURNAL

Yesterday full moon. In late afternoon practice I got up during mantra recitations to untie some knots that had wedged themselves around my heart center. I went outside into the quiet and calm evening, just after sunset, to see if I could find the rising moon. Sky clear, few clouds, sea flat. Wrapped in shawl against almost freezing air, I stood at the oval "window" that I'd recently pruned through to a view of the sea, the distant shore, and the sky. I stood below the cedars and the eccentric pine, watching, waiting... for a long time. No moon.

I went back in to warm up, then back outside to moon-gazing "window." There she was, rising behind a jagged mountain, orange, radiating brilliant reflection of sun. I watched the earth turn in the heavens against our neighbor, our one lady-lunar retinue. I felt our own earthly body suspended in space, turning in the vastness. Awe-inspired, I finished practice, happy. Happy to take the moment to go outside of prescription. Happy to follow the arc of the moon through the house window later while preparing dinner. Happy to find myself standing at the kitchen counter singing out loud, "Cold December Fled Away," a Catalonian Christmas carol. It was so spontaneous, and yes, December *is* fled away.

Dream

I was going with Rinpoche through a small town, looking for shops that might sell gold earrings, with a wish to ornament the dakini. In one shop, the man asked, "What kind of gold do you want?" I said, "22 or 24 carat." He brought out a large hand-blown clear orb, the size of a large Christmas tree ornament. Inside at the bottom was a small fuzzy, light-gold frizzle of a thing, without distinct shape. I looked puzzled. He said, "That is gold, spun gold." I took the globe. The frizzles moved inside, as if alive. It was fascinating. However, I couldn't imagine wearing this huge object as an earring, so I said I'd think on it.

The dream went on, more shops, more interesting objects, but no golden earrings. In an antique shop, a pair of dreadlocked, earth-toned, yarn-braided earrings was offered as a gift from a Buddhist friend. Really not gold. Also there was an antiquarian dharma book written by an early buddhist Westerner.

After waking and still in bed, I employed the technique that I had read about in Alan Wallace's book—not moving one's body upon waking, to let the dream memory surface without the distraction of the body jostling around. It helps.

While in morning practice, it came to me that the orb in the dream was my belly, and the golden frizzle, essence. I should have taken the orb. It was like being offered a magic talisman, a treasure, and not recognizing it. Later in the day I remembered that the frizzles also looked like pieces of dna. Golden dna of one's buddha nature.

The Map Is Not the Territory

Last summer a book came to my attention, sufficiently enticing to choose as "extracurricular" reading, anything non-buddhist being almost taboo for retreat. It was indeed wonderful, written by my friend Sheila's shamanic mentor and colleague, Bill Plotkin. *Wild Mind: A Field Guide to the Human Psyche.* Threading my way through his dense conceptual world of inner work, I was sometimes delighted by the presentation, and sometimes daunted by the prospect of my own inner work yet to be wrangled with. Plotkin himself commented that his construct is complicated, but not nearly as much as the human psyche itself. He summed it up with Alan Watts' simple phrase, "The map is not the territory." I thought, how true, as I'd just been feeling his was a complicated "map," and further, only one version of how things are, one which doesn't reflect humanness *in toto.*

The map is not the territory. The phrase steeped in me. Living in the mountain forest of Oregon, a place where a map would sometimes have been helpful, I often had wished for a map of *that* territory. Maps are magnetic to some of us, beautiful—tiny replicas of the world, like cerebral dollhouses. With few words, drawn instructions: go this way and you will find... a stream, the edge of a forest, the height of a mountain, the way in, the way out, the treasure. Following our fingertip, a vivid imagination can soar over the vastness of an ocean, up a rocky seashore, tiny islands in an arc, villages and great cities. Lost in a confusing tangle of real-life country roads, the map will indeed lead us to our destination. In a pre-map world, this is potent magic.

And yet, the map is not the territory. No indeed. Useful, but not the same thing. A set of instructions for getting somewhere is not the same as the experience of being there. Suddenly, in this investigation, something came clear: The teaching of the Vajrayana is a map, and this is not the territory, not the experience of being, nor even of becoming, enlightened.

This insight hit me like a thunderbolt. Most centrally I realized that I have been clinging to the map, as if it, of itself, would take me to the destination. As if the map is a magic carpet—you just leap on, cling to the edges, and get there. However, even if headed in the right direction, even if devoting serious life energy to the endeavor, this clinging itself is an obstacle, a block in the road, one that's not possible to simply push past. It has to be dynamited, blown up, for the way to clear.

Is the map necessary for the Vajrayana path? Yes, without any doubt. The way is perilous—endless back eddies to get lodged in for lifetimes, covered ice chasms to fall into, false bays to run aground upon, exciting torrents to get swept away by. The Vajrayana is the territory of a true quest with all its trials where, if not careful, the psyche can be overtaken by false prophets, allured by egoic inflation into serious delusion, flung by inner storm into depression, and subjected to sicknesses of mind and body—all overseen and lorded over by one's own personal mara, demon of the psyche.

This Vajrayana map to enlightenment is so utterly complex, and the treasure so hidden, that one also needs interpreters for the map, those who have gone before. Not only have they gone there, they are leading the way from within the citadel of the treasure itself.

Even though the map is crucial, it's not the territory. Even though the teachings of the Vajrayana are instructive, inspiring to the point of aching beauty, they don't stand in for one's own experience. They're not meant to. But it seems "clinging to the map" could be a special problem for many of us in the West, perhaps not because of anything particular to our culture, but simply because Buddhism, in any of its forms, is so new to our culture. Even many of us with decades of experience, not yet enlightened, are still sorting through, investigating how does each element fit into one's own—the Western—psyche. We're advised not to do this, to keep the "thinking mind" down to a dull roar. But how can we not? We're not test tube babies, not *tabula rasa*. Far from it, we come with a strong cultural background, and further, are educated in secular rationalism. We're enculturated to use our intellect. Even those of us who met the dharma in their youth are also yet of this cultural context.

So, what does clinging to the map look like? It means not trusting one's own experience. It means having a narrow focus. It means holding precisely to the visualization instructions for dear life. It means going through the motions of rituals without understanding their inner meaning, their mystical function, without which we can't fully participate, we can't dance. It means not being able to extrapolate from one dharma situation to the next because everything is suddenly out of context, because the essence knowledge and understanding is simply not there.

When I look at all these examples, I see a theme: lack of confidence, and fear. Fear of making mistakes. Fear of the unknown. Fear of experiencing life. What is the result of this obstacle? It's not truly standing up and engaging. It's not taking responsibility for one's own spiritual path. It's not owning one's own life path, one's life essence. How crazy is that? It's remaining always in awe, as if enlightenment is out there, not something inside to be uncovered. It's stuck on the instructions, as if they will save you from falling into an abyss, or as if they're magic talismans.

So, where do the mantras, the mandalas (now *there* are maps!), visualizations, and rituals lie? It seems they may straddle both map and territory—tools to be used in the territory.

But more centrally, the territory is the experience, the personal realization, the unfolding development that we must let flourish. We must take the stopper out of the bottle, and with a wild cry, become the experience of the Vajrayana. In this way, we can explode that obstacle on the path, the path at our very feet. And make it our own.

JANUARY 22 – JOURNAL

A package arrived about a week ago from my brother and his wife, all wrapped up for Christmas. A puzzle—of the Tibetan Wheel of Life! Oh what fun, a thousand pieces. I immediately started it that day. Then quickly saw how it raised my tendencies for addiction, easily spending too much time at a single, mind-engaging task. Uh-oh! For several days, I enjoyed the sorting and hunting and matching, while considering what to do about the distraction. I finally came to the decision that I really didn't *want* to spend this delicious opportunity of retreat on a puzzle. I found it really impossible to limit myself to a half hour— and more than that, well, there aren't really extra half-hours in the day. It was a good decision to put all the little pieces back in the box, feeling almost relieved, more virtuous... and happy because it was coming from within.

I've been recording myself reading Longchenpa's *Chöying Dzod, The Precious Treasury of the Basic Space of Phenomena*, and then listening to it. I'm reading the words at a slow walk, softly, so that when I listen I can really take in the meaning, using it like a guided meditation.

Listening is such a different experience. When one reads, even to oneself, there's a whiff of performance. One says the words aloud to oneself, using correct cadence and rhythm, plus the visual perception of the words on the page, too, so that the information is absorbed in a particular way—with a division between two selves: the giver of the information and the receiver. But by listening only, one's mind can really relax, is able to "not do," and thus turn toward absorption all of itself. I'm finding that experience to help move toward a meditation away from conceptuality (at least in some small increment), which is the crux of the content of the text, and really, of this retreat. It gives a great degree of stability, confidence, nongrasping, uncoiling, space.

I also have in mind that the recordings could be there when I'm in the process of dying, if I have that circumstance. I've heard that many Tibetans do this—listen to someone reading them this very text while they're on their way out. I thought, yes, that's what I want, too.

JANUARY 23 – JOURNAL

Dipping into a commentary on *Tsik Sum Ne Dek, Hitting the Essence in Three Words,* this while meditating, a section on grasping, with the mind being the source of all problems. It got me thinking about how this works with conceptualizing.

We want to understand something new, so we automatically go to the act of conceptualizing. At that moment we grasp it, thinking we've understood it. Our mind has grasped it—in fact that's even a figure of speech—but we haven't truly understood, or "seen" it, as it truly is.

However, in feeling we *have* understood it—which has now become an icon of the thing, in order to compartmentalize it—we now take "ownership" of it... in our minds. Now it's really grasped—and more so, it's "owned." And then we can go on to the next thing. When we encounter this thing again, it's almost like we can say, "Been there, done that—what's next?"

The problem is, what we just grasped is a symbol, a concept, a representation of the thing itself, which is based on layers upon layers of similar concepts built up over a lifetime. So it's not ever again truly encountered, we're not really present with it again, and actually lose the present moment awareness, not only of the thing, but of the experiential moment, too. And of the opportunity.

This is just the outer level, but I wanted to write it down, this juncture of grasping and conceptualizing, which are often taught separately... though with much more refinement than this.

Yesterday I saw a hubbub of hummingbirds. It was seven! I guess that makes a hubbub. First one flew upward from behind bushes in front of the deck, at a slight angle toward the north, swift like a fighter jet. Zip! Then hovered. Then it dove in an arc, downward and continuing north, to behind the big pine tree. One breath later, the second hummingbird followed, making the same tracing in the air. Then a third... all the way to seven! The seventh had a similar pattern, but less extreme, less high up.

Later on, I saw another, or possibly the same, seven doing the same thing. Today, more hummingbird activity in the same territory. And a huge flock of robins. If it was a hubbub of hummingbirds, perhaps this was a riffraff of robins?

Barbara came to get the mail. We had tea. She talked and I listened, since I'm in silence. I had some pre-written questions for her, like, how are you? How's the family? What about the gutters? It was lovely and we managed well. Then we went on a silent walk to the beach. A sunny day, beautiful. She's doing well, and said I seem awfully good. Must be all this non-talk, although I can't say it's non-thought!

Then at dinnertime, Tracy came with groceries. We had another lovely time—her talking and me listening, nodding, and writing little notes.

It's an excellent practice, this silence—no holding forth, no being opinionated. Being actively present, *with* the other, but not taking over the situation. Not really passive because it's still interactive, but quite different, feels mindful. I'm glad to be doing this non-conversation.

2nd Year, According to the Days: 730 Completed

As a little gift on this second year completion day I found a rather large agate on the beach. The bright sun at winter's low angle made it glow against the more mundane beach pebbles. Still cold, barely above freezing—but the unobscured sun's rays warming. Lovely.

A lone heron for a long time was standing in shallow water, fishing. I stood nearby, a lone yogini, hands resting on staff, meditating. A pair of beings, looking out together, to the sea and the eastern sky.

I've been thinking of the little boat out in the middle of the ocean, on this voyage. Looking back, toward the east (the direction that got set in those childhood dreams), I see I've covered a distance of two years. The shore hasn't been visible for a long, long time, in some ways, a lifetime. But I can still recall the shore's shape, its smell, its familiarity. The surface of the ocean has held every kind of formation: calm undulations, slow eddies, glistening ripples, reflections of stars, moon, and brilliant sun; also, choppy whitecaps, stormy swells, cascading waves to disappear in, and typhoons with giant whirlpools from which I barely escaped.

All that is now behind me, and I turn forward, to the west. It no longer gives me nausea to look down from inside my tiny boat to the unknowable depths, to realize that I'm still quite in the middle of this great ocean, this epic inner journey. The far western shore is still beyond easy reach. If I called out, no one would hear me. I don't know what the depths of the ocean will stir up between here and there, and yet I feel content. I don't know if this state of acceptance is due to having crossed an imaginary mid-point in the journey, or if it's just that I've grown accustomed to being out here. Either way, whatever it took, I'm grateful. In the middle, and yet arrived. Cutting a path but leaving no trail, bobbing along in the immensity.

In all this time, it's been barely a month that I've been able to go really single-handed. I've been on my own in most ways since the beginning, but a lifeline has been some communication with others, through phone or email. It was clear that I needed that. Originally I never imagined that I'd be on solitary retreat these three years, since it's most common to do a first three-year retreat with a group. But circumstances prevented this. So to give balance, stability of emotions and psyche, I communicated in some form with someone almost every day. Then, a couple of months ago I suddenly felt ready to go solo.

Now here at Margi's house, safe and sound, at the turn of the new year, I dropped that stabilizing anchor, and without any problem, it's been smooth sailing. I'm finding myself to be happy, stable, and disciplined. My days are full. There's not a part of the day or night that I dread. Every day about the same. Ocean, and more of it. But the interior world offers much to chew on, to observe. And then there is the turning of the earth in the starry sky, Jupiter to track in the eastern twilight, the rise and fall of the season, the surprise of flowering bushes in mid-winter, the hubbub of hummingbirds, cries of eagle, sand messages on the strand, and meditation of heron in still water.

JANUARY 25 – DREAM

Location was a retreat center in the forest. There were bears. I was with a young man caretaker and a young woman retreatant. At one point a massive bear appeared, acting angry and coming our way. The other two debated if it was huge (the woman's opinion) or just full-sized (the man's). We decided to move away for safety. I got stuck, that dream-like experience of unreasonably not being able to move, kind of captured by the earth, as if the earth, golden-colored, had welled up in a clumpy way and was holding onto me. I looked to the other two for help, but they were—we *all* were—looking at the menacing, approaching bear, and trying to get away. That's when I partially awoke, and told myself to morph the dream. Then I returned to dream sleep, staying in a cabin, and had further, less frightening encounters with the bears, more interactions with the other retreatants, and finally, a walk into the nearby village.

JANUARY 30 – JOURNAL

Retreat is well... except Tracy was in a car accident last weekend, with concussion. She left a completely lucid phone message regarding groceries, and it sounds like she's fully functional. But gosh!

My dreams lately have been busy. A little wakeful, but not so I stay awake all night. I've certainly been sleeping a lot—nine hours most nights, even with alarm on for eight. So it seems wanted or needed, or at least, it's happening.

If there's a dream theme, there are two: dharma and groups. Lots of people, organizing or doing, or interacting. Last night, similar but with a unique spin: on another planet! People were bouncing around with less gravity than earth, but more than the moon, as noted by someone in the dream. It had a desert-like environment. Everyone was arriving, exploring, enjoying, and bouncing around. I only remembered the dream while taking a shower this morning. Contemplating the properties of water in a non-conceptual way triggered the memory.

Joy of solitude. I never thought I would arrive here. But I have. I don't want to be disturbed. I feel satisfied with the day. I don't experience a special sense of a vacant, echoing house in my head at the end of the day when I don't speak to anyone—now silent every day. However, the couple of times I've had to speak to someone, it's fine—no big aversion or attraction, regret or pull for more.

Still sometimes inner turmoil arises, and regrets over things in the past. Dzogchen meditation is quite an antidote for the flotsam that drifts in.

I've been continuing to record the *Chöying Dzod* and then listening as a meditation springboard. I love this, and it's truly helping. Other texts I'm reading are dovetailing beautifully, too.

FEBRUARY 1 – JOURNAL

Something began to emerge over a month ago, as a faint tapping on my shoulder. I had occasionally been adding the practice of the 21 Taras to the mix, but I felt that something within it was missing. Here were all these pages of black text on white paper, describing twenty-one unique goddesses in four lines of verse each. I had a good sense of a handful of them, but the information contained in each stanza just wasn't enough to inspire connection for me. Kilung Rinpoche had in the past given in-depth teachings on the twenty-one, and I knew there were books out there, but with a daunting number—twenty-one—it was hard to keep them straight in my mind. I felt a need to find a solution, a way to expand the sadhana somehow, to help myself, and possibly others, develop meaningful relationships with each—not while reading a book or in a teaching, but while inside of the practice as it was happening.

One idea after the other came, and finally I settled on one: The sadhana should be illustrated, but how could I do this, since I'm not an artist? The only option was collage.

Short threads of this self-conversation had emerged over a number of weeks, and in every instance I thought: I can't do this, I'm in retreat. The faint tapping on the shoulder escalated to a whisper, then more loudly, and by the time the idea of collage illustration emerged, a loudspeaker was amplifying the message: You have to do this. Now. In retreat. It would require going online to find imagery and then printing them out. I could devote an hour a day to the project, so it would be a devotional and intuitive activity for my daily break.

And that's what I did. I knew it was marginal for retreat, but I felt I'd gotten the sort of intuitive call one shouldn't ignore, and if I didn't do it now, I knew it would never happen out in ordinary life.

As the book progressed, its validity only increased. Not only did I think the project itself had value on several levels, but more: in taking the step of listening to my own intuition, hearing it lucidly, discerning its value, and then with a kind of self-authority and authenticity, taking action based on that. It was an action that was clearly personal, slightly outside the structure of retreat. Yet it felt completely inside the spirit of retreat. I had now gone to another level: I was making the retreat truly my own.

FEBRUARY 2 – JOURNAL

In a short and light phone conversation with Rinpoche, I talked about the process of remembering dreams, and mentioned having some good, or "nice," dreams. He advised, "Nice or not nice—that's ego. Don't think like that. Just observe without hope or fear."

One dharma friend forwarded news of Mingyur Rinpoche on his three-year retreat. He had been found by a lama-friend of his in the Nepali Himalayas, who then stayed with him for some months, giving him money, food, and things to keep him warm. He also took photos and brought back a letter. His story, photos, and Mingyur Rinpoche's letter were put on the web. Taking it all in, I burst into joyful tears. I don't even know him, but I'd heard a little of it around the same time I went into retreat—how he had to "run away from home" basically, because as the baby of his family of well-established tulkus, it seems he felt overly coddled, and needed to break away to experience further, meaningful development. His family was said to be distraught.

But here were these glowing photos of him, with bushy hair and eyebrows, looking super-healthy and happy. Quite free. His letter also glowing. He's been wandering, from cave to cave, valley to valley. And somehow I found it glorious, inspiring. And from there, to happy tears. I've been thinking of him since, and prayed last night, a particularly frigid night, that he was warm, in his winter mountain cave. (Wow, am I ever safe, fed, warm, and coddled!)

FEBRUARY 5 – JOURNAL

Oo-ee-ah... Today feeling like crying with regrets and guilt about mothering and the job I did for my wee ones. In so many ways stellar; in other ways falling flat on face.

Why oh why does our culture point the finger at the mother? Western psychology encourages that, for one thing. Historically I think it's not always been like that, and certainly not for other cultures. So, it seems it's my job this year (besides realizing the nature mind!) to forgive myself everything, and forgive all others, too.

Last night I awoke to a nightmare that seemed related. I and some others were being held captive by hooligans in a school gym. It seemed they had it in for me, and the others were more innocent bystanders.

I woke up frightened, stomach knotted up, and felt that I was being punished for bad mothering, or bad anything! Then in my half-sleep, thought: I could manipulate the dream so that there would be no problem, nothing worrisome, no punishment. So I went back in and dissolved my body down. All that remained was a hat on the floor. I did this for all the other captives, too. The hooligans were surprised, and then they dissolved, too, along with my anxiety. No more problems, so then the dream itself dissolved, and I fell back into a deep sleep.

In afternoon practice reflecting on the *Chöying Dzod*, the regret, guilt, negativity all dissolved away... into beauty, love, calm.

FEBRUARY 8 – JOURNAL

There are some days down at the beach that the small waves pound in. Not such a big wind, but the rhythm is fast, up and down the strand. No discernible individual waves, but all piled up atop each other. The noise is loud, the energy pushing, pushing, as if you fell in, it would take you, pulling, pulling.

Today was such a day, and I admired this watery urging, without intimidation. Instead, I received it, and without forethought, merged. It settled in my solar plexus and heart, as if each overlapping wave were a sob of my own body. I strode along just at the edge, and without any perceptible tears or crying or any sound, had a great cathartic cry, a hidden one. Not even any sadness could be found, as if a big bellows were breathing for me, or my body's subtle levels were being pummeled by a resounding, relentless drum. This inner sob had been massaged out, an effective interplay of the elements and today's awareness, and I felt cleansed, refreshed, and appreciative.

FEBRUARY 13, FULL MOON – JOURNAL

Beautiful full moon. It figured into my sadhana practice this evening, amplifying with its misty illumination, like a halo, all white. It began just after sunset, so the sky still quite light, a light eggshell blue with clear, white moon. Then as it rose up, it became misty. And pulled on, pulled out the inner rising of my own essence. These inner traces are as yet mild...

During morning meditation, looking out at blue sky with large expanses of thin clouds, at one point one luminous cloud came in with the shape of a Buddha's head, in Thai style, with a tall, pointy ushnisha. At the tip was a nada, like at the top of the Tibetan letter Hung, a teardrop shape.

Working on this collage book, taking my time, working it into my daily break. It's great to see all these dharma and other images online, like looking through a book of someone else's dreams!

My practice has been good. Still in seclusion, not talking. Meditation seems to be spilling over, into meal times, walks—not as a dreamy state, but bringing everything into meditation. Or sometimes applying the questioning-inquiring into mundane life, like, "Enjoying a meal? Is that attachment? Where is the attachment? Who's attached?" It changes things. The edges are gone, the edges of the extreme of the samsaric view. But the experience remains. Also, enjoyment.

Today was quite warm. I sat on a pile of pebbles right at water's edge, paying attention to the waves and wind, aware of the words "dynamic energy"—applying them to both the elements and my mind. Beautiful.

Then the waves started approaching, tide coming up. I stood up and had to back up, chuckling, enjoying, watching time pass in tides. Like the thin clouds covering the moon tonight. Was the moon rising into them? Or were the clouds falling? It was like watching an eclipse, slowly the celestial bodies move, but sometimes faster than you expect, if your mind has become patient enough.

FEBRUARY 16 – JOURNAL

Out for meditation on the beach this morning. Big wind and rain on its way, but at that moment, sunny and beautiful, so I decided to take advantage of the moment: the rain had kept me in all day yesterday. Many people with their dogs passing me on the beach, most nodding to me in pleasant acknowledgment. I smiled back, sat there, fully meditating. Wind and sun churning up sea, air, my hair and skin. It was cold but I was bundled and cozy, enjoying it all. Meditation good, present, simple, no thinking mind.

After about an hour, the beach had emptied of walkers because the wind had begun to batter a light rain down at an angle. When I stood up to return home I noticed a distinctly blue stone near my feet. I picked it up—not really blue at all, but ordinary. Put it back down. Walking along, in a hurry on account of the rain and wind, I noticed more unmistakably blue, egg-shell-color stones. I thought, my eyes are seeing blue. Then the countless white shells and pieces of shell, all were radiating, or was it reflecting, this eggshell blue. They were everywhere. Blue everywhere—all over the beach.

Were the sea and sky that blue? Had I been gazing so much and opening so much to them, that they had entered my perception through my eyes? But even the sea and sky had been only a bit blue, on and off, this morning—mostly grey—so much dynamic activity of clouds and waves, and even sprinkles of rain. Maybe I had absorbed the essence of sea and sky. Vajra family, water element, is blue. Sky, vastness, is blue. Maybe I was carrying essence of vajra-sea home with me.

Later, Rinpoche said, "That was lucidity and emptiness with dzogchen inspiration."

FEBRUARY 19 – JOURNAL

In morning meditation, sitting perched on the deck bench in sun, after an hour and a half, still another twenty minutes to go—had to pee, but settled my body back down. I began to see my daughter in a halo—no, a radiance of light—before me. She was a little distant, so her image was small, a different way of holding someone in prayer, a beautiful feeling. This happened spontaneously, without forethought, not even thinking of praying or healing anyone. But I took that opportunity.

Then it all morphed into a samadhi state of clarity, being able to move the mind around within a "space," with calm and confidence, and nonattachment to the outer world... yet present to it.

Then the trees down below started to move in a unison of dance, a kaleidoscopic display, like seeing choreographed patterns of their overlaying intertwining branches. And it looked like they were all proceeding to the south. Beautiful. I stayed in this samadhi for some time, moving my mind a little—to perceive insubstantiality and nonduality, but mostly just watching and enjoying. And seeing it all as a display of my own mind.

FEBRUARY 21 – RINPOCHE TALK, NOTES

I've been wanting to talk to someone about this practice of silence. (Ha, that's funny!) It seems that when people in the West are in a group situation in silence, they think they're supposed to not relate at all with others, to try to ignore the presence of others, to pretend they're alone, but in a group. I wonder about that. Sure, it could be fine, but if there's too much of that, then it feels like a shutting down of the psyche, with negative results.

So today I did have the chance to talk to someone about this—to Rinpoche. I shared this kind of experience with silence, saying I found that some others on retreat tended to be flustered by any interaction, looking downward, avoiding eye contact, almost a coldness, a shell, to protect them from "infiltration." I said that this seemed not so healthy to me, and at least not how I'm doing this. I said I want to maintain natural warmth, care, and connection to others with whom I come into contact, without losing joy or a sense of humor. Rinpoche agreed wholeheartedly, and I was glad of that.

One time I spent a week in Samye Chimphu near Lhasa with a Tibetan nun who was in silence. She wasn't insulated like that at all. She engaged, but in a silent way, and I thought, how wonderful. We adored each other. I spoke in Tibetan and she listened, mimed answers and questions. It was beautiful. She "told" me that the reason she was doing silence was to keep out of the gossip circuit at the nunnery. (It's amazing how much can be communicated without words, and how at times the barrier of foreign language can be com-

pletely transcended.) I suppose she could have "gossiped," too, with her body language and hand gestures. But the practice of silence cuts all this down, way down, to the essentials. One becomes more thoughtful, mindful, present.

In these one-sided conversations with anyone (them talking, me writing notes), I'm more mindful, as in the technical meaning: not inside the movie, but watching with awareness. Certainly more present for both myself and the other person, almost the role of a therapist. Interesting to be aware of the other person's response while I'm writing a longer note to them: they have to exercise patience that they're not used to in conversation. Perhaps good for the other person, too, and certainly novel for them.

Rinpoche pointed out how being in retreat and this whole development points to the meaninglessness of normal conversation, how there's almost nothing to say. I agreed, and said that I'd been thinking that lately, too.

Then, when I said that retreat has become almost like not being on retreat, or any special circumstance, just doing my life, Rinpoche replied, "Being on retreat *is* life."

Related to this, I had also been thinking recently how pointless it is to hurry toward some goal—you get there and then what? ... and then what? ... endlessly... I realize this is classic Buddhism, but somehow the veracity of it has been sinking in in a new way.

FEBRUARY 27 – JOURNAL

Outside for meditation in a beautiful morning, calm and sunny. I glanced down at the pond and noticed a reflection of rainbow colors near the sun, which drew my eyes up to the southeastern sky. Such a display! Wide irregular bands of iridescence. Red to blue to purple and back to red again, showing off the delicate, subtle traceries of thin clouds, morphing ever so slowly, showing off this, becoming that. I oohed and ahhed—for half an hour, shifting my meditation perch to a place that obscured the sun from my eyes behind branches of the weeping birch, but with a large portion of the display still revealed.

I noticed that when my eyes would look, at first the colors weren't as saturated, but when I let them rest there a moment, then whoosh! the display became magnificent! Probably my pupils constricted with so much bright light, and then could see not only color, but also tiny details of cloud patterns. It was like looking into a huge red jellyfish, and being able to see indescribable designs and formations within the fish's body. Or like minute dancing designs of Italian marbled paper.

The colors were beautiful too, this iridescent morphing, not in usual rainbow order. And also not like a sundog, which is usually fairly uniform. This one even seemed to include green, definitely blues, and the reds and pinks were glorious.

I merged with it, opened to the wonder of it, felt grateful for the way it completely popped me open from my ordinary thoughts, even meditative arisings—now out and beyond that, beyond any internal conversation placed in conventional time and concern.

FEBRUARY 28, NEW MOON – POEM

Tactic of Spring

The earliest blossoms, daffodils,
Came into the house,
Insisting spring, winning the debate by the tactic of yellow.
Pungent scent morning till night,
A tonic seeping down to my cells,
Talking to my essence,
Seeding uncivilized ideas in these vacant ovaries,
Nudging, hey, it's time,
The lovely ache of the inverted pyramid,
Lasting a whole day, welling up,
A reminder of ancient lunar stirrings.

MARCH 5 – DREAM

I was having a lucid dream based on the sound of the rain outside. I awoke slightly to realize I was reciting a poem about the rain—in meter and rhyme! Something about silver drops... I tried waking up enough to remember it, but no luck. The dream and the moment were full of bliss and happiness. Then fell back to sleep. Awoke again with an intense sexual dream. This time couldn't reenter sleep. Finally got up for early practice.

MARCH 7 – JOURNAL

We ran out of heating fuel yesterday, so last evening and now this evening, a fire is going in the woodstove. Lovely. It's nice not to have the furnace noise. Sometimes I've been turning it off during practice for just that reason, wishing for further quiet.

I've noticed when I eat now, I'm so audibly expressive about the food—enjoying enthusiastically the flavors, making noises, leaning over my plate, kind of shoveling it in! It's a picture of someone who's been living out in the woods too long by himself (hehe—him), not an ascetic hermit who perceives all experiences and sense objects as equal. More of a wild-eyed one wandering on a desert island, in a Robinson Crusoe tale, who's lost all social inhibitions.

Creativity has also been welling up, in the form of project ideas. I even had the idea of becoming a wandering yogini inside Seattle—if I don't have a retreat place this summer. I could walk, pack on back, from one friend's place to another, stay a few days, then move on. I know—too distracting to be practical. But could be fun post-retreat.

MARCH 8 – DREAM

Just after falling asleep an image came. It started as an ordinary object, which I can't recall, mostly red. Then it pivoted in midair, turning until it showed me its face—a mandala! Beautiful, super-detailed, like an exquisite 3D fractal, in shades of red, pink, and orange, like a Joseph's Coat rose. It was like a city, a tiglei, a dakini realm. Uniform in its basics like a mandala, and in the four directions, but infinitely detailed and varied. I felt deep joy and bliss. I awoke slightly, so it was somewhat a lucid dream.

The heating oil was replenished today, so the heat is back on, though I kept a fire going since morning when it was quite cold.

MARCH 11, GURU RINPOCHE DAY – JOURNAL

The frogs are out in full force. I'm reminded of Margi and her love for frogs, symbol of fertility, their sound somewhat an aphrodisiac for her, she has said. I hear that's not unusual.

The other night just after turning off the light for sleep, I realized I'd been listening to the chorus as if it were music. My perception had shifted. The sound wasn't "frogs croaking in a group," nor "sounds of nature at night," which can be lovely and peaceful, comforting. This was something completely different, a direct experience of the "true nature" of a thing. I was hearing it as if it had a different value, a truer, deeper value. And yet this was not actively placing value upon it, nor lending it that thought at all, but "true value" was one result of this special perception.

Normally when conceptualizing perception, you get to the point of "yeah, I know that, that's [*fill in the blank with name of object*]." Then you've owned it, and move on—in this discarding maneuver—and it no longer has value, no longer "seen" for what it is.

So, the frogs' chorus—I hadn't done that; instead, without intention, held it in my attention, lightly, and without concentrated effort or forethought, and for the first time, really heard their song.

It was more than song! It was a thing of beauty, truly musical, a symphonic composition, melodic. Brilliant, yet natural. Modern, but of course ancient. I hummed it during one of their breaks. It was polyphonic. Somewhat repetitive, but not completely, with different singers weaving various melodic lines.

I then shifted my focus back and forth, between "frog chorus" to "beyond-concept-listening with true value." Yes, there was a big difference in what I was able to hear. The latter led to a feeling in me of deep joy, happiness, bliss. And appreciation for... these creatures, the present moment, the ability to perceive in this way.

And with the latter I also heard *actual music.*

These experiences are as yet still unpredictable, arising whenever and however they like. Even with all the practice, not stabilized in clear awareness. My mind is still mundane much of the time, involved in patterned thought, following lines of thinking without mindfulness.

MARCH 17, FULL MOON – JOURNAL

I awoke around 2 with a merging experience and awareness of dreaming. The window had been cracked open, full moon night, and the sound of frogs (again) had entered my consciousness and dream. I had merged so completely with the sound and frog-ness that—it wasn't that I had become a frog, nor did I even dream of frogs—but their presence and my presence were one, creating a stirring and a bliss, a profundity. That was my dream experience.

Then my wakeful consciousness started rising up, gradually, so at first I had contact with the dream state. And found the frog to be sort of inside me, and remembered and continued to experience the bliss of union. Again, it wasn't union with frog, but with essence of presence that the frog somehow represented—not symbolically, as an idea, but something "not me" that then merged with "me." It was loud, like next to the window—a single frog. hehe!

Then I woke up and continued these sensations, but at a reduced level. And couldn't go back to sleep. So at 4 I sat up for practice, and the day began, but slowly, after a morning nap later on.

A day or two before, I had a rather depressed day. Some thoughts contributed, and also the dark, grey weather. I felt like my little boat had become becalmed in a fog—not the calm of a lovely picnic day, but one where you want distraction to lift out of it. No distraction here, I realized that this was just the sort of deep winter day that I often relish, enhancing inward steeping, deepening.

So I deepened, merged with it, rather than tossing and turning and struggling against it. It was lovely! Almost immediately. The grace of one's own mind, attitude, can truly transform, if one remembers just the right thing in the moment. Although these things are not always transferable, I realize. That is, perhaps, where grace comes in.

So, the fog lifted after awhile, the forward movement of my boat started up, toward the west, and in spite of the continuing grey and cloudy weather, or in concert with it, another day passed on my journey.

MARCH 28 – JOURNAL

Buddhism is sailing in on an incoming tide, onto our western shore. In order to be ready, we have to see how to welcome, to accommodate. In order to do that, we have to know what we have to offer our guests, to know what we are, who we are, our capacity. If we were to make room as if there were simple empty spaces in which to build metaphorical Buddhist towns and cities, these would be false-front movie sets, not an offering worthy of the great richness arriving on our shores.

No, we have riches of our own to share. Many are buried in our misty past— but they are there. Like social archeologists, we have to dig them out, wash them off, lay them out to be acknowledged, re-assimilated, and admired. And then we can truly appreciate and assimilate the richness coming from the East. It would be a proper potlatch—continually gifting back and forth. As things are now, there's often a missed opportunity here.

I've been reading *This Is It*, by Alan Watts. Finally. It was forty-five years ago that the book came into my hands at an opportune moment. At the time I only read the cover and perhaps the short introduction, then put it down and went off with a friend to drop acid—the first and only time. I was fifteen.

The message of the book title came through loud and clear on my psychedelic trip, and influenced me profoundly, perhaps for my life.

> *It was an exhilarating time, the 60s. We were looking for the deeper mean-ing in life, the classic quest of my generation. We were certain it wasn't to be found in the materialism of our elders who had struggled through the*

Great Depression and then World War II. With varying degrees of rebellion, we looked elsewhere—Eastern religions, music, nature, and famously, in psychedelics.

One rainy Saturday in November of 1968, my best friend and I accepted an invitation of a classmate to try LSD. It had been a big decision. There were stories of people whose psyches broke into pieces, never to be put back together again. On the other hand we had many friends who had entered this experience multiple times and returned fine, speaking with a light in their eyes, of magic and expansion and depth. The intrigue was compelling and I knew I had to travel there, too, just a matter of when.

I went to my friend's house, and while waiting for her to do a last household chore, I sat on her bed and noticed a book belonging to her older brother: This Is It. I turned the paperback over in my hands, thumbed through it a bit, and set it down. On an ordinary day, I wouldn't have remembered it at all. But on this fertile day it was a potent seed that got planted.

We walked through our neighborhood to a street leading to docks where our friend was spending the weekend on a houseboat. He gave us each a tiny pill, and we quietly went outside, and hung around on the docks. The rain was dripping down that day, the usual in Seattle. Then the drips became more than water, and actually the air itself expanded into floating, multi-colored orbs. Okay, nothing frightening, everything to ponder, and more than that, to experience.

Then, the simple sentence, "This is it," flooded my mind, and I began to understand it to its fullest extent. To write about it now, decades later, barely covers it, but my best shot: The present moment is the most important aspect of life... and supersedes all prior understandings, all the striving and expectations set up by family and society. Present moment—understood as not only time, but also what is arising, what's happening. Then, present moment understood as a deep NOW, continuous, moving, dynamic—not one moment before, nor one moment to come. "It" being the culmination of all effort, all that one might otherwise put one's mind to. This is the end point, this is the every point... the whole point.

The message that stayed with me: Don't put "it" off. Don't strive for externals, nor indeed, for anything. Everything you need you have, here and now. And there's nothing to be afraid of.

My mind had been expanded. I continued mulling over the discovery in the days and weeks that followed. I thought, if this was true, then wouldn't one have to take it to its logical extent? If this moment is all there is, then what of striving to even feed oneself? Or to do anything at all? I felt profoundly that I could accept this radical life for myself. But then suddenly while standing in the kitchen, I realized the next logical step: the only thing that mattered was compassion... because if I gave up on all levels of conventional life, it would break my mother's heart. Out of compassion then, for my mother, I knew I had to step back into ordinary life... as the daughter who participates in a family, who goes to school, and shows up at the kitchen table for meals every day as someone fulfilling my parents' vision of the future... at least on the outer level.

I took my discovery to some friends, who understood it, and we would laugh sometimes at the meaningless antics of, for example, guys trying to pick us up, those who didn't have an inkling. For years afterwards, I was re-minded often of my experience, when the visual field would begin to morph, the grainy grey surface of a boulder in a river, for example, undulating, expanding and contracting, and I remembered that the world isn't as solid as our perceptions lead us to believe, that numberless sub-atomic particles are zooming around in even those stones, and that everything is in a state of change.

I hadn't realized at the time that Alan Watts' book was, in large part, about Buddhism. All that long time ago, then, without knowing it, this was my introduction to Buddhist philosophy and experience. What, then, had I discovered, on a profound level, independent of Buddhist teaching, that turned out to be Buddhist? The present moment, intrinsic nature, impermanence, and ultimately, compassion.

I found the formal Buddhist path decades later through a different route. And now, in the present moment of writing, this thought comes: this experience and knowledge doesn't "belong" to a religion, but to the human experience and human potential. Buddhism is a path to this treasure, a sure and trusted path, but not the only path.

Within the book, one of the essays has the same title: "This Is It." It con-tains a quote by a medieval mystic, Dame Julian. When I read it I felt sudden recognition, as if I'd heard it before, and perhaps so, as it is indeed famous. This recognition was accompanied by a sense of almost a location, ancient and mys-tical. I even heard music, as if the words were part of a sung liturgy.

She wrote that these were the words of God: "But all shall be well, and all shall be well, and all manner of thing shall be well." These were preceded by "... It is fitting that there should be sin, but all shall be well..."

Alan Watts wrote so beautifully and aptly about its meaning. Combined with my current reading, understanding, and meditation of the *Chöying Dzod*, I feel I understand this, deeply, including the sin part.

> *Here's my translation of that problematic word: Sin = samsaric mind, or, the fog that separates us from Enlightenment. The fog—the habitual patterns and thinking. Sadly, the western tradition bundles in guilt so tightly that we can barely hear the word "sin" without cringing. In fact, we usually pass by the meaning and go directly to guilt. But in the quote of Dame Julian, message from God, there is no context of guilt. It just is—and all shall be well.*

Tonight I brought this into the meditation session, and both elated and awestruck, have just been sobbing. Still, tears are streaming. Struck with the many:

1) Truth. I see the similarities between her Christian revelations and the revelations of Buddhist Longchen Rabjam, both of them alive at the same time, the 14th century, on opposite sides of the globe.

2) Availability. That God (or God as personally translated) is that available. That in spite of all the possibilities in samsara, "all manner of things" are included—it's taken to its logical extent. No holding back. That my own culture's deep spiritual roots include this, and healing, even for me, for one on Buddhist retreat, healing is there.

3) Love.

4) Her beseeching God for more inwardly experienced compassion, more connection. Me too. This evening, my tears beseeching for the same—connection, in my case, with Dharmakaya and nature of mind. And yes, always, compassion. This is from where her visions arose.

5) That she had these visions, then much later went into retreat to meditate and reflect on these very visions—not to have more visions! But to more deeply understand their meaning. In other words, her initial experience was enough, rather than grasping for more. I was moved by the humility, simplicity, and gratefulness of that. She had written twice, once at the time of the visions to put the bare messages down; the second time in her subsequent retreat, she wrote her commentary.

6) My own retreat, and the sense that I'm at this place now—one year and one month left—with a fresh resolve to pay clear attention to my intuitive inner compass, to follow that internal north star. In my current array of reading,

contemplation, writing, solitude, several types of meditation, the basics of Vajrayana practice, and communing with nature—I'm resolved to not get off track with bells and whistles, or grasping after further and more esoteric practices.

7) Karma.

Recently, my back went out and my teeth hurt; then digestion problems with not much sleep last night; and earlier this morning, gas pains. But everything is resolving and I've been happy (except the back pain day). These are vastly minor compared with people in my prayer book. My fears around my own minor troubles just point out my small mind. Small mind = samsara, yet part of the whole.

So why the sobbing? Maybe because there is so much course correction—of outside and inside both, of culture and my own psyche, as it is. As it is—there it is—Oh, this is IT!

I've felt a little mundane lately: This is life! Satisfied, calm, stable, ordinary, lots of inner chatter sometimes. I think that's also why the tears: it's too small, and this evening's experience, in fact much of the day, has been far beyond that, larger, and not so mundane.

Where's the map? Is this the territory? Or is it double maps? Sobbing while praying is definitely somewhere in the territory—without a map— and happy.

APRIL 13 – JOURNAL

Lately sea mammals have been visible from the deck through the oval tree porthole to the sea. The first time the sea was calm and flat, but quite a large area not far from shore, the water was turbulent, coming from just beneath the surface. I thought, herring, many of them, or something. So I kept my eye out for sea mammals that might be feeding on them. Sure enough, dolphin fins appeared. Wow, fun to finally spot them from the house!

A couple days later, while meditating, just as my gaze fell on the water, a plump seal surfaced and turned back into the sea in a quick flowing motion. Then next day, more dolphins.

For a week I watched a crow couple coming for nest-building material. Many times each day they flew to the tall weeping birch right in front of the deck. They pulled off strands from the swaying branches—not too big, not too small, just right—then flew off to a nearby evergreen tree. It seemed one of them was less experienced, probably the blushing nubile bride, first year. I made that up. But it was the smaller of the pair who seemed slow to understand what to do. After a couple of days she got the idea. Then, they were gone. Nest must be done.

I had spoken to them, asking them to please take their pick from a certain branch that's obscuring the sky view, getting thick with new spring growth. They seemed to respond, flying to that branch, and ever after, always going there. I kept encouraging them with positive words. There's a new group lately who also have been picking at some branches. But they're not so suggestible.

APRIL 14, FULL MOON, LUNAR ECLIPSE – JOURNAL

Intensity. I sat outside for afternoon meditation. The day had been beautiful, spring warm; I covered myself with my shawl. The wind picked up. Shawl came up over my head. I stayed out for two hours, increasingly chilled. By the time the session was over, I almost stumbled into the house, felt sick, like I was coming down with something, weak, almost nauseous.

I made a nice supper: mushroom-cottage cheese omelets, with kale and English muffin. Plus hot water. But when finished, still chilled, weary and ill. I lay down on my bed for half an hour, and improved a little. Thought: maybe that had been too much wind-*lung* energy for my current state, so the antidote: more earth. So I went back to the cushion for evening practice with the Buddha of Compassion, in which the moon is prominent.

Full moon. I watched it rise as I was doing mani mantras—misty, *huge*, ethereal, just hours before the eclipse. I felt this amazing intensity. As I had begun the sadhana the weariness had lifted, and yet a residue remained, only there as a subtle flavor. Watching the moon, thinking of all the shamans and neo-pagans (hoping all were benevolent) also doing their practices that same moment... and me and those like me, Buddhist hermits and practitioners, connecting with the Lord of Great Compassion, magnifying and multiplying on this full moon eclipse night.

All lights in the house were switched off, save the xmas lights—atmospheric—the midnight blue sky, the misty moon. My body, heart heating up, rising energy, sending loving kindness, seeing the beautiful Chenrezig Avalokiteshvara's form, his face, the moon's face.

By the time I finished the sadhana, it was late, around 10, and moon was obscured by thick clouds. I checked the forecast—no chance of seeing the eclipse from midnight to 1. I was relieved in a way, now totally spent. Again, I was stumbling, as if I'd just woken up, or as if 80 years old, not 60. And chilled again, too. But grateful for the compassion practice, and grateful for a warm bed to catch my fall.

APRIL 19 – JOURNAL

Remembering the first couple of retreat years, whenever I had a day of total silence, nor of seeing anyone, I would experience it like an echo in a large empty room. It was like someone was walking around making noise by rearranging the furniture. The non-sound sound would bounce around, echoing off the bare floors and walls. Or, like a large temple bell that had been ringing, suddenly the ringing stops and there's a vibration that continues, on and on, reverberating inside my body, all day long.

It was neither good nor bad. I just noticed it, with some enjoyment: I was sustaining this minor austerity, this evidence of retreat, as a physical and psychic sensation, even slightly sensual. In its subtle presence, of non-company, it *was* company. (Maybe only to a Gemini, who gets companionship through her own multiple personalities? ha.)

But since New Year, in solitude (mostly), the transition was so smooth, this presence was gone, replaced by a normalcy. The bell hadn't rung recently, so nothing to reverberate, except my own thoughts, plentiful enough. This normalcy seemed almost *too* stable, without the sense of sacred space-time that the reverberating empty room used to give.

But the Zen people, the Taoists too, I think, would say, chop wood carry water—ordinary is the right direction.

Stable, and quiet. It has certainly been *pleasant*—and that is something I wasn't expecting on retreat.

Further thoughts about one of the advantages of being "in silence" while in long retreat:

We can shift away from the linguistic structures that solidify concepts, and through declarative statements, bind us and trap us in the fix of having a defensible position on anything and everything—"This is that, and here's why." —the dualistic paradigm. This is not what is borne out through contemplation, which is the realm of paradox and merging. The former is the Western state of mind, imbedded firmly and then nailed in through language. Not speaking while in retreat gives it a rest, so we can separate from it, and let meditation pervade, let it have a chance.

These thoughts were reinforced by retreat reading: Alan Watts: This Is It, essay number three, and Philip Richman: Karma and the Rise of Buddhism in the West, page 146. Later, out of retreat I came across this from James Low, a dzogchen teacher from Britain:
"The fewer ideas you have, the more you're likely to taste what is going on. The function of meditation is to release our addiction to ideas as the vehicle of truth." One then can hold both the true-nature "taste," and simultaneously, the samsaric way of perceiving.

APRIL 21 – JOURNAL

Periwinkle blue butterflies, small, are appearing now in the garden. Hummingbirds still around, but on the periphery, nothing in this little garden to entice them at the moment. Two of them doing their maneuver again: one shoots almost straight up thirty feet, then down at a diagonal. Then the second one follows almost as high, same trajectory. You can almost count off time in heartbeats between the disappearance of the previous bird and the appearance of the next—about two beats.

APRIL 22 – JOURNAL

Barbara took me to a doctor's appointment, and afterwards Diane B. took me shopping for groceries. Ordinarily I don't step foot in a grocery store, but today was different. I made two lists, one for Diane and one for me, to split up the task. I was looking around in the bulk nuts and oats department, trying to figure things out, when Diane shows up—her part done! We regrouped the list and finished up pretty quickly. I had this sense of being so utterly focused, surrounded by *all* those *people*—passing them quickly by, without a glance, and sensing the strangeness of that. I felt like I was driving on the freeway suddenly after being used to solitary country roads. And everyone else was rushing. At noon, on Bainbridge. All these people who had retired to an island to get away from it all, were rushing with their heads down. It felt very mistaken.

And yet, people have reasons for rushing sometimes. Diane needed to get her new, large and cute, fluffy puppy, Chummy, back home after her nap—for a poop! We didn't make it in time, but it all got cleaned up in the end, and all was well.

APRIL 23 – DREAM

Last night's dream was difficult, with people grilling me about my retreat. I wanted people's approval, recognizing this as a wrong-headed refuge in the eight samsaric dharmas. But the bigger part, I wanted to get the hell out of there, back to my own authenticity, my authentic retreat. Singular, independent, solitude.

It's raining cats and dogs right now, comforting sound, tucked into bed. Oh... fleas again.

MAY 2 – JOURNAL

I'm in a period of surfacing—doctor's appointments and checking in with family. When I talk I feel like the floodgates have suddenly been opened, it's all rushing out, gushing out, in endless, entertaining chatter.

One year to go now. I don't even know where I'll be.

MAY 8 – JOURNAL

Beautiful spring. With fleas. I've been working hard every day to vacuum, doing laundry, saying prayers for them, and still getting bites. For awhile I thought they might be gone. I must be missing something.

JUNE 1 – JOURNAL

It's been on my mind for awhile to write, but things in a way uneventful. Just putting along. May was lovely, garden beautiful every day, practice schedule the same every day.

I finished recording the *Chöying Dzod*. The 21 Taras book is coming along—just finished number 19.

The fleas are gone, I'm quite sure. That was more than three weeks of being on a "campaign."

Right now Jeanne is with me for a few days of retreat. We're doing practice sessions independently, not speaking until dinner. She lost a close family member recently, so undergoing a hard time. Drained and exhausted when she arrived, she's doing better now, with practice, rest, and companionship here.

The weather has been lovely, so, mostly in silence, we've taken long beach walks at extra-low tide three days in a row. The tide reveals sand bars, delicious against bare feet. We've been running and playing up and down in shallow wavelets, and kicking up splashes of water, watching the refracted sun in the tiny droplets of jettisoned fluid. We're imagining we're in Hawaii. I think I haven't played on the beach this freely since a girl.

One day after I did tai chi at the water's edge, Jeanne espied a spectacular sky display: a huge, multi-colored streak of shimmering cloud shaped like an arrow with feathers. Not normal rainbow colors, but brilliant turquoise to green, and others. We were held awestruck; I offered sand writing of *Om Ah Hung* in Tibetan. The arrow and other surrounding shimmers of cloud-light stayed a long while as we picked our way across a mile of beach, the miniature islands of sand, the knee-deep dark abysses of slimy seaweed lakes, as the incoming tide quickly filled warm tide pools with cold. We held our silent retreat space and warm friendship connection, back to the house for late lunch.

JUNE 5 – JOURNAL

Some remarkable happenings. Most significant is that I get to stay in this house through December! This feels really miraculous, the continuity in one place excellent for retreat. I realized I'll be able to go into silent seclusion again by the end of this month until I make the next shift. It also makes possible an intensive practice I'll soon be starting—without interruption for five months. I'm deeply grateful to this family. Skip said, "It's a win-win."—a point of happiness.

Somehow I caught the flu! It's mild, the first while on retreat—achy, sore throat, lungs, GI tract, tired, and dingy in the head. Yesterday I took a break from retreat... and vacuumed! because fleas are back! Diane B. brought chicken soup ingredients so that kept me busy in the kitchen. The night before I had one of those beautiful non-sleep nights of retreat, lying there in a kind of reverie, relaxed, happy, deeply resting. I didn't feel sleep-deprived after, but altogether, vacuuming, soup-making, flu—I was quite tired. In the middle of cooking, chopping onions, I chopped into my thumb! So yesterday felt a little hard, but in another way, very fine. And having the flu in the context of retreat just felt... a bit novel!

Today I'm a little better. Gratefully back to a full day of practice, including evening sadhana. Just as I was reciting mantras of the wrathful practice, that huge tree branch, right before my eyes, broke off! It was the very branch of the weeping birch that I'd asked the crows to prune—because it was way out of proportion to the rest of the tree, overreaching into the large available space—and was blocking the view of sky and light. I had thought *many* times, how great if there was a laser pruner, to take off that one giant branch; even wondering if it would be dangerous to climb up and saw it off! So when it came down, with a great noise, ripping off at the trunk, I felt horrified, as if I'd caused it. I had been asking for this precise thing, and then it happened. Most Americans would say, of course, that it was an unrelated coincidence. What shall I think? Only that I should be careful what I ask for.

JUNE 6 – JOURNAL

I've decided that the tree branch wasn't my doing, but a cosmic coincidence. However, like with a significant dream, you have to look at the meaning. What did I write yesterday? It was "overreaching into available space, blocking the view." Its weight couldn't any longer be supported and it fell.

The meaning? Overreaching beyond what's supportable. Overreaching blocks the view? Now view and light has been revealed, naturally, in its own time?

Who knows. And be careful what you ask for. All well.

JUNE 22, DAKINI DAY – JOURNAL

I knew this trip was going to come, but not so suddenly! Today, Rinpoche called to say now—today—is the time to introduce a new practice, before he leaves for Tibet. So all in one day I made instant arrangements to get to Whidbey Island and arrived here same evening!

Door to door, the phases of the trip included two ferry rides, two public bus trips, car drives with three friends, and a walk through downtown Seattle! Arrived exhausted, but happy to be once again in Jeanne's gracious home, a place that I lived, once upon a time.

JUNE 28 – JOURNAL

The following days on Whidbey were filled with transmission, teaching, and consultation. Then, a much easier return journey, because Karen drove me all the way from Whidbey to the Bainbridge ferry. A huge help.

I had recorded the extensive teaching sessions, so now back at home, I've been transcribing, almost full time. I can feel the transmission received from Rinpoche in my old practices, and can sense the trajectory of the new, not-yet-begun practice, as freeing. After recovering from the flurry of the outer world, I'm quite perked up! The new practice is complex, a rich set, like starting Ngöndro from ground zero. I had kept myself pretty pure for years, intentionally not nosing around it ahead of time. So, now slowly entering, happily.

JULY 5 – JOURNAL

If you think the world has gone crazy, does it mean you are crazy? Or is the world crazy? Last night I went down to the beach at twilight to watch the fireworks. It really sounded like the whole world had gone crazy! The wind and sea were calm, warm, overcast barely, but the humans were making up for it!

Everywhere up and down the Sound explosions reporting, echoing—BAM BAM—in all different calibers and distances and notes. Rockets going off everywhere. Huge ones across the way over in Seattle, and beyond.

There was the big Seattle display visible behind Magnolia Bluff. But beyond the whole line of the harbor, rimmed by its hulking white shipping cranes, you could see another lineup, way beyond, of mammoth fire bursts, one after the other, not just in one place, but stretching north to south. Plus of course West Seattle and Edmonds and Kingston, and neighborhoods in between. It was a surprise, that's for sure. And I, a sole observer, at the edge of the encroaching tide, enjoyed the insanity.

I saw a mouse today running through the garden. I picked tiny strawberries from the garden and ate them with some raspberries and ice cream. You could barely taste them—so teeny.

So much coming up in the new practice, one insight after the other so that I can barely recall them all. One topic was delving into the nightmares I often had as a young child where I was frequently pursued by evil, murderous men. Now I'm thinking of them as perhaps demons in the Buddhist-psyche sense. And out of this came, for the first time, realization that something quite positive came from these dreams:

The dream experience brought out my own resourcefulness from my child-psyche: teaching myself to fly. In the dreams it seemed the only option and came spontaneously. In the beginning it took some effort to get aloft, and there was tremendous fear that I wouldn't be able to make my escape. I would wake up crying in the middle of the night for my mother. But as the attacks continued over the years, I kept at it, to the point that not only could I confidently fly in self-defense, propelled by need, I could also do it anytime, by choice, and for enjoyment.

This resulted in the demons after some years not visiting any longer—so I was ultimately victorious, no longer a victim. And a new sense that I could be the master of my own consciousness. This development is perhaps common since so many people fly in their dreams.

JULY 13 – JOURNAL

A magnificent sky at sunset tonight. Sitting eastward on my cushion, as always because the house faces that way, I noticed the sky turning unusually pink just after the sun set. I finished practice, then went outside. A gigantic rainbow stretched across the sky—no rain—with a backdrop of vivid pink. This was after sunset! I walked to the western side of the house and was wowed by bright, brilliant red sky. I didn't know which way to turn, east or west, pink or red.

JULY 23 – JOURNAL

A book came my way, *Prison Angel,* about a Catholic nun named Mother Antonia, a kind of American Mother Teresa, her object of service an overloaded Mexican prison near the US border. When I first read about her, I just cried— her tremendous fearlessness and the impartiality of her love while living for thirty years right inside the prison, ministering to *all*—from the petty thieves to the drug warlords, to the guards and their families.

One might think I'd be interested in taking ordination. I've always been profoundly moved by the ordained, Catholic or Buddhist. And yet, for myself, it is not for this lifetime.

There's something noble and inspiring about ordination, sacrificing personal needs for the ultimate, the mountain peak of inner human endeavor—the ineffable, sublime, and sacred. The putting on of robes declares this interior commitment to the outer world. This can be deeply inspiring to others, and I think must continually remind and inspire oneself.

However, to me, joining an order, a nunnery, smacks of hierarchy, systems, and sexism. Placing external strictures on oneself may be inappropriate and therefore counterproductive, not to mention the risk of becoming a monastic goody two-shoes.

Further, how could one, while contained within a hierarchical system, follow one's personal process—a delicate, intuitive matter, one's unique path through the inner wilds, and in the case of Buddhism, toward the awakened state of awareness?

Giving up one's identity, including sexual identity, and how one freely expresses in the world, seems like undesirable interruption in the dynamic interplay of life.

Living with the constraints of exterior disciplines placed from above, and a list of ancient rules (many additional for women!)... well, I understand the purpose, but feel discipline should arise from within. All the above leads to a firm knowledge that ordination is not for me.

But what about going without, accepting austerity? Well, in a way I have done much of that already, during the work with Rinpoche, in Tibet and in the West. Giving up a conventional career path and the comforts that come with that, I threw myself instead into the humanitarian and sangha work with utter joy.

Now, on retreat, another austerity, I'm only occasionally joyous, but at this point content and happy, yes. As for fearlessly putting my life onto the front lines, without a safety net, as some friends have noticed, I've done that too.

And all of this to the same service—the ineffable, sublime, and sacred.

AUGUST 12 – JOURNAL

Beautiful full moon display two nights ago. Again that day I felt twinging in ovaries, or was it womb. Beautiful. Lasted an hour perhaps.

I could never remember, which is it at full moon—bleeding or ovulating? So I looked it up. One source said it could be one or the other. "White Moon Cycle" bleeds on full, which is most common, more for procreation. "Red Moon Cycle" ovulates on full, more as healer, or where sex is useful for other purposes, such as spiritual path… more in the case of older women.

In my case then, far past menopause, a phantom visitation of ovulation, signaling time to watch and see.

And then the next night came a clear dream, an important message with retreat instruction.

AUGUST 16 – JOURNAL

I've been thinking some of music lately. The new practices include singing quietly, really a kind of humming, to be done "melodiously."

Out of a music vacuum for the last two years, these simple, evocative melodies come. I'm reminded of some old movie with Alec Guinness, where the character is in his old childhood home, a humble place, and he's humming to himself, simply, not an integrated or recognizable melody, just a meandering, unself-conscious musical sound of contentment. I feel I may have made this memory up, but my own humming keeps evoking this.

Another image is of a lonely woodwind, perhaps a clarinet, at night, on a street corner, a jazz musician, after the performance or the party, all played out—but not quite—in this meandering and unself-conscious way, playing simply, quietly the soul, creating, improvising, alone.

Tonight at the end of the session, it sounded so beautiful to my ears, I cried. Not many notes, nothing earthshaking, but I hit some profound "chord" with myself. Simplicity, like a Zen poem or haiku. I'm musical, but realize I'm not currently in any shape to have perspective on this. No matter. From the time I began this practice, the humming has helped to transcend some recent yoga-induced physical pain.

I'm reminded of being sixteen at the piano, sometimes improvising, most times playing classical pieces. I would often get into a zone of deep rapture. I felt bliss throughout my body and simultaneously experienced transcendent spirit. I felt it was special and thought of it as combined spirituality and sexuality. There I was, a quasi-atheist and a virgin—but it didn't matter, I knew these things, deeply. I was creating it and at the same time worshipping at its altar. If my mother would occasionally interrupt me, I felt like exploding, wanting to say (perhaps I did say?), "Don't you know I'm in the middle of prayer, Mom?" ... of worship, of devotions, of union, communion, of a profound mystical experience?! Ah, the indignities of being a teenager at home.

My wish for post-retreat: to be reunited with my piano.

AUGUST 21 – JOURNAL

Now almost too late at night to write, but I wanted to record something about anger transformed into openness and then an insight.

I had gotten fixated for days on Rinpoche's apparent irritation with some of my questions during the recent trip to Whidbey. I could hear this irritation clearly in the recording while transcribing.

Then I thought: Better to apply some dzogchen advice of dear Patrul Rinpoche via that text that's been sitting on my puja table, the one I'd used a time or two in the past. I pulled it out. It says, don't look at the content, the story. Look at the "you" who's feeling the anger, look directly at the anger itself—and see the nature of your mind. Anger into patience. It worked. It wasn't a big emotional deal, no catharsis. It just dissolved.

Then from that vantage point I decided to look directly, without fear, at Rinpoche's irritation—I considered the possibility that he was justified in being irritated at some pattern of mine—and I found it. The recording revealed my display of a poverty mentality that has been lurking around, and in fact, about which he had spoken to me a couple months ago. There it was, on tape, caught. But previously my fear and engagement with the "eight samsaric dharmas" had prevented my being able to make a shift.

Once I clearly saw this, my mind went to Rinpoche's recent encouragement to use my own intuition in making big decisions about my practice and external life. He was encouraging me to counteract a sense of personal lack, to have confidence. Yes, it's about time, I thought. And then even the root of the anger was gone, a gift received.

AUGUST 22 – JOURNAL

I've patched a lot of clothes on retreat. Slippers I sewed back together with leather thong. Favorite old faded khaki work pants I put iron-on patches in four places, and this morning wove with thread a place at the knee where the patch was pulling apart from the fabric. Old leather work gloves I sewed a couple of finger seams back together. Tank top undershirts were too binding so I clipped the bra elastic at the side seams. A summer nightie was too big so I stitched it closer at the sides. Darned some socks. Widened the waist on a long skirt. Completely created one short skirt by copying another. A friend patched one old shirt for me with her sewing machine. Glued some shoes back together—twice. And it's not over yet!

SEPTEMBER 5 – POEM

Counting Retreat

How many months left? How many days? How many butterlamps burned? How many sticks of incense in a day? How much incense needed to the end of retreat? How many mantras breathed and how many sung? How long to accomplish a sadhana? How many accomplished?

How many full moons seen? How many stars? How many shimmering airplane lights at night? How many rainbows? How many torrential downpours? How many passing ships and rowboats? How many hummingbirds in succession shooting up in an arc and then diving down again? How many seals lying on Goose Island? How many vultures feeding on the beached seal carcass at Cattle Point? How many deer? How many bears, cougars, foxes, coyotes, scorpions, elephant seals, martens, skinks (blue-tailed), frogs, pollywogs, hares, horses, elk, squirrels, eagles, and osprey did I see? How many flea bites? How many agates found?

How many conversations with Rinpoche? How many words spoken? How many strangers passed along the beach? How many words spoken to strangers at the beach? How many dream lovers did I love? How many babies?

How many visions? How many signs seen in clouds? How many lamas did I meet? How many blessings melted into me? How many minds thought of my retreat? How many realizations graced me? How many tectonic shifts of psyche? How many lifetimes?

SEPTEMBER 5 – JOURNAL

One person entered my retreat sphere on and off for some weeks. He was working outdoors at the house sporadically, which led to some conversations, which proved a bit intense... he was intense! Two days ago I came to a point of telling him that I needed to, for the sake of my retreat, end our conversations.

When I awoke yesterday, I realized his voice was still happening in my head, its inflections, its pervasiveness, and his relentless energy. I recalled the dream that I'd just had: There was a room with a tv that was on. I went to turn it off and found it to be complicated, with a lot of extra electronic gear attached. I tried pushing all these different buttons. Sometimes the channel would change, but the problem remained—it was loud, disruptive, unwanted, and was disturbing the serenity and dharma teachings about to happen in the adjoining room. Finally, I found the main switch to the whole apparatus and switched it off. Ahh!

After I awoke, though, the presence of this person was still resounding in me, like the tv noise. I sat up for my Ngöndro session. And the solution came to me: to understand and see myself as space, the space of the dharmadhatu—as pervious, like a membrane that anything can flow through. And it happened instantly. He flowed through me and it was released. I wasn't blocking it any longer, which turned out to have been a form of holding on (even as I had been trying to push it away). I had been attaching to something that one would rather release; but one's reification of it, even the reification of oneself, prevents that release. It sounds so ideal, even impossible to have dissolved this so instantly and completely, but it happened.

Today, he came to the house for further work, and I was calm, even pleased to see him for a moment, but without complication (or words) of any kind. All's well.

SEPTEMBER 8 – JOURNAL

In three hours the moon will reach fullness. My womb is speaking to me again, answering the moon's call. Who knows which it remembers, its readiness to receive life, or to drain away, lifeless, to begin again. This time it must be the blood exit, the menstrual side, because it feels most like that. The other, ovulation side sensation, used to feel more a twinging of ovaries, a subtler ping. Menstruation was more seismic and central, and it is echoes of that experience once again. Life! It's good.

Now, three hours into the moon's wane, I can still sense the faint waves of my responsive womb. It began subtly, without any forethought. I was surprised, again! But that's not what I intended to write about this time.

My afternoon session outdoors was energized by the full moon, to an unusual extent. The moon hadn't yet risen, but I knew the timing of fullness, 6:38 pm. I felt I was riding a wave of its waxing power, and, for several hours of practice, intentionally used it, even without its usual visual inspiration.

In the first part, simple meditation. I kept coming to Suzuki Roshi's words that "we sit not to accomplish something; we sit to express our true nature." The intention of these words has frequently been in my practice these days. Riding on the moon, I continued with the meditation to the last moment.

Then, I began a sadhana. Again, especially potent, but without seeking any special energy, nor affect, nor anything. And yet it naturally arose, expansive and specific simultaneously. I could feel the specific lunar power, too, the final dissolution, coinciding with the time of fullness, magnified.

There was a sense of confidence, too. A grounded kind of knowing, unshakeable, of true importance in the path, my path, this path.

Today I wrote something new. A friend's mom died and she wrote to friends requesting prayers. I replied, saying that I'd do "prayers for the 49 days, part of my tradition." *My* tradition. I'd at first written "*the* Tibetan Buddhist tradition," and then changed it. This felt like a big step. The former says that this path is one of many possibilities in our culture. I'm following it, but with a kind of professional's distance. I can still talk to others as equals: "You know, we understand each other, there's this Tibetan Buddhist thing that I'm into…" But saying "*my* tradition" communicates that I'm an actual practitioner of something. I'm not selling it, but I can represent it. I'm in it, *of* it. It's my tribe.

After I sent the message I truly wasn't sure if the syntax sounded weird or not. It may. I'm obviously not as sensitive to what others think, how they perceive. In some ways extra-sensitive, but maybe less in a predictive way and more of a present-moment way.

So I ate dinner, then went back outside. It was warm, dark, overcast. The clouds tonight are obscuring the full moon. I sat and meditated. Teeny raindrops began to fall. No matter. Beautiful, calm night. Clear, uncomplicated. The drops increased from heavy mist to actual drops, and I was eventually covered with a sheen of water. Decided to retreat indoors with the aspiration, "And may all beings find shelter when they need it."

I haven't been writing much at all about experiences or dreams for months. Rinpoche advised me to stop keeping careful track of minor experiences as part of an effort to give up on striving for achievement. Yes, Longchenpa wrote much about that, and also Suzuki Roshi. Part of the paradoxical nature of Buddhism, this journey without goal.

SEPTEMBER 18 – JOURNAL

A couple weeks ago I sent off for a deluxe camping pad, three inches thick, and with the last halcyon days of summer, no rain, I slept out in the bug net tent for at least a week. Just came back inside two nights ago with drizzle. Every night stars and moon. Every dawn awake, then back to sleep till sunrise-sun. Sit up in tent, zipper open, fresh air, sky blue, sun rising up, doing Ngöndro looking out at sky, sea, and crab apple tree.

SEPTEMBER 21, FALL EQUINOX EVE – DREAM

I woke up this morning early, around 4, for a pee. Then recalled a dream: Kilung Rinpoche and I were serving Dilgo Khyentse Rinpoche while we were readying for a journey somewhere. There was deep devotion, and the steady, enlightened Buddha presence of His Holiness. He was aware of everything going on, and he knew me, but nothing extra was needed. He was like the hum of a powerful engine deep within a huge tanker ship. Just there, you know it with confidence, nothing needing to be done. Wherever we were going was beautiful and serene. End dream.

After awhile I realized it would be better to sit up and do my practice, thinking I could sleep after. So I did, but when finished, about 6:30, not tired. The dawn was lightening and the chance to watch sunrise on a clear morning at equinox beckoned me out of my nest.

Warm morning, rosy sky, in nightgown and slippers, I made tea, sat down in front of the door-window to watch, warmed by my wool prayer shawl.

Yes, right at 7 am (without daylight savings, that's 6 am), a small red glow appeared through the trees, exactly east. I felt triumphant! for some reason, silly me. But it felt like, yes! it works. Either the sun and the earth work, right on time and directionally; or our clocks and calendars, their predictions, and our compasses work. So simple. You spend a whole lifetime in our modern world— indoors, or surrounded by tall buildings, and in a place more often overcast than not (Seattle)—and you miss these validations. One could be appreciative of what it took and continues to take, the astronomy, etc, to be operating in this pretty good system.

Then I meditated, utilizing the rising sun, the blue sky, connecting the inner and outer light. Quite beautiful. Many wonderful thoughts appeared, like morning stars, connecting in a constellation of perfection, and Buddhadharma. Now here I am to write them down, and yet they're elusive...

But here: it's about how open I've become. Like an impressionable young girl, ready to fall in love—with the universe. This openness is partly the permeable membrane of being. Meeting everything naturally with tenderness, love, joy, curiosity, and appreciation.

Anything that's neutral or better is Wow! taken inside in this way. Anything sad or upsetting, Wow! also taken in—with sympathy or anguish, as if happening to myself or my family, as if everything and everyone has become my own family! A family I'm not the head of, nor the mother, but more of a sister to everything, or a lover.

Everything I read is "it!" Every idea becomes central. Every person I speak to is "the" one, reflecting love back and forth. It's like I've lost normal discrimination, which could be good—or great! But also seems that enlightened Discriminating Awareness Wisdom isn't quite operating.

Remember, the young girl still needs guidance from her wiser kin, to keep her on the safe side, protected, until she can gain perspective, some wisdom, and life experience. I feel there could be such openness these days, I'm quite vulnerable, so absorbent. So, simultaneously, I have to be my own wise kin, my elder sister, my own grandmother.

Then I thought, now it's getting serious, the need to learn and practice letting-it-flow-through, rather than absorbing like a sponge, which is in danger of holding onto and becoming stagnant, then grasping and solidified. Or becoming besieged. Instead let's go for diaphanous, permeable. To contact and connect, in joy, love, and compassion, and to remember the fourth immeasurable: impartiality. All phenomena are equal in reflecting off of one's consciousness—none of it truly existing as we ordinarily perceive. And so, like space, phenomena can flow through, without leaving a trace.

I think this is the key point, from which wisdom, clear perception, and health all arise (as well as those Four Immeasurables) with expanded ability to be of help to others.

I feel attached to having this continue on past retreat, while realizing it's still just a phase. But wonderful to appreciate what is happening now.

SEPTEMBER 23 – JOURNAL

Up and down, up and down. I've been for some time noticing that my discipline for getting onto the cushion is still not what I had in mind. Once

I'm there, I'm (usually) fine, or much better than fine. But getting there is the challenge.

It's partly habit. The mornings since beginning of retreat have been good. It's the lunch and dinner breaks that I usually want to extend too long. The 21 Taras project filled that need for something of interest to my mind, spending an hour after lunch. Now that I've put that aside, the habit of looking forward to that distraction continues. I've been unhappy with myself about this form of addiction. It's not really laziness, not quite. Today I experienced it as boredom and restlessness.

The thought came that I feel like a cosmonaut, up for months in a space station by himself. (Why a male Russian, I do not know.) Busy with small tasks, communicating via satellite with humans on earth, taking care of his daily needs for food, water, washing, sleep, exercise, writing perhaps, reading, being patient. There must be a sense of privilege to be up there, something wished for since he was a child, and so he might feel gratitude for all the factors and people that made it possible. There's an end date, and for that he is also grateful: It's hard, an inner challenge to handle the kind of solitude, the sense of immense distance, unable to make a change—more than a commitment—he's stuck! And some pressure to perform, to accomplish his assignments, to maintain the necessary stability, to prove himself worthy—for the success of the mission.

So, I'm a retreat cosmonaut, checking my oxygen supply: Will there be enough to sustain me for another seven months?

Seven months still sounds like a long time. Diane B. delivered groceries this evening. We talked about how slowly time passes for us, something unusual that we share, so she understood this completely: It could be another lifetime, these months.

This boredom. I feel it almost physically, my muscles achy today. I wanted to throw something! I'm tired of repeating the same practices every day. Except dzogchen meditation—always a salve.

I added in a different practice recently, and I'm already tired of it, too. In order to make room in the schedule, I took away other practices, and should probably fit them back in now, but can hardly bear the thought of adding more practice time! But what am I doing with my extra minutes? Nothing of substance, not even writing, or any kind of "project"—because retreat isn't the place for projects. So I'm not. What am I doing? Becoming bored. And restless. I hope it's in the stars because then this may be short-lived.

I need to make a new plan, or even just alter some minor things, like do practice in my nightgown, or take a bath, or practice in different rooms. Or take a day off to write.

I'm also aware this state is a big hint that something deep is wanting to emerge. I need to find out, watch, or dig.

Tomorrow my long fingernails are coming off. I've been growing them for three months at a time, which is about as long as I can withstand. In a way they're pretty, but once they get beyond two months, it becomes difficult to do many things, and sometimes one will bend backwards. Last time that happened twice to the same nail it bled—excruciating. Such an immense pleasure to cut them back to pianist length.

> *While in retreat it's recommended not to cut hair or nails. One will see this on many yogins. It's part of conserving the blessing energy which is thought to extend to every part of the physical body, and retained even in the hair and nails. Then, if and when one does trim, it's better to ritually burn, rather than casually discard. While one's cut hair is put into the fire, one can do compassion prayers for all human beings, joining the self with the plight of our common species, and further, as a reminder not to abandon love for all sentient beings.*
>
> *It was easy for me on retreat to let my hair grow long, but the nails were a different matter. The hair that accumulated in my hairbrush I did burn though. And my nails I scattered in the woods.*

SEPTEMBER 24 – JOURNAL

Most days I do not really take a rest. I don't sit in an easy chair to read. No naps. I'm either sitting on my cushion, or sitting at table for meals, or standing in the kitchen cooking, or walking. By the time I hit the bed, my back is tired and I'm fully tuckered out.

But here's something regarding the previously mentioned boredom and restlessness. I began the process of getting back on track and already feel improved. I made a list of retreat things I'd like to do in the next seven months. Then made a calendar for them. I spent time refocusing my priorities and energy and view, putting time in for everything wished for, including a couple of "projects" that are slightly off the straight and narrow of hermitage. However, they are actually helpful for retreat. I will be doing them in a carefully limited way, and including them so that the unrequited need for them doesn't become a shadow that's dealt with in the form of the addiction to distraction, or depression or self-loathing. Wow—just those words written so directly clears it up!

Here's a story. I had been on the toilet, then flushing down a poop. Out of the corner of my eye I noticed a piece of poo was on the side, near the water line, and it wasn't going down with the rest. Suddenly it flew up and out of the toilet! No, wait! It was a jumbo-size brown moth!

It all happened so quickly that my first, instant impression was that this poop was flying! Because of my open state of mind, it was wondrous! Not horrifying, nor even impossible.

In the next split-instant I recognized it as the moth—but it didn't become any less wondrous. Instead I was absolutely delighted that the coincidence had happened that way, to lead me into being fooled for one instant into believing that turds can fly! Turd into moth.

There were extra delight points because this particularly Berger-esque event happened in the Berger house, and I know it will delight that family no end to one day hear about this.

OCTOBER 3 – ESSAY

Musings on the Mantra of Interdependent Origination

Om ye dharma hetu prabhawa
hetun teshan tathagato hayavadat teshan tsayo nirodha
ewam vadi maha shramana soha

All phenomena arise from causes;
those causes and what puts an end to them have been proclaimed
                                    by the tathagata himself.
He who truly speaks such words is the great shramana.

Tracy popped out with a question while here to bring groceries. She had given me a short massage on some tweaked toes, and then, as a return favor, asked for an explanation of the Mantra of Interdependent Origination. She said she'd been doing this mantra for years, but with no teaching or understanding. Kilung Rinpoche had once said in answer to her query only this: nonduality.

I immediately sprang to the task, answering as best I could. Here's something of what I said, with amplification:

It's an ode of appreciation to Shakyamuni Buddha, for his discovery of this important nugget: that everything arises due to something else. No thing has been "created" out of nothing by a creator god. Everything comes into being from something that preceded it, or as a result of other factors.

This was of such utter import, so many other truths branch out from it, and enlightenment itself can come directly from deeply realizing it, that it's a central, originating truth of Buddhism. And therefore when we say it, we are hearkening back to our roots, and making a sweeping bow to Shakyamuni, who discovered and then taught it.

Tracy asked, is this the same as Indra's net—yes, it's highly related. Not precisely "the" nugget, but one of the immediate truths that extends from it. Tendrel, auspicious coincidence, is another one, and of course. Nonduality is another one, not quite "the" central point, but immediately appears as true. And so is emptiness. And impermanence. And grasping. And suffering. They each are like the petals of a flower with interdependent arising at the center.

Tracy and I talked about emptiness, and the mantra's connection to the Heart Sutra, where it's pointed out that there are no eyes, no ears, no tongue... no dharmas, etc. I tried to explain how our concepts get in the way of realizing the true nature of things. How, since things have originated from something else, then they aren't really what our concepts tell us they are—our concepts which have a hard shell around them.

This then brings in impermanence, too. I used the example of the ring on my hand. Here's this ring... where is the "ring-ness"? If you took it apart, which part is the ring? From where did it originate? The metals came from the earth, the earth came from the universe, the universe doesn't have an originating point, but is timelessly existing, predating the Big Bang. So, then, someone made the ring-object. They did that with tools that they bought or made from somewhere, and learned to make from someone else, who learned it from someone else, with energy from somewhere... infinitely. Interdependently.

Then I said, but undeniably here's this object, and it's not permanently a ring. Even right now at this moment, its teeny atoms and subatomic particles are vibrating and zipping around. Little pieces are sloughing off, and someday it will disintegrate or melt down or break. The subatomic particles are so tiny, that in fact it's mostly made of space. As is everything. Then Tracy talked about how she sees this space all the time in her psychic body work on people, that we're all almost entirely made of space.

So our concept of ring as a permanently existing object isn't accurate. But someone could say, well, it's convenient. Yes, but we can take that apart, too. For everyone the idea of "ring" is going to be a little different. It might be imbued with emotional or meaning associations (e.g., marriage, social connection, heritage, precious metals, money, aesthetics, etc.). Or, going even further: for a human, it's something you put on your finger and it signifies something (social connection, style, etc). But for a crow or a monkey, it's something attractive because it's shiny. For an insect, a ring embedded in the ground could be a territorial boundary. So, for all these different beings, and even among humans, there won't be perfect agreement on this object. So "ring" doesn't exist as a perfect object in the universe. If we use the concept as a convenience, which we humans do, it's because we have shared concepts, at least within cultural groups. But still, that doesn't make the concept "true," consistent, permanent, or originating independently of anything. It means the object, "ring objectified," is just a concept in our minds.

And further, utilizing concepts such as "ring" leads us to discard what we're actually looking at. Instead of considering the true nature of things, we grasp it through the concept, then discard it. *Yes—we "know" that, we've already "owned" it, and now we're done with it.* In other words, the first time we ever saw a ring, perhaps as a wee child, we wondered about it, found out about it, and came to understand it. Then we transferred that to "ring" as a label and concept, and in so doing, we became attached to the concept (oh, attachment raises its head now!). Then, the next time we saw a ring, we understood it and so didn't need to investigate it. We could move on without spending time on it. Convenient, but... we've now gotten to the "been there—done that" phase. So we don't fully experience it in the present moment. And we even miss the present moment altogether. But if we can get beyond concept, instead truly experiencing objects, we can experience their true nature... which is beautiful, astonishing beyond words.

In the example of the ring, I'm using an object, what's commonly called a "sense object" in the texts, because it's contacted by our sense faculties (five senses). But all these ways of deconstructing concepts, and nonduality, and arisings, are also to be applied to what goes on in our minds: our thoughts, emotions, actions, reactions, relationships. And that's where the real fun begins!

This then takes us to the next step, to nonduality, where we see that what we're experiencing is none other than our own mind. That when we look at (or hear, or smell, or taste, or feel) something, it's not actually "there" and we're not really "here." It's just our own mind that has conjured our concept—has put it onto a visual screen (or sense receptor), has even turned it upside down in the "photographic camera room" of our brain, has applied associations to it (the five *skandhas*), and has separated "it" from "I."

So then, we say this mantra ultimately because it's stating the nitty gritty of reality, it's bearing the essence truth kernel, and thus it has great power.

It's like the moment when Shakyamuni Buddha proves to Mara that yes, his enlightenment *does* count, that it *will* be noted. And he puts his hand down so that his fingers contact the earth. At that moment of witnessing, the earth responds by trembling. Flower petals fall from the sky. Then Mara, knowing it's been defeated, dissolves away. The power of truth.

There's a line in the Heart Sutra, too, about this being "known as truth since there is no deception." I had always thought that line was a little obscure because of course, *all* the sutras must be "truth," so why does it say it especially here? I think it's because there's something so crucially important in this particular message of truth, connected with this originating point of Buddhism, and through this mantra—this kernel of truth—that gives great power. The power to awaken.

OCTOBER 7 – JOURNAL

Sitting outside this morning for practice, the fog on the sea spread into our trees and all around. Sublime quiet. I began a practice of sending mantras to the animals. Shortly into it, here came a flock of juncos, flitting into the trees and bushes. I was perfectly still, quietly intoning the syllables in a quick way that ends up sounding like a low drone. I put on my glasses.

Then, the juncos came out, to the ground, the pond. Oh, some robins were then in the pond, tentatively bathing and looking around, young ones. You can tell by their innocent look, the still-fluffy "hair," and smaller size. Then the juncos started zooming around, with each other or here and there, near me. Came onto the deck. The robins were stirred up, too.

Then a sparrow showed up. And thrushes. And a somebody with bright yellow streaks. Everyone was chirping, singing, talking, looking, trading places, butting each other away, fluttering. I thought, the jays would come, but they didn't. Who did were the flickers. My! Must be their winter duds: two flaming red ovals on their cheeks, and gorgeous speckly stripes all over, beautiful tans and black. They took over the pond, and then the crab apple tree, and pretty soon they were gone.

I felt I was a privileged guest at a fairy dance, lasting more than half an hour. Beautiful meditation throughout. Joyful, while maintaining a stability of inner quiet.

OCTOBER 13 – JOURNAL

Oh boy, I ordered a smart phone, which turned out to be not so smart. Even opening the box, I could tell there was a potential for days and days of exploration. The red flags were up. However, I was reminded of the nifty app that Rinpoche has on his: a compass! One where, with the flick of a switch, it toggles between magnetic and true north. The app for me, I thought.

I looked around in the phone and couldn't locate a similar app. Then thought, if there's one person who would have this app, it would be Andy. So I called him up. He said, "Diane! What are you doing? You're in retreat. Why do you need a smart phone? If you need a compass, just get a compass." It completely stopped me. I said, in a weak, chastened way, "Gosh, I needed to switch phone companies, and thought as long as I'm doing this, I may as well graduate to my first smart phone. I was thinking the novelty would wear off... It wears off, doesn't it?"

After a little more of this, I realized Andy, not even a Buddhist, was absolutely right. In fact, having the phone made me feel slimy. Wonderfully relieved, I put it and all the little booklets back into the seductive box, sealed it up, and called the phone company. Without even asking why, they said they would ship me their most basic flip phone right away. I walked the little box up to the mailbox, and returned to the house, light and joyous.

Here it is, viewing how it is. Not easy to be in retreat. Third-year anniversary coming in a few days.

I've been wishing for some long chats with Rinpoche, not formal consultation, but informal talking about my retreat state of mind. But he's just returned from Tibet, and tomorrow teaching a retreat for a week.

OCTOBER 14 – JOURNAL

I've been aware of an undercurrent of anxiety lately. This afternoon was more of an *over*current. It came up spontaneously during practice. Lately, lots of thoughts about coming out of retreat. I feel that I'll be asked to explain everything—about my retreat, about the form of the retreat, about my state of mind before, during, and after retreat. I'll have to do another retreat immediately, a book-writing retreat, that will explain it all.

Then, there's the subject of what shall I do and where shall I live. All unknown, and now beginning to raise its head: Post-retreat anxiety!

So, I've been looking at it in dzogchen meditation—or, not looking, but resting in nature of mind—and dissolving it. Today, the sadhana finally dissolved it. That was two hours, though, of feeling like I was on the hot seat. There's kind of a child's fear that it won't pass but will worsen. However, it did pass. I had an absolutely delicious dinner just now, and feel better. Up down up down.

OCTOBER 16 – DREAM

Rinpoche and I were traveling together, then in a house. While he was busy I was called away to do something—a statue of Guru Rinpoche needed to be consecrated, so I went ahead. First I filled it with grain. Then taking a small *Kuntuzangpo* statue I slowly pressed it into the grain inside the statue. Then Rinpoche was there and I told him what I'd done, which was fine. He was busy setting up an altar. I said I like having the Kuntuzangpo statue inside the bigger statue, but now it's not there for the altar. Of course that didn't make sense on a deeper level, because it *would* be there—inside the Guru Rinpoche statue. I realized that and Rinpoche looked at me funny, like didn't I know that?

Then I said, what else is needed, I've forgotten. He said, the prayers. I thought he meant the consecration puja that would come later, but he meant the tiny scrolls with prayers. Of course. I went to find some, wondering how it was all going to fit.

When I woke up, I felt the sacredness of the dream, and that oneself becomes consecrated through the practices, the practices I'm doing on retreat.

I recently read Sera Khandro's autobiography. Her life as a *terton* was difficult. She was encouraged by many visionary messages from the dakinis. Even *she* needed encouragement.

OCTOBER 17, THIRD-YEAR ANNIVERSARY – JOURNAL

Otter visited the house again on this good rain day. Intentionally, it was a different sort of day, to rest and observe, observing self over this span of time, even making an observance of the anniversary. After writing a long reflection, I organized my retreat notebook, created a table of contents, typed up the scribbled notes that I'd taken from some of the rather serious dharma reading, and glued those pages into the notebook. It's been wonderful to review that material.

Reflections on the Third Year of Retreat

It's been a whole new department. Right at this time a year ago I came to Margi's house on Bainbridge Island. By December I'll have moved again, back to Cattle Point. So one of the themes for this third year has been the location: a big, cavernous, open-plan, dark-paneled house from my past, filled with antiques and art. Just by being here I've been reminded often of family, with its interactions, expectations, disappointments, love and warmth. The mixture of one's personal samsara. But it was really so good to be back here. I wrote about this in January as "safe and sound," and I felt real holding and care, by family and by my loyal and loving retreat attendants. Not much externally to complain about, so anything coming up was clearly from my own *ma-rigpa* (read: deluded mind).

I write that as if I was deluged by difficult arisings, but actually what characterized this past year was stability. Stable in practice, emotions, location, health. So stable, in fact, that I've just barely felt "on retreat." It's become more like being in life—retreat as life. A comfortable routine—I half-wake recalling dreams, then sit up for in-bed Ngöndro, visit bathroom, get dressed, eat breakfast, refresh altar, do prostrations, sit for a couple hours or so of meditation. Then take a long break for lunch, business, and a walk. Then do an hour of study, followed by three hours of sadhana practices. Break for dinner, an hour of practice followed by reading in bed for an hour, then say night prayers, and sleep. It's extremely comfortable, easy to accomplish. I still wish to break some habits, like being a little bit later than I wish (for everything), but even that one is so old, since childhood, perhaps perversely comfortable in a relaxed and stable way.

My mornings are still sacred time, when I have no trouble getting down to it. It's there, it's morning, and that's what it's for: sustained and effortless practice. It's where dzogchen meditation lives—my favorite practice of the day. I'm still immersed in Longchenpa's *Chöying Dzod*, using it as inspiration and guide in my meditation sessions almost daily. It's been golden. If the Nyingmapas have a bible, that is it.

After lunch I'm drawn into the external world where my samsaric mind feels this lovely dance, and addictions abound: Food continues to beckon, as does really anything! Email, though nearly nil, is a Call of the Sirens. Paying my monthly bills is even delicious—seriously. Doing the laundry is a diversion. Reading at lunch, usually a serious philosophical text, makes me feel I'm accomplishing something. Walking out to check the mailbox satisfies my gemini need to facilitate connections—doesn't matter that it's junk mail for Margi. Sending off my grocery list is something to do. There aren't many things, but they have become potent in this relative vacuum of retreat territory.

It's because of this great attraction that I scheduled the study first thing for afternoon: I'm drawn to the cerebral, so yes, another attraction but at least it's on point. Then, easier to transition to the hours of sadhana practice. Dinner, and then some shorter practice to fill out the evening until bedtime. Sometimes I just go straight to bed.

There's really no time of the day now that I feel anguish at being alone, or torn about being in retreat. This even includes dinner and evening time—part of the great stability. Of course there have been occasional moments, but very few all year.

I spoke to a family member the other day who said he thought where I am right now in retreat, toward the end but not quite, would be really hard. It would be like his experience of college where in his senior year he found it almost unbearable to stay put and finish. But you had to. I said, yes, it's like that. You really want to be there with all its opportunities—for going into further and further deep places and understandings, groundings in philosophy and in experience, which can be quite joyful. But the limitation of not being able to spend time with my young granddaughter especially, or the rest of my family, is the hardest part for me now. I don't mind missing the rest of the world, don't feel such a social need.

But what is to come after? Questions pertaining to that are surfacing and feeding some anxiety. All of which is right there in dzogchen practice, a particularly good place to be with it, move through it, letting it dissolve, unknot.

As I enter into this fourth year of retreat, it seems apparent that I need to adopt a new level of self-confidence, of trusting and listening to my own intuition, of valuing my retreat experience, and my spiritual experience generally. Of valuing who I am. I know that Rinpoche would agree with this. At some point we all have to do this, after enough time in the dharma, we have to have integrated it well enough into our core, that we can speak from a place of experience, of knowing. That's part of what three-year retreat is all about. And part of my anxiety is this question: Am I ready for that? That's my small mind at work. For me, I think I have to rely on joy, conveying my deep inner joy out into the world. That's been there from the beginning, and will continue to carry me, and others with me, wherever we need to go.

OCTOBER 23, SOLAR ECLIPSE, PARTIAL – JOURNAL

It's been stormy for a few days, looking like no chance of visibility. But then a dynamic sky today with clouds rushing by, turning this way and that. I went out just before maximum eclipse, to the beach with three pairs of sunglasses. One pair was super-dark, the kind they give you after they've dilated your eyes. All three together and it looked like darkest night.

The rain was coming down from a big dark cloud going by. But there, just at the fullest eclipse moment, the sun and moon were visible through passing clouds. I looked a little—wonderful! The crescent sun was at the bottom, a cup turned up, drinking the moon in. It disappeared behind clouds, then appeared again. I didn't spend much time direct looking, wanting to be careful, even with three layers of sunglasses. Then it appeared completely unshrouded by clouds. I glanced for three blinks—quick! It was indescribable, but I will try.

The intensity of the sun was not like light. It was like a sword, like molten metal, like an object, not like clear space that emanates light, but an object with density, the density being sharp but without edges. Formless and incisive. It is, after all, the source of light. But not just a bigger, better light bulb, not just a bigger, better fire either. It has substance, mass—which we know from science class, but this was visible. Its quality is something beyond any earthly fire, and not just a matter of magnitude.

I saw the sun as an object with unique properties, in the way that liquid mercury is unique. The sun's amazing brilliance was seen as similar to mercury's reflectivity—which is not just a surface thing, not like silver coating on a mirror or of chrome, nor is its reflectivity caused by a specific attribute. Rather, mercury's quality of reflectiveness is an intrinsic attribute of its nature.

The sun isn't reflective of course—it's an actual source of light. But in the same sense as for mercury, the sun's attributes—light and heat and energy—come not from a response to, or outcome of, something internal (like the fire that results from combustion of a material here on earth), but are its very nature, the nature of its very mass and its makeup. This is also what I saw.

My impression was that the moon was putting a squeeze on the sun, like a huge boulder moving to block an immense river—you can't really block something that big and relentless, but you can affect the flow. So the flow of the sun's energy was blurching out the crescent side, like the large bosom of an ample woman wearing a tight corset, spilling out, surging out. This was my impression in the blink—three blinks—of two eyes.

Then I thought, the sun is constantly in a state of eclipse. It just depends on where you're standing in space. Both the moon and earth are eclipsing the sun constantly. Night in a way is a state of eclipse: the other side of the world has eclipsed our side every night. So in some ways one might question if an eclipse is special. But just knowing that dispassionately isn't the same as seeing the sun blurching out of the corset of the moon, here from one vantage point on earth.

My morning meditation just beforehand had been wonderful. Looking. Healing. As I walked down the lane through the woods to the beach, all the birds were quiet, forest quiet... that pregnant pre-eclipse hush that comes: what's happening? what's happening? Now the crisis has passed, the crows cawing, airplanes humming, little birds tweeting.

I was careful not to overdo the viewing. More rain came. In the opposite sky, a rainbow. I heard myself saying *om mani peme hung*. When I'd finished looking, thicker clouds settling in, raindrops falling, I went walking back up to the house. I noticed a sensation across my forehead. Empowerment? Or, was I careful enough? But each time I had glanced or blinked at the sun, there was no imprint on my eye screen of just having looked at a bright light. I think my eyes must be okay.

Now back at the house, it's still eclipsing, and wow, a long clap of thunder. What a magnificent display. My description barely touches the immense import and power of what the sun actually is. Of course people have worshipped it!

Only at partial eclipse is the full glare cut down to a level where one can view the sun in this way, that and all those layers of sunglasses filtering the remaining bright streaming rays. Proper eclipse glasses would have cut down the light too much for the risky but perception-changing observations I made today. Which seemed made possible also by the clarity and subtlety of mind brought about by this retreat.

OCTOBER 25 – DREAM

I was awakened in the wee hours this morning with a dream of a demon, the first appearance on retreat. I don't remember anything about the circumstance or interactions, just a deep fear which awoke me. My awake state was just barely, but I responded to my fear by reciting the yidam mantra, which came automatically.

Then I thought, maybe I'm not ready for a showdown by invoking this powerful and wrathful deity, so I switched to the compassion mantra of Chenrezig, for pacification. I recited in this way only about three times, felt sufficiently confident, and submerged back into the depths of sleep.

Now at night we're having a big wind storm. The power may go out. I'm tucked into bed, everything ready for an outage. Many branches have already hit the roof, and the lights have flickered. We shall see...

OCTOBER 26 – JOURNAL

Three years ago, in the darkest part of my retreat, I realized I needed to refocus on myself, to shore up my belief in my own intrinsic spiritual value. I feel this strongly rising up again now, in need of a voice. Many people with confidence in me have encouraged that voice. And yet I feel often I don't have permission to speak. This is old-old, from childhood.

Now, I've been on my own mission, so far from my ancestral home that my family of origin can't even imagine it. I have to stop longing for that home that didn't really understand what my life was going to be about. "You have to leave your people..." That five-year-old's dream perhaps came too early, as a trauma, and I felt flung out of the nest early, then many times seeking a way back in.

This is only partly true. Is it true at all? Or just story?

So where am I in this self-discussion? I'm seeking independence. And also seeking my next step in the world after retreat. How can I be of service? How do I want to express?

Sometimes I think I'd like to be like a Taoist master, hidden, and clean washrooms for a living. And yet I'm excited to teach. What a stewpot of contradictions. When Tracy asked me the dharma question about the mantra of interdependence, I'm all set to answer her, with conviction... and joy.

Maybe I just need a focus and a niche, and then everything will fall into place.

OCTOBER 27 – JOURNAL

I was elated to read an email from my friend K, that she and her family are offering me their Orcas house for my last two months of retreat! She sent photos of a grand and modern log cabin high up on one side of Eastsound, with big views. Really, this is amazing. She is a most splendid person.

How to repay all of these kind, generous friends?

OCTOBER 30 – DREAM

I was awakened last night with my own laughter. I don't remember the content of this humorous dream, but was filled with utter mirth right in my heart center, and it was burbling out. I was laughing not in a facial way or with my lungs, but from my heart, a deep, warm mirth spilling out, giving expression. Wow. Fell back into sleep.

NOVEMBER 9 – JOURNAL

On a short break this morning, watering the big geranium in the dining room, my eye was distracted out the window by commotion in the pond. An otter was bathing! She got out, wiping her wet face on the flat stone landing, and shuffled off, around the house, to the stairway, the best route to go uphill here. Up the steps she went, as if she lives in the neighborhood, which she does. Wonderful!

Now November, finally cold and crisp, or cold and soggy. It's been an unusually warm fall till now, way, way warm, past Indian summer. Hummingbirds still here often, bees buzzing, tiny insects flying. The eagles just returned recently, from their fishing up the rivers for salmon during spawning time. The osprey seem gone. Huge flocks of birds massing and storming the sky, sometimes with unbelievable speed during a wind storm. I imagine they're soon to fly south, and now I see how they can get there in no time!

NOVEMBER 18 – JOURNAL

I'm eating granola that I made. About a year ago I started making it from scratch. It's healthy, lots of seeds and nuts, less sweet than what can be bought.

Retreat Granola

Mix in a large bowl: 8 cups old-fashioned oatmeal, 1 cup sunflower seeds, 1 cup chopped almonds, 1 cup chopped hazelnuts, 1 cup pumpkin seeds. In a separate bowl mix together: 1/4 cup vegetable oil, 1/4 cup honey, 1/4 cup maple syrup, 1/8 teaspoon salt. Mix the wet ingredients into the dry. Spread the granola out on some baking sheets or pans. Bake at 275 degrees for 45 minutes, taking the sheets out every 15 minutes to stir and re-spread (to prevent scorching). Add 1 cup raisins and 1 cup chopped walnuts at the end, so they don't get baked. (Buy the seeds and nuts raw and unsalted.)

My left pointer finger has been twitching lately. It comes and goes, more so with anxiety, that's increasingly clear. Anxiety about post-retreat. It also seems connected to counting mantras on the mala.

An image lately that recurred many times while doing compassion mantras: Each bead, each *om mani peme hung*, was the rotating wheels and surge of a fast train hurtling across the plain of India to Bodhgaya. The sound of the mantra, the physicality of my arm and hand and fingers, my heartbeat, an intensity of traveling, forward movement, to the end of retreat.

I loved this, but it apparently embedded, with the anxiety, as a twitch! So I've been working it off by physically shaking it off, with awareness of anxiety, letting it pass through, welcoming the future, affirmations—everything I can think of, and—"Where is the nature of mind?"

NOVEMBER 22 – LETTER

Getting ready to shove off from this house, I wrote a letter of appreciation to Margi. An excerpt:

I've loved receiving the beauty of the little pond, the two tall cedars, the leaning birch, the whimsical pine, and the arching crab apple. These friends have all become part of my interior landscape since I've spent hours out on the deck almost every day for meditation, even in midwinter.

They, along with all the mobile creatures—otters, coyote, deer, raccoons, and squirrels; herons, hummingbirds, hawks, osprey, and eagles, of course; and jays, swallows, sparrows, robins, chickadees, juncos, finches; flickers and woodpeckers, crows and ravens, the neighborhood cats, and the frogs... have I left anyone out? They've all become my companions on this journey while at your house. Sometimes I did speak to them, but most times stealthily quiet. I think you know how that is.

All the while your presence remains vivid in the house. Your warm heart, generous spirit, truly wishing for good for others—what a wonderful ripple you created with your life, and still so clear everywhere in and around your house. Thank you for all.

NOVEMBER 23 – ESSAY

Expressing Our True Nature

Explaining Buddhist retreat to the outside world comes with challenges. Does one adopt the polite stance, the retreatant's version of *How are you? Fine, thank you...?* Actually, for a three-year retreater there is no polite version. Once you let the cat out of the bag, the very idea of spending three and a half years away from society in religious retreat provokes automatic eyebrow raising of one kind or another. I heard one person, in explaining it to another, emphasize that my retreat and silence were *self*-imposed. I wondered if they were looking for the ankle bracelet. Especially in our time, instead of desert pole sitters, we have dessert pole dancers. People hardly know anymore why someone would choose to become a religious recluse, a silent hermit, devoting their life's hours to meditation, contemplation, and prayer. It's unimaginable—to most, but not all.

In the first year of retreat, in Raymond, Washington, a chiropractor surprised me by exclaiming with excitement, "You're doing it! You're doing the real thing!" An elder doctor in that same town was amazed at my youthful appearance for my age, attributing it to my spiritual path. He appeared deeply touched by hearing a little about my life—humanitarian work in Tibet and now Buddhist long retreat. He had devoted his whole life not to exotic, but to *local* humanitarian work—in severely underserved parts of Washington state—and I was, in turn, touched by that.

Then the other day, in the third year, I explained my life situation to my puzzled Bainbridge doctor as "extreme Buddhist retreat, like extreme sports." I have no idea where in the far reaches of my mind *that* came from, but somehow the modern but absurd comparison seemed to satisfy her since the mystified look on her face instantly disappeared. A couple months before, in response to a Bainbridge chiropractor's question, "So what's the end goal?" (the end goal?!), I laughed and said, "Enlightenment, of course!" Then, trying to accommodate his sincerity, I added that I was taking the opportunity to delve into the diversity of practices offered by this "path of skillful means," as Tibetan Buddhism is often described. It would have seemed offhand to brightly toss off the truth: *It's a journey without a goal.*

Or it's supposed to be. All our striving that races automatically to the fore—through our cultural genes, from family, and really as part of being human—is ever-present in the psyche, on retreat or not, standing as a thick wall between oneself and the Buddhist task at hand. One is strongly advised to drop all striving and expectation of outcomes. And yet, paradoxically even from within Buddhism, the goal of Enlightenment shines brightly, like a neon sign flashing outside your window at night, hard to ignore... while you're also dealing with your thoughts and emotions, trying to develop equanimity and concentration—okay, let's have more compassion—while trying to maintain just the right balance of discipline!

So really then, what's it about, this endeavor that I've been involved in for twenty-five years, and completely immersed in for three? My favorite practice, from before retreat until now, has been meditation. "Resting in the nature of mind," it's called, in the dzogchen tradition. It's akin to a zen style of extreme openness, awakeness, unfabricated, allowing but without following, looking at awareness itself. Then, not looking. Vivid. It's beyond constraints such as watching the breath or focusing on an object. Non-meditation meditation. Potent, it's said to be the direct way to Enlightenment. And yet, the desire for attainment, niggling quietly at the back of the mind...

In the third year of retreat I read Suzuki Roshi's famous book, *Zen Mind, Beginner's Mind*, which I found beautiful and helpful. In it he wrote:

> *Our way is not to sit to acquire something;*
> *it is to express our true nature. That is our practice.*

Thank you, I thought. This is what Kilung Rinpoche has been trying to get through to me, and is what's stated bluntly over and over again in the writings of 14th-century Longchenpa. But by coming through a side door, from the Japanese Zen tradition, somehow the power of these simple words expressed "journey without goal" in a way that struck me with final authority. I printed it out and have looked at it every day since. Weight drains off, anxiety melts away, and I shed expectations that are part of the approval-disapproval, success-failure, hope-fear polarity.

It's so simple. In all my meditations, all the hours of practice, in pouring water into offering bowls, lighting candles—in fact in all that I do—I'm just expressing my true nature. That's all. That's what I'm learning to do. On retreat. And I hope to continue to do. That is my practice.

Lastly, I offer this artifact, retreat advice from a Western mystic.

> *You do not need to leave the house. Remain sitting at your table and listen. Do not even listen; simply wait. Do not even wait; be quite still and solitary. The world will freely offer itself to you to be unmasked; it has no choice; it will roll in ecstasy at your feet.*
>
> −Franz Kafka

NOVEMBER 24 – DREAM

Lucid dream with awake, living quality, more than clear remembering. And yet many details are not quite available to me. It was long, with two main parts in different settings, but the main point was the same. I was engaged in both listening to and speaking on a commentary on "pure perception"—as it pertained to the situations and relationships in the dreams. It was logical discourse, and also a kind of transmission.

Both dreams had a dynamic and interactive quality, not passionate exactly, but not dull or pedantic. It was clear and present, connected to life. The dream woke me up early, around 4:30, then I let the dreams steep in my gradually clearing conscious mind.

NOVEMBER 25 – JOURNAL

So many dreams coming at this time. I'm about to shift places again, and the dreams seem to be highlighting the ordinary world I'll encounter in the move. There's a theme of my disconnect from others' samsaric concerns, such as controversy, or exterior appearance, or jealousy... giving me the feeling that I had mistakenly entered an entirely mundane world, among people who didn't value sacred outlook, or who couldn't appreciate the path I'd chosen.

Yesterday, Penelope the gardener made a special trip over to say goodbye. She brought some things she wanted to give away, like cowboy boots (which didn't fit me) and a whimsical purse that I accepted. I gave her a card and piece of my writing, which she loved, and a houseplant that I'd nurtured back to life. We enjoyed our time, with mutual appreciation, kind of the opposite of my recent dreams. The dualistic hope and fear at work.

Chapter Eight

San Juan Island, III

All appearances are divine.
–Jamgon Mipham

Yesterday nonstop, continuous movement packing up the Bainbridge house. Barbara came over to help, and then Karen from Whidbey Island. We all worked together in a cooperative threesome, the way the Tibetan monks and nuns work together, without second-guessing each other nor hesitation.

Then today, a grand adventure to San Juan Island—Karen and I woke up to snow on the ground! Setting out early, we traveled over sometimes icy or snowy stretches, and passed two different pickups in ditches. There was a calm watchfulness in the car as Karen skillfully negotiated around curves, two-lane back roads, and higher, snow-packed crests. In Port Townsend, less snow, but the wind suddenly extreme. However, the ferry passage to Whidbey Island was quite okay, not as rocky as the wind had promised.

The Whidbey roads were dry as we drove north, but winds were again wild, even pushing small dumpsters across parking lots. Our second ferry ride through the archipelago of the San Juans was surprisingly fine. We arrived at Cattle Point just at dusk—to no electricity! Not because of the wind, but because of the freeze, too much power use had strained the system. So Karen, Tom and I unloaded all in the freezing cold and increasing dark, with headlamps. But the house was warm, and my folks had put many candles around, so it was special and glowing with golden light. When the power later came back on, it was almost disappointing to reenter the electrified world with its sharp edges.

After dinner, we all sat around the warm woodstove. Karen was draped over an easy chair, exhausted, and I was, for some reason, on a comedic roll, so we all four were laughing. At one point I was asked what I might do after retreat, and I mentioned the possibility of writing a memoir about this experience, expressing uncertainty if anyone would want to read it. Tom said, "You should write it and let others decide that." I thought, that's an interesting approach. But we shall see.

DECEMBER 2 – JOURNAL

How will I handle the world after retreat? Let's see how I'm doing so far: Karen left day before yesterday, back to her own island of Whidbey. I set to unpacking and moving in while my folks completed their packing up for another winter in southern California. There were two errands for me in town: groceries and the bank.

My bank is right next door to the big grocery store in Friday Harbor, so it seemed an easy task to open a new account, though I hadn't visited a bank in some years. I sat down across the desk from a smiling dark-haired young woman who wanted to engage in light conversation. She asked what I was doing on the island. Oh boy, I realized this was not going to be simple after all. In retreat, one should speak to others as little as possible, if at all, and if it couldn't be avoided, to certainly keep the matter of retreat private, going incognito as best you can. So I said I'm doing a writing retreat—partly true since I'm doing some writing on my retreat. Ah, a writing retreat! She really lit up. It turned out that she loves to write, so she wanted to know all about it: what kind of writing, had I been published, would I like to share my writing at a local writer's forum in town, etc.? I thought: What happened to the common courtesy of privacy when doing business at a bank? Now on top of it, I also regretted having white-lied... which had exploded into even further investigation. I felt like fleeing.

With a sense of relief, but also vulnerability, I exited the bank and walked the short distance to my next stop. Entering the huge supermarket hit me with the riot of color and commotion of a carnival. I felt simultaneously like crying and throwing up. I hurried through the open produce section, and made a beeline to a more quiet aisle, where I slowly settled into a sense of anonymity and calm.

That's where I ran into a friend whom I hadn't seen for some years, but I knew that she had recently suffered a tragic loss in her family. She looked pale and needed to talk. We spoke about dharma—her Hinduism and my Buddhism. She implored, "All these years of *reading* about philosophy, I'm tired of it! Now's the time to *do* something with it!" I wanted to help her, but all I could do was encourage her to return to meditation, which she said she had dropped. And I inwardly hoped that meeting someone (me) engaged in full spiritual life might encourage her a little. I was left with some sorrow, extending silent prayers, and also the hope that our meeting gave true reason for me to be out in the world.

The reentry report: mixed.

This morning Mom and Tom took off in their RV, pulling their little jeep along behind, setting out on their long but enjoyable trek to the warm desert world and community of friends there.

Turning back toward the house I dove directly into all the rituals of re-opening retreat, with love and confidence. Actually at first a little tongue-tied supplicating the deities, but it warmed up. And then there was intensity and heart connection and earnestness—even in a quiet voice, a voice that I own. And also repeated many times, "for all sentient beings." Even though freezing, it was sunny, only a little wind, so I took my time.

Now, while writing and thinking about what's to come, I'm in this wonderful bed overlooking sea, eastern sky, out to Lopez, and the other small islands.

DECEMBER 4 – JOURNAL

Big family news: Sophia will be having a second child! I had a feeling there was some game-changer news out there, and here it is. Wow, another family member, whose arrival will happen soon after retreat is over.

Today retreat feels almost back to normal—a relief. I did a tsok all afternoon, and feel really ready for this next phase, internally, externally.

DECEMBER 6 – JOURNAL

Four otters on the front lawn were rolling around on the grass when I came into the dining room, accidentally startling them with the sound of my hard-soled slippers. Half of them ran into the bushes, the other two hung around, cautious, but still a lot of energy. The other two reappeared and all four wiggle-walked down to the edge where they pranced around for awhile. One of them repeatedly sprang up and down onto its belly, like a kid flinging himself onto his bed just for fun. A couple of them ritually peed, sniffed the ground, ate a tuft of grass, pawed around, stared at the house. Then all disappeared over the edge, back to the water. I had just watched an exotic tribe of others.

During one puja, at the moment that I boldly pronounced one line, and stood up to offer incense, a multi-pronged buck walked into view, close to the house, in a stiff-legged, highly energized way, not fast but cautious, the body ready to flee at the slightest noise.

Two days ago while outside for smoke offering puja, a flock of quail passed through the garden near me, not shy.

And the seals are back.

Dream

At the Berger house I had made a fire in the woodstove. I'd been in another room packing up to leave and realized I'd better check on the fire. Somehow all these logs that had been stacked around the stove had caught fire, some smoldering, some burning. I thought, geez, I've really neglected this! Then went around putting the burning wood into the stove, which wasn't easy, but I had good gloves and fireplace utensils. I wasn't terrified or panicked, mostly alarmed at my own mind for having neglected the fire for so long.

What am I neglecting—some aspect of retreat? or psyche?

DECEMBER 7 – JOURNAL

Otters back today, coming up from the beach. One had a skate-like fish in its mouth, the size of a large man's hand. They hustled off into the bushes when they saw my head pop up from behind the windowsill to look at them. It all seemed highly comical, we peering at each other. After a little while a red fox also came up from the beach sniffing around, and followed their trail. Looking for skate scraps?

DECEMBER 9 – JOURNAL

Huge wind last night until nine this morning. Crashing waves, relentless, onto the low bank here, the ledge now closer to the house than it used to be. Then dead calm this afternoon and evening. A second storm is predicted for tomorrow, stronger than the first. Yes, I can hear it picking up. It requires some grit at first when you're not used to it. This is my annual initiation.

Today as I returned from my daily walk, the sole of my hiking boot came unglued, most of the back part. I was suddenly walking with a clown shoe, ka-flump, ka-flump. It struck me as hilarious—great enjoyment from that.

John came with my groceries. This was our first meeting, having been arranged by a mutual Buddhist friend on the island. He had actually attended a slide talk I'd given in town ten years ago, about my first trip to Tibet. Today he asked about retreat and how he might apply some nugget of this to his personal practice at home. I gave advice about that and meditation. It was all sincere, humble, relaxed. He's a gentle person and it will be a pleasure having him help me in retreat.

DECEMBER 11 – DREAM

Nyichang Rinpoche had come to visit Kilung Rinpoche and I was greeting him, along with Inomoto and another Japanese man. This third man was sitting playing a lute-like instrument, beautiful, ancient Japanese music, and somehow familiar as if mixed with western modalities. I was entranced. He was robust, swarthy, a country-looking fellow, also the look of an advanced practitioner of Vajrayana or Taoism.

Inomoto and I went out to see about the space where the two rinpoches would meet. Then we were serving tea. But it was black and too strongly made for Japanese taste. So Inomoto and the other fellow were making adjustments with hot water and explaining it as if part of their green tea philosophy—more subtlety and delicacy.

Then I needed batteries to make a recording. Someone brought double-A's but triple-A's were needed, so no recording. No power... which is how I feel this morning.

I just finished outdoor morning sang offering and it all seemed in a great fog, or the molasses of a dream state. I realized it's extremely low pressure this morning. I tried finding the nature of mind—in this murky, foggy, ordinary mind-cloud. Whew! Where is it?... Time to meditate!

DECEMBER 15 – DREAM

At this point in my journal, so much of the writing is of dreams, revealing anticipation with some anxiety about post-retreat life. I later wished I had written more about my awake-life spiritual experiences, though that would have been contrary to retreat instructions! This reminds me of several conversations just before I began retreat. When asked if I would be posting to a blog during retreat, I said, "Why would I do that? It would only go something like this: 'Yesterday I meditated, today I meditated, and I'm planning to meditate tomorrow.'" Here it is then, toward end of retreat, and that is exactly the story.

Dream

There was a big retreat filled with my Buddhist friends. Even though I was still on three-year retreat, I wanted to attend, so it was worked out for me to stay cloistered in my room with Jeanne as a go-between. However, I kept getting glimpses of friends, and it was clear that everyone wanted to see me. At one point I had to go do something important in a different room and, deciding to go for it, I dashed quickly through a large room filled with people I knew. As I went I could see and feel all this love pouring out toward me, and it was returned, me to them. Some people tried stopping me to say or ask something, but I responded with a look of love and "gotta go."

The dream left me with a sense that any shyness I had been feeling about returning to the sangha after retreat was ridiculous. Instead, whatever I exude will be received by them, reflected back to me, transcending anything needing to be transcended.

DECEMBER 15 – JOURNAL

Yesterday I was out sweeping leaves off the stone pavers near the house. I was about to go return the broom to the garage, when I turned to look at the prayer flags hanging from the porch, thinking to straighten them out. Slipping on a wet railroad tie, I fell and crashed onto my hip. Uff da! A perfectly round, protruding welt popped out on my hip. I'm much better today, but creaky in my shoulder. Grateful that was all.

A red fox just ran up the lawn, and after a couple of minutes, back again, marking the corner of the porch with his scent on the way.

I've been making fires again in the woodstove. The weather has become calm and colder, fire cozy.

You see how it is? And then everything not a dream, seems a dream.

DECEMBER 20 – DREAM

I was at a group retreat, sitting in the shrine room as people were arriving. I realized I'd forgotten to bring a cushion and felt a little embarrassed. Suddenly one well-known practitioner behind me called out to me in a loud voice so all could hear, saying something demeaning and petty about my lack of a cushion. I turned around and with hands together, bowed toward her, as if to say, thank you for pointing out my faults. I realized the bow was only halfway, and that internally I had a sense of irony and subtle sarcasm. So I bowed deeper yet, sustaining it until all resentment and ego melted away.

DECEMBER 24, CHRISTMAS EVE – JOURNAL

The glittering, glittering night, my gratefulness knows no bounds.

My appreciation for the dark solstice, the inner stillness of winter, gave rise today, Christmas Eve, to an integration of my chosen path of Buddhism and my Christian roots; the latter having paved the way at a young age to sublime mystical life at Christmas, now crissing and crossing between traditions, unifying them, and reflecting.

Quiet, so quiet today, but allowing music into retreat, music and the flexibility to meet my spontaneous and natural inclinations. So much joy in one day.

The integration point lit up in reading Anam Thubten's book in which he wrote, "The greatest miracle is Enlightenment." Yes, this I believe. And, but of course! And it struck me, having read it at this Christmas time, that that is what Christmas is—celebrating the miracle of Enlightenment.

The Christians see Enlightenment in their Christ only, as a reflection of God's light. His birth—he came that way, like a tulku. But the miracle is that anyone—someone—manifested as an expression of the ultimate—full of profoundest love, wisdom, impartiality, compassion. And light.

For Buddhists this possibility is everyone's birthright, and has manifested countless times. When this manifestation happens it's a reflection of the Dharmakaya, like the Christian God, full of light, pervasive, and beyond conception.

In either case, the once or the many, the miracle of transcending the mundane, or awakening into super-reality, is so awe-inspiring, we're called to celebrate. Even we mundane ones recognize it, long for it, can nearly define it. Why? Because we all have the same essence, we're programmed somewhere deeply inside, to also wake up.

So Christmas is a celebration of this bright light of Awakening that sleeps in everyone's heart. In all this music, the words sing in the language of poetry, which sometimes allude, as poetry does, or point to without saying, like art does. Sometimes that's the only way to get to the heart of the mystery, the paradoxes, where the linear cannot go. Lo How a Rose Ere Blooming, Christ the Apple Tree, The Counselor, Lord of the Dance, Holly and Ivy, Three Ships. And Hallelujah, Hallelujah, Hallelujah, a hundred times.

I think without these ancient songs, this poetry and this praise, we can scarcely begin to comprehend it. It's why the quite ancient pieces speak especially to the mystical, magnifying the vicarious experience of this enlightenment, or at least, the awe.

It is in the dark of winter that the mystical landscape, this tapestry, can be spread. It is in the dark of this glittering night that the miracle of this glorious light's brilliance can be most appreciated. And in the holy moment we fall to our knees.

This morning began early, grey clouds with light entering around the edges. Dead calm. After breakfast I felt called to walk the deserted beach. I felt integrated in my body, with the sand and rocks, the air, the sea, the seals and birds. Back for meditation. Then for lunch break I put on Christmas music, some of it striking me as so sublime I cried. Afterwards I walked the forest and up the small mountain for a good hour. Coming back, more music, drank a little eggnog and opened some gifts that had come for me, enjoying all.

With Christmas music going and darkening day into twilight, I felt called to meditate, even though I'd given myself permission to take a break. I noticed, for the second time recently, that my automatic response to deep feeling, sensitivity to the sacred, was to sit in meditation. Today I did this with music playing, some of which was sublime, some very familiar. It was wonderful, staying present in all, staying with my inner experience while being fed with the outer. Meditation continued after the music ended, until dinner break. Then, more music, a fire in the stove, reading some short things, including, from the house's bookshelf, Rilke's *Letters to a Young Poet*—the one he wrote at Christmas time. He writes much about solitude, profoundly. I feel I'm getting there. Today spoke to no one, and it felt perfect, not an austerity. It's the sublime at work.

"In this time of dark long nights but inner light"... the words of the Canadian radio announcer, just now, nearly midnight on Christmas Eve.

DECEMBER 31 – JOURNAL

I'm on a break, down in Seattle. The trip is twofold: Sophia has had debilitating morning sickness, the kind where you can't get out of bed, and you moan. I thought my presence at Christmastime, though brief, might be of help. And secondly, for an in-person consultation with Rinpoche.

Yesterday I took a floatplane ride from Friday Harbor right into the heart of Seattle. Door-to-door, far fewer hours and interactions than the ferry and car rides. It was a most glorious clear and calm day. The experience of flying was vividly present, including my slightly nervous responses to the sensations of dropping, lifting, surging—the gaps in smoothness that inevitably come with small plane flights. But I enjoyed it, though sometimes a little too determinedly—normally I'd rather be on the ground than aloft—but happy and delighted nevertheless.

While waiting for Sophia at the small floatplane terminal, a dreamlike scene unfolded. A tall, frail, elderly man with Navy insignia had come off a different flight and was wandering around a bit lost, wondering where his driver was. He came to me and asked questions about where he should go. I said, "I'm not one to know," but then got him some help.

Then, his young driver appeared and was confused, even suspicious, about who was I and why was I helping. It seemed I had flown into a foreign country where strangers aren't allowed to speak to each other, certainly not to help. What was even more odd to me was how comfortable I was talking to this re-tired military man, with such warmth, and he with me, and odd that my helpful actions didn't seem to fit with the culture of my own hometown. It made me aware there will be some adjustments coming up. And yet I don't want to lose this spontaneity and lack of self-consciousness, self-editing, in order to fit. I'm quite happy to not entirely fit.

JANUARY 5, 2015 – JOURNAL

Ahh... Lovely to be returned to Cattle Point. Wonderful time with my children in Seattle and beautiful meeting with Rinpoche on the way back. I feel renewed and refreshed, ready for the new year, and the final part of retreat—four more months.

The metropolis really felt like entering a storybook place, or a science fiction story, like *Brave New World* and *Blade Runner* rolled up into one, with some hope thrown in. Is this because it's now so far outside my common experience, or have things really changed that much? Is it internal or external? Probably mostly internal.

Then returning to retreat. Since the holidays are over, the loud, pervasive sounds of the "growlers" are back—the Navy jets that take off from Whidbey, and sometimes fly over this island, controversial for their noise. I think of them as wrathful deities, Vajrakilaya, or protectors, and I harness their power sound to a pervasive intention for positive change in the world. When my mind strays over into "aggressive military disturbing natural and human life," then I send aspiration prayers "for the pacification of our military." Either way, good. Either way, internal realm of appearance and emptiness.

I've been thinking much about nature, of being a natural person, in the state of natural being, or more simply—of being. Not forcing, not anything. Thinking about how that looks and feels, from the inside out. It feels I'm approaching it.

JANUARY 6, TWELFTH NIGHT – JOURNAL

Spontaneously, this twelfth night, just as the moon was rising, I took nine big pillar candles, the battery kind, and set them around the circular brick terrace with one in the center. Walking many times slowly around, within the circle, I sang the mani mantra. Then with mantras flowing, sat on the stone bench watching the moon rise behind clouds. The candles I left out for a couple of hours, though not as late as midnight when on twelfth night, it's said, the heavens beam bright light to the earth. Tonight the nearly full moon shall be outshining that light, I think. But a big moon circle appeared later, greeting my minute candle salutation.

I've been taken aback lately at how fast the afternoon break disappears. It seems there's no time to do anything except eat and walk, and then suddenly the sun is almost setting for early winter. I must be taking extra time, entering some other realm, or a dream state, where I'm gone for awhile.

This evening delicious though. After the candle circle (à la my buddhist friend Cary), I came inside and finished reading the beautiful *Letters to a Young Poet*. Very apropos to retreat since much is there about solitude—its importance, its difficulties, how patience is key, and how to do it. Direct soul wisdom. I thought of my son while reading.

JANUARY 6 – POEM

Luminous Winter Expanse

The night in deep winter meditation,
    even the seals silent.
A slow steady respiration
    of the sea's breath,
        a mammoth being heaving in bottomless slumber,
And the wind at rest.
I switch off the light to signal my own descent.

Soft luminosity glows through the window,
Full moon projecting its light into fog,
Each particle of space amplified, magnified.
What before was invisible, now defined
    In its full dimensionality,
        by teeniest water drops
Of gentle lunar light.

The sole, bare, beachside tree
    Cloaked with white glow,
No Goose Island, no Lopez, no horizon.
All disappeared, replaced,
    Erased into light,
        For one night.

JANUARY 11 – JOURNAL

Last night I made a new schedule for the next weeks, perhaps until retreat end. With Christmas and the break, followed by tying up loose ends, and finally by Rinpoche asking me to look over notes for his book—with all that, my schedule had been too lax and a little unfocused. So I quickly sketched out a plan and began it today. It felt easy and fine.

This evening I finally did my releasing-at-end-of-year ritual: writing on paper all the things to relinquish from the past, and burning it, all the negative thoughts still held onto, the things to forgive, and ask forgiveness for. Before setting it to flame, I read it aloud in front of the altar, sometimes teary. It felt sincerely cleansing, heartfelt, in spite of it being eleven days late. *Late.* I can release that concept, too, eh?

JANUARY 12 – JOURNAL

Following the new schedule, and happily so. I passed a couple on my daily walk, up on top of Mount Finlayson. The woman said, "How did we get *such* a beautiful day?!" The man, a bit portly and puffing to keep up, burbled out with, "I wish I could bottle it!" I laughed at that as they passed. I thought, these people are happy ones. Someone else might be complaining today: cold, overcast, the clouds completely obscuring the Olympic Mountains.

Ah, but it *was* sublime for a Northwest winter: calm, with the hint of a breeze clearing the air, the cloud cover quite high up, letting light through; the color of the sea, almost lilac in its grey, matching the sky; the water's surface with faintest ruffle, going, going, going, out the straits to the ocean; and from our small mountaintop, surveying down on the small islands around Lopez and in the pass; and on the point, the old white lighthouse. Maybe they were on holiday. I didn't want to tell them that every day is beautiful if their hearts are beautiful, as they are today. Sounds corny and preachy, but it was what I thought.

JANUARY 14 – JOURNAL

Clear sky, the workup to sunrise, sublime. Intense colors infuse the light clouds near the eastern horizon. Almost directly east, clouds form the large head of a Kwakiutl thunderbird, its long beak slightly open, facing the imminently rising sun. The clouds so still, thunderbird remains there after one hour. Also, the outline of a heart, its point directed at thunderbird. The sun rose right into the heart of the heart, which is still there, too, as I write, and sun still within heart's boundaries... all throughout first practice.

JANUARY 17 – JOURNAL

Anniversary of three years and three months of retreat today. I've been hunkering down into the practice in a truly solid way—with enjoyment. Doing five formal sessions a day, plus evening reading, plus nights included as a sixth.

Ken H, the old sweetie, sent me a packet of texts which recently arrived. They include, along with a sweet letter, the Diamond Cutter's Sutra.

This evening I enjoyed reading this sutra, which I had become familiar with at Williams, during the weekly gatherings of Lama Jamie. Then I sat in meditation, reflecting on the direct similarities between the sutra and a dzogchen text of Longchenpa. I thought, this sutra must be Mahayana, second turning of the wheel—so much on emptiness. Beautiful. I love the ceremony of it, too, the ultra-formality. And it should be: It's presenting the truth of the universe!

Big storm coming, started. There may have been a big tree down. Loud thud out there through the sound of waves and wind, in the dark.

JANUARY 19, MARTIN LUTHER KING DAY – JOURNAL

Today marks three years, three months, three days! I look at the page and barely believe it. But here are some things to verify it: Eve of new moon. A dream. A gift.

Dream

Rinpoche wanted to order some new calendars for the new year, actually to create them and have many copies made. I said, "But look, we already have all these calendars ordered, many coming." I showed him one which had a nice, brown leather cover. With all the added info, such as Tibetan lunar calendar and quotations and astronomical data, it was hard to tell where one year stopped and the next began. But Rinpoche could tell and he pointed it out and explained. Then I understood.

When I awoke I realized that the last "official" day of retreat is actually today, not tomorrow as I'd been thinking. It seemed auspicious to have received that nudge—a sign on the ending day, not to be diminished as happenstance, but a dream message received.

And that is how I received the gift of this morning. I was out meditating on the deck, a lovely morning with sun sometimes and billowing, passing clouds. Unusually, I'd brought out the binoculars. After about an hour, a small open boat was passing Goose Island at a slow crawl. There was just one person aboard, who seemed to be looking at the small island. Then a larger boat also came slowly along. I looked through the binocs and saw a woman with a huge camera shooting photos—it seemed at houses on the beach. I thought, oh strange. Then large letters on the small boat came into view: "Whale Research." I still didn't get it, and thought he must be out researching the seals on Goose Island. How dense!

I swiveled the binocs back to the large boat just as a large dorsal fin of an orca broke the surface of the sea. Oh! Oh joy! A pod. There were many, maybe ten. A full family, at least two large males. They went slowly, surfacing many times through the pass, and close to the small boat. Then I could see them for a long time straight out the pass into the straits, finally curving around this island to the west. By the time it was over it was noon. I said dedication prayers. With huge love in heart made many gestures from heart outward, drawing out, sending love and encouragement, saying, "May all beings take care of their Mother Earth, and all of her beings, container and contents." And I wept big round, love-filled tear drops.

So, after absorbing more warm sunbeams, I headed back inside, full of this gift, this sign of encouragement for the ending of retreat.

But wait, no! It's not over yet. Three and a half more months to go, to make up for all the days taken as rest days, or doctor's appointment days, or breaks. And yet... Rinpoche said: Now rejoicing, now free. Okay, I shall take that then, and go on.

Reading Anam Thubten Rinpoche's book, *Magic of Awareness*. It's truly beautiful, perfect for this phase, perhaps any phase. Hard to summarize, but... drop all concepts, expectations. Go straight to love and joy. Sounds like nothing new. But he's emphatic, and the message just wants to loosen all constraints, including Vajrayana, or *any* dogma.

JANUARY 19 – REFLECTION

On Arriving at 3 Years, 3 Months, 3 Days of Retreat

Today I was thrust into the fact that this is flag-waving day, completion of three years, three months, and three days. There are three and a half months of retreat to make up for time off, yet there's a pause inherent in coming to this day, stopping to take the temperature, looking around at the scenery, glancing back at the starting point. Posing questions like: how's the pulse? Sniffing the air: where are you now? Taking depth soundings: how far off the coast, the one you've been headed toward?

Here are some answers. Temperature: in the pink. Scenery: lovely. Weather report: rain or shine, beautiful. Location: not quite arrived, but close—still pulling on the oars, but stopping often to drift and gaze down through the blue water, or to lie back in the boat, looking up at the vast sky, or sensing the off-shore breezes ruffling my hair, caressing my skin, lulled by the gentle rocking of the small boat on the calm and boundless mother ocean.

The pace has vastly slowed, without urgency about anything at this point. I almost wrote "any longer," but realized that things could seem urgent in the future, that I could feel all kinds of things in different circumstances. For the here and now though, it seems I'm truly beginning to drop the striving, and just experience *being*.

The natural state of being. A year ago I made a drawing of a fortress on a wide, open plain. There's a waving flag proclaiming the name of the realm: The State of Genuine Being, with the motto below, "Just As It Is." Longchenpa writes much about this state, simply and obviously. Many of the masters do. And yet it has taken me this long in a rather extreme situation to begin to have it absorb into my... *being*. It's probably in the "people are funny" category, but it seems that part of getting to it is understanding that one truly has permission—to simply *be*. Yet in this tradition it's way beyond permission—it's direct instruction, even admonition. It's one of those paradoxes in spiritual pursuit. No Pursuit Allowed!... on your journey. Yet a secret voice still whispers, "But do I actually have permission?" In my case, the permission certificate was delayed by a few years, but finally showed up, was it a year ago?

Sensing how the quality of things has changed, I feel I've dropped, yet again, further into solitude. At some point in the last year I received the great gift of not wishing for something other than that. At any point in the day there's a lack of agitation, or expectation—however subtle or gentle—about being alone. I will always prefer companionship, but this preference doesn't talk to me any longer, doesn't complain, advocate, or scheme.

So, what is this deeper level of solitude giving me? Well, for one thing, it is truly peaceful. It certainly has created a space for the unfolding of practice, the expansion of mind. Somehow it has also given rise to a greater measure of self-acceptance, and acceptance of external circumstances. And self-confidence: I have the feeling that I'll really be okay, no matter the interior weather, whether angry or sad or afraid; it seems that my inner resources have increased, both in strength and number, and so handling future disturbance feels less daunting—on my own and without numbing distraction.

In thinking about going back into the wider world, I've been realizing it's not others' feelings and negative expression that I'm sometimes leery of, it's my own feelings and responses that I'm afraid of. This is of course obvious as philosophical and psychological truth. But to have it become so visceral and crystal clear is something new. In other words, I now have a keener grasp that when something arises, anything at all, it's of my own mind and nowhere else.

So how do I feel about reentering that wider world? I still love the world. That's as it ought to be, and more so, especially if the definition of "love" continues to expand. But how renounced am I of that world? I'm not sure yet. The world around me every day while on retreat is so splendid, beautiful, and wondrous, and the wider world is, I think, the same. But more intricate, at a faster pace. So much to love.

I can see the possibility of losing some of this openness, love, and calm after re-entering normal life. It seems that some booster shots of retreat now and then would be a favorable tactic to maintain it, or even better, to keep this journey going.

But where am I going, you know, if there is no goal? Perhaps that's it. To keep up having no goal. I like the ludicrousness of how that sounds. So much effort into... nothing. I was reading today Anam Thubten's book in which he writes that we need to *enjoy* life, not get so caught up in the serious business of spiritual pursuit, trying to be perfect—and lose years, decades, of the possibility of *enjoying our precious lives*. Yes, I thought, simple enjoyment, of the essence. So, to keep it simple and deeply enjoyed, some effortless effort is sometimes needed—the goal-less journey.

Of course many teachers also stress the importance of a daily practice, and someone who has brought it home so inspiringly to me is the poet Gary Snyder. He's a Westerner and a writer, not a buddhist teacher, and isn't promoting a buddhist agenda. He teaches though, by example, through that beautiful life of his, including the essential ingredient of daily meditation—in his context, somehow noble. And now through the magic of retreat its necessity has come in through my cells. Perhaps that's one of the important pieces of three-year retreat—Kilung Rinpoche did say that to me—that always from here on out I'll feel compelled to do a daily practice, will feel really incomplete without it, and will be drawn to the cushion.

That is another new quality. At all kinds of times of the day, it's now so simple for me to sit down and practice. This sounds, again, quite ludicrous. What, I went into solitary retreat without that? Yes, I did. Even though previously I did sit for practice, it just wasn't always so simple. I would often feel there was something drawing me away from the cushion. There was a sense that something else was more important, more interesting, more compelling. Or something yet undone, some errand to complete, some conversation left to finish. Always something. While on my first personal retreat decades ago, I discovered to my chagrin that that "something else" wasn't at all exterior, but rather, interior. Surprise, honey! My own mind wishing to avoid my true self. And now, somehow, perhaps that is the big miracle after these three years—it has become simple to sit for practice. No underlying diversionary pull, no addictive ideas, no something else.

All these forces, working, working underneath. There was no agenda, no pronouncement from a mountaintop to "become more peaceful, be happy in solitude, go with ease to the cushion!" They've just happened on their own, as a natural result of long retreat. Does my mind still wander in meditation, and do I still have interior conversations about long-standing (and dumb) issues? Yes, sometimes. Am I still subject to emotional responses to bits of news, allowing them to infuse my mind and body for some time afterwards? Yes, definitely. But now the options for dealing with these feel more practiced and effective.

Now that the end of retreat is looming, some of my interior conversation has been related to how I will relate to people after. There are questions that I know people will ask me, and I wonder how I'll answer. Are you glad you went on this retreat? I truthfully don't know how to answer that yet. It's been my life. It was a huge challenge, often not easy, but like the life I had before retreat, rewarding and fulfilling, rich and illuminating. Both based on seeking interior growth, and for the higher good.

So then, the question becomes, were the years of retreat worthwhile? Yes, I think so, but also the process is so deep, on the level of myth or dream, the subterranean realm of the psyche, an indefinable journey, sometimes exquisitely subtle, even as yet unknown to the conscious levels. And it's also ongoing. So it's not a question that can or should be quantified or qualified, not a question that ought to be wrangled with for a definitive answer.

And yet it's an understandable question because for one thing, people who ask it may be wondering about three-year retreat for themselves, which brings this further question: Do you recommend it for others? My answer: Who knows? I think it could be good for some, given a beneficial set of outer and inner circumstances. In talking about this with two lamas, one Tibetan, the other American, it seems that traditional three-year retreat needs some adjustments for Westerners.

Lama Jamie openly expressed his non-enthusiasm about three-year retreat for Westerners. He'd noticed that too often it resulted in actually leading people *away* from the dharma, maybe due to an overkill of intensity, and longitudinal exhaustion by austerity. When he took me on at his retreat center, it was with some initial hesitation, and he recommended that I take a serious break once in awhile.

Kilung Rinpoche also said for Westerners a long retreat of real seclusion could be detrimental. During my retreat he mentioned that it was good I wasn't becoming crazy as was known to sometimes happen in Tibet. Adding to that, we Westerners have a particular set in our psychology—of over-involvement, perfectionism, goal-orientation, and achievement, which, together with isolation, gung-ho austerity, and meditation, can potentially result in permanent psyche-physical damage or out-and-out mental illness. Or just in exacerbating instead of loosening long-standing, uncomfortable mental and emotional dead-ends.

On the other hand, with wise guidance and keeping all the aspects in balance, I think there *are* ways to do this so that the intended results bloom.

But then again, what *is* possible for us? What's the intention? What is blooming?

The possibilities are karmic.

The intention is our birthright: enlightenment, pure and simple.

It's always blooming. Everything, everywhere.

JANUARY 20, FIRST DAY OF MAKE-UP PERIOD – DREAM

I was wearing, more like swimming in, a lime-green gown, frothy, covered with sparkling things like sequins, with overlapping ruffles of stiff satin taffeta and netting, a train, and petticoats. It was some kind of costume, really over-the-top, but without a stated purpose. So the purpose was playful, as self-expression, actualization of an inner pulse.

We were traveling, my daughter Sophia driving and her daughter in the car—and me in the chartreuse green dress, with all the ruffles swathing me in a profusion of chaos in the backseat. Suddenly we needed to go to the dharma center for my end-of-retreat celebration, and no time to get changed. I felt mortified to go in this unseemly extravaganza. Then I realized we also had a basket of unwashed laundry in the back of the car, and I felt relieved that I could wear something of my old retreat clothes. But it turned out there were only tops, so that idea wasn't going to work out.

When I woke up I thought, Oh, I'm really hiding my true self, hiding the flamboyant, the outrageous, the humorous, the colorful and playful, the feminine, the beautiful... in order to fit into the pious and reverential and spiritual. GAK! Uh oh, I can see what's next here—Breaking through. I wonder if I can come up with a new and expressive wardrobe, make some things. What would they look like? The new pink suede boots, a gift from a friend, are a good beginning.

It's more than exterior. I'm still afraid of judgment of all kinds, of people judging my retreat. I feel I need to hide my truth, and in the dream I was wearing a big outer sign proclaiming the truth. Hey! I'm me! Not a theoretical person in a theoretical retreat. I need to come out! "Proud?" Well, that would be over-doing it, over-compensating. No thanks. But lime-green taffeta, crinoline, and fru-fru—Sounds good!

FEBRUARY 1 – JOURNAL

Rainy, grey, sunk in, hunkered down, beautiful.

I picked a book up off the shelf here, quite wonderful and apropos to retreat, a story filled with Jesuits and agnostics, deeper inquiries into the inner quest, union with God. Over breakfast I read these lines, which were the Father Superior's answer to the agnostic doctor's query about vows of celibacy. The priest said, "It seems to me that sainthood, like genius, is rooted in a sort of inspired persistence. It's a consistent willing of one thing..."

There are several parts here to mull over. One is monasticism, which I'm not considering for myself. But the austerities of this retreat do form a kind of monastic life, which I've come to embrace, as it clears the way for further and further inquiry.

Then, persistence. This is similar to determination, an absolute requirement in long retreat. I quite like persistence. But it must be combined with an inner flame—the inspiration part—in order to be intrinsically motived so that it may become something true: the bodhisattva, saint, or genius, or even something approaching that.

Inspired persistence. The thought injected today's wavering self with resolve, and inspiration.

FEBRUARY 8 – JOURNAL

Outwardly, nothing much. Inwardly, little ups and downs, enjoyments and boredoms, peace and agitation—but nothing in the extreme. I leave in two weeks for Orcas Island, so in one week will be packing, organizing, and cleaning, as usual. But all that mostly put aside until it's time.

K and I had a good phone call a couple weeks ago about her log cabin. I wanted to be sure she understood that this is a Vajrayana retreat, not only meditation in a broadly understood sense. Because she's not buddhist, she really had no idea. I thought she should know since the energy of place is centrally important to her. I said I wasn't worried about it, only had a concern that if, at some future time, she came to know this is what I'd been doing, including perhaps some wrathful (yet compassion-based) deity practices, she wouldn't feel deceived. She had to sleep on it and next day wrote a beautiful email welcoming me fully. And so my mind was put at ease. All well.

Then, Jeanne and I had a happy conversation about the retreat end. We discussed plans for her and Rinpoche to come to Orcas, to retrieve me out of retreat, followed by a celebration on Whidbey Island at the dharma center.

We also talked about what to do after retreat. We wildly threw ideas around, like going together on the road, teaching Buddhism out of an RV like itinerant preachers! I said, "I want to unleash myself onto the landscape of the world."

A few weeks ago I wrote a reflection about how I felt sort of home-free at this point, and that it was so easy to go to the cushion for practice. Then almost immediately, as if backfiring, it's become *difficult* to sit for practice, at least in the afternoons. There's some major resistance that I've been looking at, but still don't understand. I'll have a wonderful practice, heartfelt with tears one day, and an opposite almost-rejection the next. I keep feeling: I'm done with this! I'm done with retreat! Ready to launch. And yet I can see how much more is needed after the end comes—that it's just a continuum.

Two days ago it was Longchenpa's anniversary. I'd finished reading his autobiography months ago, but at the time had left one small section untouched: his parting words right before his death, his last testament. It was in verse and lengthy. I had thought I didn't want to read this in the same storybook way as for the rest of the book, but to take it into meditation sometime later. So that suddenly came to me on his anniversary day. I spent four hours with it, reading each stanza, then meditating, reflecting. It was so beautiful, utterly caring, warm. I felt like he was talking to me directly. Quite overwhelming. In the last line of every stanza was the word *please*. Please remember this, or please hold your mind this way, etc. How could there be any tension to dissolve, any resistance? I wept that day.

And yet the next day, resistance. Hmm. I must be a hard case!

Right now I'm sitting in the car at South Beach. My folks asked me to drive their car once a month to keep it in proper working order. Lovely, calm day, so I took a sandwich which I ate on the beach, and have been writing in the shelter of the car. Nice to be "out," but perhaps this is as far as I ought to go. In two weeks I'll be driving this same car myself to Orcas, laden with my retreat "household."

FEBRUARY 15 – ESSAY

Giving Birth Out of Retreat

An analogy came to me. It's like I'm about to give birth. The gestation was 3.5 years. The birth is looming. What will it be? There's some anxiety, and also joy and happy anticipation. Whatever it is, it's going to occupy my life for many years to come—it will be my life itself, of course, but the form as yet unknown.

So, the birth, the narrow point of an hourglass, where timing, flow and atmosphere are important. I've been planning on, assuming a home birth all along, and now with Rinpoche's suggestion to do the unsealing of retreat back on Whidbey, it seemed the doctor wanted a hospital birth with its platoon of nurses and aides—feeling impersonal, like it's not really happening to you. That wasn't what the pregnancy was about, the nourishing, beyond-concept experiences, the growth and development.

Just as the embryo has been hidden away, protected from outside bustle and distraction, the birth wants to take place in a private, quiet circumstance, with no chance of interruptions.

What would a home birth uniquely provide? Continuity, timing, and context. The continuous flow with the rest of retreat would be there, in an inspiring space. The timing is instantaneous, there would be no holding of breath, no gap, no travel. The context of what has built up over the years, the inner elements, the blessing of the retreat altar, the atmosphere, and the presence of the local protectors and guardians—all are there, blessing, magnifying and encouraging sacred essence to go forth into the world. This is potent, like the energy of vajra, pointing outward, lightning into sky, into the vast clear ringing empty space of the matrix, the bell, the mother.

All this sounds quite overblown, overstated, as if real enlightenment is taking place. I don't mean for that impression to be made. Only that the potential for that, through the symbolic potential of this retreat, might be unleashed.

> *The unsealing was eventually set for the retreat house on Orcas with Rinpoche and Jeanne in the intimate setting I'd hoped for. And then two days later, a coming-out celebration at Pema Kilaya's center on Whidbey with sangha, friends and family would be like bringing the brand-new baby to meet its tribe.*

FEBRUARY 20 – JOURNAL

Calm morning, overcast with beautiful cloud sections, low, some distant fog, and sun playing with openings and clefts in the clouds. Startlingly brilliant overlays of silver sea reflections of sun in pockets and stretches, weaving between mist, small islands and reefs. Tide low and still outgoing. Utterly quiet.

Eating breakfast, noticed a massive mammal arise on the sea's placid plain. What? No dorsal fin, it was black and distant. A gargantuan seal? No, it was a whale, or more than one. It surfaced two or three more times, going out toward Whale Rock, out the pass with the tide. It would be a grey or a humpback. Never saw one here before today. The sheer size of it was awesome. Lucky, just before departure.

FEBRUARY 21 – JOURNAL

Big packing day, and here it is, 7 pm, with time to sit back and write. For the record, it takes six hours including a half-hour lunch break, to close the sacred space. That includes outdoor puja, leisurely, taking everything down, putting away all the texts and images, and carefully wrapping precious and fragile altar items. Also, putting boxes into the car. I know I'm slow, but precise. House is clean, put in order, and plan in place for traveling tomorrow.

I'm leaving here three weeks early, the request of my next host, K, so that we can overlap at their house and she can transfer house information to me more easily. My practice has settled in here so well, part of me wishes I had delayed going until my folks return. But plans are set into motion, and here I am, leaping again into unknown environment.

FEBRUARY 22 – JOURNAL

I had been following a special packing-up schedule for the last five days so that there would be time every day for practice among all the preparations. A little anal, but it helped to pace the process and relax without wondering if I'd forgotten some essential task. I even had an extra hour on this travel day, so I walked to the beach to meditate. Finding a log to sit on, left by a not-so-high tide, I rested. A couple yards just in front was a huge moon snail, over on its side. Wow! Hard to tell if still alive, a little worse for wear, perhaps snagged by a "sacred enemy" and then abandoned. I went immediately to pick it up, washed the sand off its foot-tummy, and put it back in the water. But the tide was outgoing, so it would soon be revealed again. However, I was curious if it was even still alive. I went back to sit on the log. After some time, on the way back to the house, I searched for it. You would think such a huge snail's house would have been easy to spot. But that part of the beach, covered with large cobbles, was a great camouflage, and at last I found it, left high and dry by the receding tide, sucked to some stones—alive! I was glad and rejoiced.

This is my life.

Then, I did all the last house things, turned the water off at the road, locked up, looked back at the house with a little nostalgia, and climbed into the car. Turned the key. Nothing. Actually, a little something and click-click-click. Starter working but drained battery! Oh no, everything done just right, with fifteen minutes ahead of schedule. What to do? Slightly panicked but not wildly so. But... a ferry to catch!

In this neighborhood of mostly vacation or retirement homes, hard to know where a neighbor might be found. Fingers crossing, I walked briskly next door. No one home. I heard a voice over by the main road and followed it. A neighbor was on her phone on the back balcony. I interrupted. No husband at home, why don't you try the neighbors with the blue truck? she said.

I had no idea about a blue truck, but I found it, and then, which building was their house? Yes, there was the door, and yes, they answered my knock. Could he help me with a dead battery? Yes. He drove me around the block in the famous blue truck while chatting about his experience in India in the Peace Corps. I thought, how did I not meet these kindly folks before? He jumped the dead battery in no time. I was half in a super-alert state, and half-calm and quiet. We could have continued the lovely conversation, but I had to be off. Then got to town so on time I was first in line for the ferry. I wondered, will the car start again? Yes. Will it start to get off the ferry? Yes, it did.

A lot of excitement for one hermit.

CHAPTER NINE
Orcas Island

> Simply trust—
> Do not the petals flutter down,
> Just like that?
>
> *—Issa*

FEBRUARY 25, 2015 – JOURNAL

Three days ago I arrived, utterly welcomed by K. We talked deeply, and at other times quickly when she showed me around the house. I helped her late at night at the ironing board while she finished a sewing project, and then we both fell into our beds near midnight.

Next morning I was up early, and while making tea in the kitchen, getting some breakfast food, I had disturbed her sleep. Her bedroom is directly above the kitchen, which I hadn't realized. She came out of her room and from the balcony called down to me, saying that guests always erroneously think that the kitchen will be the safest place in the house to keep noise from floating upstairs, and she apologized for not warning me ahead of time. Ooo, I'd felt so sorry as the last thing I had wanted to do was to be the cause of annoyance. She went back to try to get more sleep, and I decided the safest place would be outdoors. So I sat out on some stairs while doing practice in the beautiful sunny morning.

Finally K woke up again—on her own this time—and hurriedly made her final preparations to leave. She said her goodbyes to the spirits of the place, alone and outside. We had a warm, loving goodbye, and off she went. I slowly turned to my own sacred presence here, greeting the spirits of the place, the buddhas and bodhisattvas, all the deities and protectors who have come with me on this retreat. And the local and family spirits and guardians. In this way I asked permission to be here, and for their help and protection for my retreat—for the benefit of all beings. One leaving, one coming. A busy place in the spirit world.

Then slowly I unpacked and set up. As the hours passed, exhaustion increased. Every time I looked out, at the mountains across the sound, the new view, I felt a welling up of tears. The origin of this was mysterious and so, so subtle, not poignant enough to actually cry, as if it were too far away, or too deep to contact.

Perhaps I was too exhausted. If from that cause, exhaustion, like a tiny baby who just needs to be put down in her crib in a dark room for a nap, but instead must withstand just a little more stimulation. So fragile, or frail.

If, from being in a new place, looking out the window at a remarkably different view of the world, now up a thousand feet in the air, among trees, facing south and west—if from that cause, then so sensitive! Or aged. Having imprinted on the last place, one that I know indelibly, my folks' house—now to be uprooted and facing a different screen, imprinting on a changed landscape—could my psyche be that susceptible to ossification? With scant outer stimulation, each imprint has taken over my available perception capacity, which has now apparently shrunken? And therefore any change is a sea change, a 9.0 earthquake. Could it be that?

I didn't notice with the sense of tears any sense of joy. More like grief—but of what, I couldn't say. It was just a tiny squeak, an echo. But every time I looked out at the view it was there. It was part of something else, a sense of being in a dream, too. All was good, all beauty, even the distant grief (let's call it grief)—all good.

My final theory is that something of this place uniquely evoked this—a memory, or a deep familiarity triggering something. And my exhaustion, and the dreamtime, helped me to be susceptible to it. I wished it had remained for another day or more, so I could come to understand it through meditation. Instead, I continued moving through the space of the dream, taking a few rests, no nap, and the process of adjustment continued to unfold, to morph.

At one point I saw a mirror and thought, oh I should look at myself, maybe that will help to know who I am, to reassure myself that I'm not lost, not on a spaceship out in space, gone forever. It did help, even though my image surprised me. I looked some kind of beautiful that day, not tired, deeply peaceful, like who I am, without affectation of any kind—who I am now, not before. I look changed, a serene look, with the presence of a Native American in an old photo, something different that I didn't quite recognize.

Now today feels quite normal. I realized I'd switched off the alarm this morning without any memory whatsoever, must have been that tired, even though plenty of sleep. But a very fine day. Cloudy and misty, atmospheric for the first sang offering this morning. It was one of those mists that envelop so thickly, almost a rain. Quiet. At one point a small flock of tiny birds flew nearby. They must have knocked down a large fir cone onto the deck, which hit with a bang and startled me in the quiet and the fog. I jumped, then laughed.

I've been getting the last bits into place. Tweaking the positions of images, colored lights, texts, thangkas. The sunroom has become the shrine room. There's a great huge overstuffed chair in one corner, bright lime green of ultra suede, new and sumptuous. I propped a large image of Guru Rinpoche on top of some pillows on it, like they do with empty lamas' thrones in temples. This is quite the throne! And a beautiful shrine room.

... In a gorgeous house! Everything is extra-large. K is really tall, which I'd forgotten, and her husband, too. So this house seems sized just for them. Log walls with extremely tall living room ceiling. K's sense of design is elegant. Colors! The art on the walls beautiful and touching and sensitive. There's a Christmas tree that's been up for years. Well, just right for me—the Tree of Life! I've been turning the lights on at night, honoring that universal pole, covered with five-colored tiglei's, and precious, delicate offerings.

FEBRUARY 26 – JOURNAL

I met Anne today. She came as retreat helper via a mutual friend, Thrinley, the temple-keeper on San Juan Island. Anne and her husband, both Buddhists, work as therapists here on Orcas. For this first grocery delivery I invited her to stay for tea so she could get to know who she was helping. She told of her work on the island, her wish to retire soon, and an exhaustion made worse by physical ailments. I was fascinated to learn of a group therapy she and her husband used to lead, Holotropic Breathwork, which, aside from psychological healing, leads to mystical experience and insight. Great fortune to have her as my resource person for these final two months.

MARCH 4 – JOURNAL

Many clear, sunny days, mild. I've lately begun a review of my retreat by going back and reading my writing since the beginning. The idea came from Rinpoche suggesting I review the retreat and to rejoice. He maybe wasn't thinking it would take this form, but it's been affecting, and quite wonderful. Sometimes I feel a tender-hearted compassion for the suffering that arose. Sometimes dismay because the strength of earlier spiritual presence and experience seems diminished now, in a way coming to feel quite ordinary, almost worn out.

It's a combination of many things—wearied of retreat, wishing to relax the austerities, and the artifice of retreat. There's a holding onto a specific mental view—of nature of mind, nonduality, awareness, rigpa—I've experienced them, but not in a continuous flow. And all the reading—wonderful but containing the same basic set of philosophy—I feel worn out of that, too.

At the same time, I'm at a great point of really being fine in solitude, of enjoying the basic life, of enjoying practice. Like today, being moved by listening to two sentences of the *Chöying Dzod* recording, and being able to immediately and deeply put it into use in meditation. I enjoyed my walk, and when I returned decided to find a rake and tidy up the long driveway. I *loved* doing that, happily. And ordinary chitchat isn't at all of interest. So... what am I looking for?

Two days ago I decided I'd better attend to the car battery by taking a drive... to the top of Mt. Constitution! This was a big field trip for me. But the interesting point is that it was quite enjoyable to go alone. Where in the past I would have had an underlying feeling of awkwardness about being by myself in unknown places, where most people are in twos or threes, where I don't know where to go, what to look at—now I felt perfectly comfortable, not wishing for something different, just being and doing, utterly ordinary, enjoying the scenery, the cold icy wind at the top of the mountain lookout, and taking a walk on the sometimes precipitously scary trail along the edge of certain-death drop-offs. Perhaps that latter aspect would have felt safer with a friend, but there was no awkwardness about being there alone.

So I've come to be alone. And dropping down into solitude is, it seems, one of the main components for further journey. But now, where am I? And where am I headed? In some ways I feel, not lost, but sidetracked by being at this ending point. For most people, a two-month solo retreat would be major, just to arrange one's practical affairs to take the time away, and precious. But after these years, and the sense besides that it's "make-up" time, I feel a bit on holiday, or that it ought to be—or that now's the time to be making a reentry, readjustment. It's not that I'm impatient really, which I have previously felt, but that I feel done. Quite.

MARCH 5, FULL MOON – JOURNAL

The other day while meditating outside, a young deer accidentally walked close to me. You can tell young by the naïve face. He was extremely startled, of course, when I gently said hello. He rushed off, but not far, still curious. Then he was intending to walk into the woods, but a deer net-fence was in the way. He bumped his head into it, sending the net into undulations. No, couldn't get through. But he couldn't quite believe that, being young, so he leapt at it. Oh no! Couldn't get through. Got stuck! Went wild, struggling! I put my hand over my mouth, feeling somehow responsible, or, what would I do if he were truly stuck, how would I help this frantic beast?! Suddenly he detached, and just stood there, considering his options. He looked at me sitting there silently. He must have then remembered the way, for he turned and walked off. But before leaving completely he turned to me again, pulling himself up to his highest adolescent self, and made brave, stamping motions in the earth. Then turned and stiffly walked away.

MARCH 7 – JOURNAL

I've been asking lately for guidance messages in my dreams (or from anywhere actually) about my next step out of retreat. Even though I don't find a specific direction in the following dream, there's enormous auspiciousness, positivity, generosity, and confidence.

Dream

A musical ensemble was going to perform. It was beautiful music, classical and sacred. I was supporting the performers by organizing the event. I wanted to give them something in appreciation. I had in my hands a collection of jeweled rings, bracelets, and earrings. Each one felt magical, encrusted with multi-colored, large gems. I felt intense joy and invited each of the musicians to choose something. Even the men were happy to take one, including my first husband. I felt magnanimous, as if wealthy, and confident.

The music aspect of this dream I love—soul food. So I listened to music today, sacred choral music, some contemporary, and Samuel Barber's "Agnus Dei" —deeply affecting. The echoes of its lines and harmonies, coming with me into practice, evoked the word "God" in my mind. I thought: touching God; touching the face of God, by the pathway of that music. I felt this intensely, without doubt. Then looking at my Vajrayana text, reconciling two worlds, how? I thought: through dzogchen, which utilizes the symbol of a mirror—showing you your own face, your true face—*TA!*—your true nature—Dharmakaya—God. I felt this, without any doubt. Two traditions, two faces, yet the same one face.

The music continued in my mind. I began weeping. Why weep, I thought. It shows some longing unfulfilled. Some reunion dearly sought, now found. I have found my path, profound and true. It fills my body and mind. But what about soul, that Western construct? This would be filled by one of two things according to the Vajrayana: awakening or deep devotion (deeper than I have), or both. And in this path it's said that devotion is the key to awakening, to Enlightenment.

Still the piece played in my mind, tears continuing, streaming down onto my breast. Entering the door of the wrathful liturgy was a little challenging because the sublimity of the music didn't seem to match the active wrathful practice from Tibet. I persevered. Then, after hundreds of mantras, I suddenly remembered the peaceful deity at the heart of the practice—pure, white, love, light, and I went there. *That* matched the sublime Western song still reverberating under it all. The purity of the Christian intention—for good, for compassion, for healing—matched the compassion deity's purity and light perfectly. They became one. And in that union my body vibrated and felt great love, joy, tears, and energy generating for all beings.

I feel so inadequate with my words, telling the story of my retreat. The words are a paltry reflection of the experience. Rinpoche is right in saying that sharing about my retreat would limit it, that myself and others thinking they have understood it through the concretizing impact of words would limit it. I felt that while experiencing this music with divine light and joy streaming in and through.

This evening's meditation outdoors for an hour at sunset—glorious. It was also inspired by the earlier music, and actual warmth of the sun, and sublime calm, intense blue of sky, shimmering sea, soft moss, craggy rocks, dark green trees. Afterwards when I got up to go inside, there stood a fruit tree covered with blossoms! Ahh!

Maybe I'm so used to being in solitude, I don't realize how open I am, but I think I am very open.

MARCH 8 – JOURNAL

Wow, three vultures just swooped by the window, doing dramatic dives, even hitting a tree. One of them soaring high, high up, while two others swiftly whirling. Mating-related?

Saw a purple finch today, among a mixed flock of beautifully singing small birds. One day saw a small hawk which flew close to me and perched nearby. Lots of vulture-sightings, and some eagles.

This evening outside for an hour meditation, felt great bliss, thought—oh yes, I take refuge in meditation. Then thought, do I take refuge in bliss? Sounds dangerous. Maybe I'd better rethink that.

At dinner, reading in a text about dzogchen, the section was exactly on that subject: Beware the mystical experiences. And beware the signs—even dreams of receiving transmissions from the lama can be put there by deceiving demons, to increase one's attachment, pleasure, and pride. But what if one is needing encouragement? Sometimes I feel I've been almost saved by grace, saved from falling too low, by the encouragement of signs.

Today saw an angel wing in the clouds—attached to a towering being with a strong, energetic central channel, and topped by a tiglei just above the head. Not many cloud signs for over a year. Demon or angel?

If one is too quick to think demon, I'm reminded of fire and brimstone fundamentalism. Not going there.

MARCH 11 – DREAM

In Tibet, I went to a shrine room where there were some lamas sitting on high seats; it was in the middle of the puja during a break. The main lama was a young Westerner, tall, with red hair. He had several third eyes, one in the normal place at his forehead, but also ones on his hands and perhaps elsewhere. I went close to try to get a good look. He played with that, bobbing and weaving around, and laughing, making it into a game. Then he grabbed me up and hugged me, kissing, or just looking and appreciating, asking me questions. Now I was sitting next to him, sometimes still trying to see the third eye in his forehead. They were like jewels, magical and precious. It felt a little awkward to be there, as it was not my place, but no one minded, these older Tibetan lamas, or others who were there.

With later reflection, it came to me that the "I" in the dream was a child, although that's not how I initially remembered it, more as simply me, as I am now. Either way, perhaps the feelings are the same, of being loved, included, and yet in this dream, slightly an outsider.

What is the experience of a dream? Who is the experiencer? Who is the "I" of a dream? Two I's, like in waking life—the I that engages and the I that observes—just the beginning of that endless conundrum.

What is "I a woman" versus "I a child"? In this dream, there wasn't perceptible sexuality, but it seems there was the male-female-dichotomy magnetism. Beyond that, just looking at the feeling content, there was love and affection, which go beyond age and gender, to anyone.

MARCH 14 – JOURNAL

For weeks since my last consultation with Rinpoche my practice day had become a little too relaxed, even before shifting to Orcas. Rinpoche had said, okay now review and rejoice—you're free to decide, to do, etc. So I thought, alright, I'll just see what makes sense. Each day I kept my morning practices, and then lessened the occurrences of sadhana, adding more meditation. But the result was somewhat purposeless, an aimless quality. I got a clear taste of where I am—and what it's not is a stabilized dzogchen yogini where the deities are present yet parenthetical to continuous rigpa, and one has gone beyond need for regular evocation of them.

So some days ago I sketched out a new schedule. It has rotations of different practices, revisiting most of the sadhanas I've done on this retreat. Meditation is there, too, and tai chi. I want to feel "full"—filled up as I leave retreat. This is a direct acknowledgment of Rinpoche and other lamas' advice about the important role the deities and Vajrayana play in supporting dzogchen. I can't explain it, but I feel and sense it—deeply. I'm not clinging to sadhanas, but am drinking deeply, with refreshment, at their well. It's all working together, as one integrated piece. How wonderful to have come to this through my own experience—because difficult to convince of this through logic.

MARCH 23 – JOURNAL

Still alive on retreat. Still alive in the world. "I was here."

Yesterday while in morning meditation I was reading a bit of dzogchen text of Patrul Rinpoche. Suddenly a song came to me from a musical: "Words, words, words, I'm so sick of words. I get words all day through, First from him, now from you. Is that all you blighters can do?... Tell me no dreams, filled with desire, if you're on fire, show me!"... I laughed out loud! *My Fair Lady* turns out to be tantric! Too many texts, books, wonderful dzogchen and tantric writing, but too much!

Then in bed last night I sang it loudly and joyfully. Now it has taken over my mind this morning. Ah, music! I miss it. And yet it's tied into the world of yearning, passion-attachment. Well good! It fed a very powerful, related dream last night, an exceptional gift of Vajrayana transmission.

My folks came yesterday to bring some things, a wonderful visit. I offered a gift for all they've done, which came spontaneously to mind—after retreat to stay with Mom while Tom takes a one-week holiday on his own. Both he and Mom loved the idea. He'll probably go camping.

So interesting to have visitors. At once intense and loving and present. Also removed slightly, with a kind of special vision way of seeing them in a vibrational field. This has been arising for more than a year. It doesn't happen except when with people. The moment I notice and the thinking mind gets involved, it fades slowly away... not because I ask it to go away. It's certainly not disturbing, and I assume could continue to develop and become increasingly informational.

APRIL 1 – JOURNAL

In a recent dream I received a transmission and detailed practice instructions from Kilung Rinpoche, and then as soon as I woke up promptly forgot all details. This seems to be the theme of retreat for the last month or so. There's a sense of already finished with retreat and being mundaned by the mundane world, and my leaning into, actual willingness to, letting that happen.

In slowly reviewing my retreat notebook and journal writing I'm struck by how sublime many experiences were, but followed quickly, within days, of a sense of defeat or hopelessness. Rinpoche is right: one of my maras—for this retreat and perhaps my life—is expecting failure at every turn, and thus easily interpreting things as signs of failure. (The benefits of having a lama who knows you thoroughly... not always comfortable.)

There's a mystery of what's to come after retreat. I have occasionally received nudges from family to find a paycheck job in something like fundraising. But really it makes more sense to me to take into account all the dharma training—these retreat years plus the previous twenty-five as a buddhist student and practitioner, including the fifteen assisting and understudying with Kilung Rinpoche. Specifically in retreat I've been training in contemplation—as a hermitess, meditator, introvert, while dabbling in reflective writing and translation of esoteric Buddhist texts. So, I have to find my way, letting the path burble up through tendrel, which can only be ascertained by intuition.

However, yesterday I found myself putting figures on a legal pad—of budgets! How much I'd need if I rented a tiny apartment in the city, groceries, etc. Uff da. I'm not sure I'll have the required resources. What to do to help the practical to happen, I do not know... yet. Patience wins the day.

APRIL 6 – JOURNAL

I finished reading Thinley Norbu's autobiography, *A Brief Fantasy History of a Himalayan*, recently published. It was so beautiful I was enchanted. As it was coming to a close, my sense of grief at this Rinpoche's passing increased, now personal, replacing my earlier grieving for others who felt the loss of him. My connection with him has become unexpectedly alive and potent for me throughout retreat—reading and absorbing his books, his appearance in dreams, photo images of him on my altar, and the memory of encounters with him in Nepal.

The enchantment of this book has also beautifully filled my practices with guru devotion, a longing which is not a negative. I realize that actually he's still alive—in heart-mind, in consciousness, in practice, and in dream life—he's available to spur one on the path.

He was exceptional, truly, and the book, disarming. When he wrote about people who frightened him, including sometimes his beloved wife, it was a reminder that even the masters live in, operate in, the particular, the individual, as well as the cosmic. It reminds me of the two wisdoms: the wisdom that knows the nature of things, and the wisdom that knows things in their multiplicity. It reminds me that even while not-yet-enlightened we can have an effect on the lamas, and in the world! But of course, why would I not know this, having worked so closely with a lama for fifteen years.

APRIL 9 – JOURNAL

My hip went into spasm the other day, probably the result of too much cross-legged sitting lately, and then earlier that day I had thrown myself into two hours of vigorous house cleaning. This was enormously painful, couldn't put weight on it, barely walking, and I felt a little panicked. Then, as I was eating supper my eyes happened to fall upon a passage I'd written last January: "I now have a keener grasp that when something arises, anything at all, it's of my own mind and nowhere else." I thought, well of course, that pertains to this, too. So I shifted my perspective and perception, and the pain melted away. I was able to walk into the kitchen, without fear.

I still need reminders in situations like this—of nonduality, etc—for them to be operative, to infuse my mind. The following day I was fairly recovered—no pain and walking normally, while aware that the hip still needs tlc.

A few days ago while outdoors for morning practice I heard a bird singing in the trees, a melody so familiar throughout my life, a song of spring. So beautiful and melodious. I thought, I know that song, but I do not know whom to thank, do not know even its form or name. But I would like to know.

Then yesterday morning while again on the deck sitting quietly in practice, there he was, ten feet away, completely in the open, perched on the railing of the deck, singing his song, over and over again. He was a stocky chap, grey, with black bands along his head, two on each side. I had never seen him before in my life, that I could recall. I appreciated him from my meditation perch, sending silent thanks with the thought that this chap was the one with the miraculous music, and big tears welled up in my eyes. I reached over to my glasses to get a better look, and he was gone. But still his voice could be heard from some further branch.

While watching him sing, I wondered if he might be a sparrow, famous for their splendid song and, I recalled, not very splendid of feather. I looked him up later—yes exactly, song sparrow.

Just now indoors while writing, a long, slender lizard came onto the deck, more than six inches in length, and looking around, curious. At one point he scratched his armpit with a back foot, like a dog. I'm not used to seeing lizards here in the islands. His skin didn't have the translucency of a northwestern salamander, more snakelike.

This evening Anne came bearing the weekly groceries. I asked her to take me somewhere to toss the tsok offerings that I had been accumulating in the freezer. Normally I would find a place to toss them nearby in the woods, but my hosts had mentioned being careful not to do anything that would attract critters, so I defaulted to freezing the offerings until a later distribution time. Anne seemed delighted to help with this dharma task, so she took me to her husband's favorite place in the world, she said, a south-facing knoll high up on the side of Mount Constitution. Beautiful it was to look out on a crystal clear, blue-sky day. One of the piebald, albino-esque deer of Orcas even made an appearance! Then I made us omelettes for dinner. Quite a nice time.

APRIL 18 – JOURNAL

Two weeks until retreat end, so consider yourself on vacation. Today I lay on the deck for sky gazing, half in the sun, feeling simultaneously happy and restless. My concentration is somewhat scattered, easily delving into mundane thoughts of all kinds. On May Day, Rinpoche will come here with Jeanne, to bring me out of retreat. Then the celebration two days later. All this and more has been swirling around.

Not sure how I'll handle the celebration party. A religious recluse goes to a party. Sounds like the opening line of a joke. I think by the end I'll be sitting staring into space with a goofy grin, humming while strumming my lips, a sure sign of having disappeared over the edge.

APRIL 20 – JOURNAL

These last days are not easy. I thought maybe it was low energy due to the new moon, but now we're waxing and I still haven't come along. In fact, today actually depressed.

Suddenly many emails, from family, and from sangha friends related to ending retreat. One set of Buddhist friends who helped me in retreat wrote to say they're coming to the celebration from Oregon! And if I need a place to stay after retreat, their house will be available for housesitting. I was so touched by both things, and also overwhelmed with the thought that I don't know how to repay, on an individual level, all these people who went out of their way for me and my retreat. And well, maybe some of the overwhelm is anticipating feeling shy and introverted.

It's the surprising feeling of: Oh! many things! So much to consider, to think about, to respond to (already), to anticipate. Suddenly life is complicated, and a depletion is the result. My practice has felt increasingly dry, distracted, and uninspired. And at the other end of the spectrum, I care little about talking to people! When I imagine conversations full of chit-chat, my eyes glaze over. I feel dismayed at the prospect, or is it dismay at myself?

In a way it's as if I've suddenly become disenchanted with samsara, which could be a good thing. The problem is that I'm also disenchanted with my practice in its current state. It's a malaise. However, a close dharma sister wrote me a wonderful email yesterday about her own recent, exquisite retreat experiences. This made me happy and joyful—a good sign, no jealousy or judgment.

Actually I am looking forward to knowing what people are doing and thinking about. Also, to music and... pie! And having no external restrictions. Retreat was to dissolve all internal restrictions—finding internal freedom and intrinsic vast wisdom-mind. I did have these experiences, many. But without continuous accomplishment, I'm still questing. Journey without goal is also a journey without end. Every day, wake up and go again. Every night, enter dreams and go again. Lifetime after lifetime.

APRIL 28 – JOURNAL

I haven't been writing during this significant and tumultuous week. What was once the ordered and peaceful and simple life has now been disrupted—to such an extent that there's not much time for practice. A lot of communication, planning, and the beginnings of moving, all adding up to eroding practice session time. It's to be expected, but the result is much internal disturbance.

As I'm approaching the shore, my destination, I'm going to have to cross the surf, the pounding waves. So I have to search for best landfall, a way to ease in. Is there a cove, an inlet, even a dock? In places, the currents are strong with tide rips and big entanglements of kelp. I can utilize the currents to carry me to a safe landing, and glide over the tops of those seaweed tangles. I find a protected cove. People are there, waving me in. I take some final strokes, and my bow touches the beach with a gentle scrape. Now tippy while standing up in the boat, stepping out on solid ground. The world begins to rock and I'm dizzy, landsick. So many hands wanting to hold and hug, wishing to help, to claim. I'm happy. I'm overwhelmed. As someone wrote recently to me, "Oh boy, Oh no!"

Another image. Being both newborn baby and mother—wanting to show the baby to everyone and simultaneously wanting to protect.

Spirit sent me a quote recently: "The universe is friendly." It hit the spot and I wept. Why would I not feel the universe is friendly? The samsaric world: full of complexity, intrigue, beguiling, treacherous even, danger, rejection. It feels there's unfinished business "out there." I've been feeling actual fear and anxiety.

I've taken these into practice every day, applying dzogchen antidotes. It helps, dissolves, then reappears the next day, sometimes intensely, or not.

Yesterday evening I decided to listen to music as an antidote, to re-orient my mind and psyche. It worked. Ordinarily, zero music in my retreat world, so I didn't know if it would layer on more overwhelm, but instead it replaced these constructions of the psyche. The music also reminded me how open I am, that naiveté, loving whatever falls my way.

I've been hearing from many people, warm emails, loving wishes. A beautiful call with Barbara before the deluge of activity, to thank her for her part in my retreat. A surprising note from a buddhist friend who wants to reestablish a connection, offering me a place to stay for awhile. Celebration organizers are expecting around fifty people. One person flying up from San Francisco, the couple from Oregon, others from the islands. How could I possibly be nervous?! It's beautiful. It will even be the full moon and a warm, sunny day. All come out—into the open, into society—welcoming with loving arms.

I had a lovely talk with Rinpoche last week, too. We spoke about what I might do after retreat. I said I wanted to do dharma work, but because of my personality I wouldn't just charge out into the arena on my own, like some might do. But I'd need some kind of "charter" or recognition—in the traditional way, permission to teach.

He said that he would never give recognition to someone just because they'd put in the time of three-year retreat, but that he did feel I'd accomplished it. He asked, Are you ready? Do you have confidence? I said, I think so, for certain things, like dharma advice and writing. He then advised me to take some time, and especially with teaching groups, to go slowly. I said, Yes, I agree with that!

He also said he was very happy with my retreat and the balanced version of the retreat form—balanced for a Westerner and for me personally—not too ascetic, and not too loose. He said even moving from place to place turned out to be a positive thing—taking me out into the world once in awhile, turning my attention outward, balancing the long periods of isolation.

After the talk, I, too, felt happy, kind of amazed, and not. And set onto solid ground.

APRIL 30, LAST FULL DAY OF RETREAT – DREAM

Just before waking, a beautiful dream. There was a conference on Buddhism being held at a monastery and I was there with Rinpoche. We were listening to a panel discussion with two Tibetan women lamas, both of them well-known. During a break, Rinpoche and I went to sit on a bench at the back of the room, and one of the lamas came and sat in a chair facing us to talk.

At that moment I was aware that I was exhausted and my inner state disturbed. I listened to them talking seriously, and noted that it was in English so that I could understand. How kind, I thought, both of them including me, even in my current, disturbed state. Then, Rinpoche was holding my hands affectionately, and the other lama reached out to bless me with her hand on my forehead and head. I thought, oh, here are two enlightened beings, one male, the other female, forming an electrical pole—the gender polarities—running energy through me, to heal, to bless. I opened to it, and received huge energy, felt internal buzzing, and pure love. Then I started to quiver inside, realizing it was the release of pent-up tension and anxiety, the anxiety I've been experiencing lately about leaving retreat.

Then the morning alarm clock went off and ended the dream. I felt quite wonderful to have received this love from two lamas, and a transmission, a healing and blessing, quite viscerally. There was self-reflection within the dream, similar to an awareness of dreaming. And great appreciation.

Devotion is an ongoing journey of its own. At the same time it seems that devotion mirrors the overall inner journey, like dreams do. My devotion to Kilung Rinpoche has only grown over this retreat journey. I've been aware of tremendous feelings of kindness I have toward him, a deep appreciation. Unexpectedly, the sense that I have of the immediacy and availability of his spiritual power, or spiritual truth, is even replacing that of Dilgo Khyentse Rinpoche in my psyche. "Replace" is really inaccurate since a) Dilgo Khyentse is irreplaceable, and b) on a spiritual level they're one and the same. But there seems to be a gradual transference. Dilgo Khyentse has been gone so long now, almost twenty-five years, and the connection has faded. This other growing devotion is quite beautiful, and I realize that all throughout the retreat in every dream where Rinpoche has appeared, one quality has always been present: Love.

Tomorrow Rinpoche comes to unseal the retreat boundaries. It feels needed, this ritual, to actualize it on the level of the unseen protectors, guardians, buddhas. I've done well, I think, in maintaining these connections through all the moves. But Rinpoche has much more ability to actualize it. So for this step, coming out, it will smooth the way for what's to follow. Smooth the way and continue the quest. I'm so happy.

Jeanne coming, too.

MAY 1, RETREAT END – DREAM

As I woke up on my last official day of retreat, I realized the central character in my dream was an old dinghy, a potent symbol for me. Someone, a not completely reliable man, offered to sell me "a seven-foot pre-1700s rowboat, for $47." I said, "What's the story? What's wrong with it? Why only $47?" He started describing it and it was clear he needed to get it off his hands as soon as possible. I went to look at it—in the water, waterlogged, half-sinking, with dry rot like Swiss cheese. But I was intrigued—the lines, its history. I decided to take it. It was being temporarily kept at a maritime museum.

I got quite excited about restoring it. I thought, well, I'll have to bring it with me to my folks' place, and hoped they wouldn't mind if I was working on it all summer while I stayed with them. I knew my shoulder would be a problem for the physical work, but thought, why, I can do it! I brought my mom to look at it, and she was excited about it, too.

One lady tourist saw it and offered to buy it from me for many times more than what I had paid. But I was firm in wanting to restore it. She was curious to look at the hull, so we flipped it over together. It was light! And didn't look so bad after all.

A dinghy—the symbolic conveyance throughout my journey of retreat, and here it was, showing up in the final dream of retreat. Both the dream and the rowboat gave me great pleasure. I seriously thought I could restore a rowboat.

Indeed, and why not?

Epilogue
Dry Land

Visitors! The car crept up the long fir-lined driveway, conveying Rinpoche and Jeanne to the house for my final hours within retreat boundaries. I welcomed them in and we stood around the kitchen for awhile, chatting informally as I made tea, and enjoying the expansive view from the kitchen windows.

Sky was clear, so it was a pleasure to welcome them further into retreat with Riwo Sangchöd. With Rinpoche here, who was to lead, I thought? Well, me, it seemed, this smoke offering having become almost a centerpiece of my retreat. So I went ahead, slightly awkward, at once hesitant and its opposite. But what can't be shifted by exactly this powerful means of dissolving confusion, this incense supplication?

Then, I led Jeanne down flagstone steps to K's cozy, handmade artist's studio, magically anchored to the nearly sheer cliffside. K had invited me to stay there as much as I liked, to meditate or to sleep, but whenever there my mind would invariably drift into earthquake territory. That, and the view was a forest of tree trunks—beloved, but preferring a sky view for meditation, I admired the cabin from outside instead. But it was the perfect place for Jeanne to sit in meditation during the couple of hours that Rinpoche and I needed for our last retreat consultation.

Back in the sun-shrine room, Rinpoche asked questions to test me, and filled with awe for having arrived at that moment of culmination, I answered. Joy was beginning to fill up the empty space vacated by dissolved anxiety. I was given advice, and we seemed to come to some agreements about what to do after retreat. But really, all had mostly already been said.

Rinpoche said words to remove the boundaries, while internally I thanked all the unseen entities who had helped me complete retreat.

So many obstacles could have arisen over the expanse of time to thwart the goal—three and a half years—but they didn't. Obstacles which did arise were met, solved, and moved through. Even the most dramatic, my father's death. When the time for each location was ending, a new one would present itself. Each was beautiful for retreat, in different ways. People always emerged, willing to help me with groceries or other needs. The source of funding—sangha and friends—was continuous throughout. Health obstacles were all resolved. The inner obstacles of the psyche, the ones that retreat in solitude predictably presents, were surmounted. And the final key, the lama, remained throughout.

It was done.

And then, we had a ferry to catch.

Jeanne and I left Rinpoche to snooze down in the car and headed up-stairs to the ferry's main cabin. Even though I had been "out" a few times before, now there was a new sense of "out there without a psychic shield." I thought, oh, this freedom, this utter permission, shall be a relief. But walking around in this way, in public, was disorienting, boundary-less, morphable, yet everything vivid, simultaneously dreamlike.

And then, the dream continued, for there, on the ferry, was my friend and sangha member, Sheila, walking toward us, with an amazed look on her face! I must have had the same look, and perhaps Jeanne, too. We were all stopped short and enormously joyful! What, what?! Of all the people I could imagine welcoming me into the world, it would be Sheila, a soul-quest nature guide. And her partner, Anne, was just around the corner at a table, setting out a feast of delectable deli items. More amazed greetings and hugs, and an invitation to sit and partake with them.

At first I was compelled to simply drink the two of them in, not saying much. For Sheila and Anne, the spread before us was a well-timed lunch. As for me, just having stepped into this sensory extravaganza, I gradually began to nibble and savor in amazement each delicious morsel of cheese, or olive, or cracker. The synchronicity of first our meeting and then the out-lay of delectables struck us further, as a serendipitous tsok feast. Offering, offering...

We spoke a little about the coming celebration of my retreat ending. Sheila had previously agreed to deliver the invocation, making our connec-tion with the deities, protectors, spirits and entities, the expressions of the five directions and elements. Though highly experienced in this role in her work, she had never stepped into it in Rinpoche's presence before, and she expressed some nervousness. But I reassured her that I had full confidence.

So it was in this way that we made our way over the sea to the main-land, and then to Jeanne's house, where I was only too happy to collapse. My assignment for the following day was to rest up for the coming reunion with friends and family.

MAY 3, PARTY, PEMA KILAYA'S CENTER – JOURNAL

The retreat-ending celebration was truly amazing, that's what people said. Love and joy were bursting out of people, ricocheting around the place, that's what I say.

Jeanne and I spent the morning at her place. I tried not to talk too much to keep from wearing myself out, but it was hard to refrain. Driving there we were stopped at a red light, and yet she started to make a left turn onto the four-lane highway. I calmly said, "Are you sure you want to do that?" She saw her error in time and expressed amazement that it was *I*, the foreigner to this land, who had noticed. We both laughed because I'd been so calm, as if there had been the parenthetical question, oh, and do people make free *left* turns at red lights now?

Jeanne had to check with Rinpoche all along the way by phone in order to get our arrival timed just right. We drove up the long driveway lined with new, tall poles and prayer flags. At the top, lines of people waved khataks—people I knew and loved, faces shining, love pouring out, eyes smiling. Rinpoche stood at a tall sang offering burner, clouds of incense and cedar smoke billowing out. He had a khatak in his hands and I walked over to greet him, the khatak going round my neck. Big smiles.

All the folks slowly walked my way as I began walking around the side of the house toward the Tibetan tent and streamers of prayer flags. I turned back toward the crowd who had all streamed behind me. No one spoke. Someone raised a tent line so I could come over to their side, but I lowered it in a playful way, silently miming, "I need some space yet!"

I stood and gazed at the crowd—my friends. They stood and gazed back. I beamed. They beamed. My gaze went from face to face, lighting up each time anew: Oh! There's so and so! Oh! It's you!... over and over, sharing love in this silent, unhurried way. Someone said, "This is a very unique situation." I was being welcomed back in ultra-present time, and I welcomed them into my heart. Finally, I stepped forward to embrace my radiant mother, and announced, "This is my mom!" eliciting an "ahh" from the crowd. Everyone had been forewarned not to overwhelm me with much talk or visiting or hugs. But they knew I would make an exception for my mother.

After a splendid potluck lunch, we gathered in the big tent. First Sheila's uncharacteristically shy invocation, but lovely—ah, I thought, instead of invincible, she's more like me, all good. Then, I began my speech, the one I'd polished over the preceding weeks. Everyone, friends and family, were rapt, some with moist eyes, and I was happy, doing what I felt meant to do.

Then Rinpoche spoke, at first generally about retreat. Recognizing that many people were understandably inspired, he urged people not to jump into long retreat, and certainly not without a qualified teacher. He said he wouldn't always give recognition for accomplishment based on the amount of time someone spent in retreat. And then, about to confer something, he stood up on his dais, and his beguiling three-year-old daughter wrapped herself around his legs, charming everyone. I thought he might lose his balance, but no. He held a paper in his hand, a kind of certificate letter, and he read it. The words are honoring, and encourage me to teach Buddhism in the world. It was recognition of accomplishment, and I was deeply touched.

This was followed by heartfelt speeches by Jeanne and Karen, and then spontaneously, my daughter Sophia also spoke.

It felt like the end. But no, everyone lined up to present me with khataks. We poured out love to each other, one by one. I think I exclaimed to just about everyone that they were so beautiful! They were. It was a radiance. Extraordinary, intense, and touching. When nearing the end of the line, after more than an hour, my energy began to flag, but I didn't let up.

Finally, most guests having wandered home, I went into the house and sat with Rinpoche and a few others as we decompressed a little, and enjoyed the echo of the afternoon together. Then we all got into our cars and drove away. Such completion, such a satisfying reunion. Happiest of days. All doubts about reentry swept away.

MAY 27 – JOURNAL

Four weeks since out of retreat and into the world, and I've written nothing. Many times phrases and sentences arose into mind, but exhaustion always plunked me into bed before I could pick up a pen. Or the siren call of my family, or simply an inability to face the inner intention summarized by the verb "to do." This was the story for a full two weeks after reentering the world—I could barely look at email, could not write a single word of reply, could not write in this journal. Could not pay bills, or any manner of serious business, not that I needed to do any of that. But I had wished to capture the full intensity of the return by writing about it afresh.

So here I am, at about the third level of reentry, doing fine, watching how things are: the high-energy mornings and the slow afternoon slides into weariness, followed by okay evenings in which I've been either watching British telly with my folks, or reading a novel to my mom, or succumbing to my solitary and quiet guestroom bed.

MAY 29 – JOURNAL

My jaw has been extraordinarily tight for three days. I think too much talking and smiling. It's been a very full week!

JUNE 1 – JOURNAL

Many scraps of phrases, wafting sentences and thoughts floating through like ribbons carried on a breeze, then reappearing randomly. Here's one: This post-retreat time so far is a bardo state, in between, a transit station.

Another: I'm transiting between "true" lives—the true life of the hermit and the true life yet to be found in the outer world. One day merged with the last, and the next, without definition or purpose, without really belonging to my self. Wandering in samsara, with little reflection.

Partly it's a matter of time. My time has been taken up with external agendas—appointments, meetings, gearing up a bit for this outer life, "practicing" it, and taking in its enjoyments, including time with my mother. But in all of it my core feels somehow lost. A vividness, and grounding, and balance have been reduced, submerged. It's not extreme, not dizzying nor upsetting. I've been happy. Happy and accepting to go this way or that, to watch and to see. But the reflection time of retreat is sorely missed, along with an inner navigation of what's important and where headed. I feel sometimes that plopping down into the American society of secular scientism is so distant from my true Buddhist underpinnings. And yet by giving this time, being a loving companion to Mom, this *is* a true path: dealing with whatever presents itself in the most compassionate way one is capable of. This is to serve.

There is the possibility of staying here for some time while writing. Would it be quiet and reflective enough? Could I regain that inner compass? Can I regain it *anywhere* in the samsaric world? That's the crux.

May through August were fully immersed in the mundane world, the first two months with my folks at Cattle Point, the latter two in the city. And all the time coming and going. Such an about-face. The advice was to reenter delicately, but circumstances and other people—and my own eagerness—pulled on me to jump right in. Many of the plans had a hint of quiet, like a beautiful week on remote John's Island with my daughter and granddaughter. Then a boat trip with my friend Andy through the islands, full of adventure, with one evening singing old Broadway songs out over a still, small bay at night. One week I nestled in at Cattle Point with my mom while Tom went off to the wilds of Canada. Then, there were warm meetings with old friends, and my daughter's pregnancy to help with. And in all this I was reminded of how much time it takes just to make the arrangements for the meetings and happenings of a complex life. I'd forgotten.

In July I moved into my mother's condo in the heart of Seattle, surrounded by high rises and nightclubs and people bustling to their downtown jobs; also drug addicts and prostitutes hanging around the streets. In the years I was away, the traffic in Seattle had become markedly congested, which had become a continual complaint in conversations, even a topic on the radio, in newspapers. I could hardly tell the difference.

For me, driving had become so completely foreign, it was all now novel, and I had to retrain myself in rudimentary maneuvers. To illustrate just how basic: As I drove up to a traffic light, I had to look directly at the light to tell what color it was, or if it had changed; I'd lost the ability to keep this awareness in my peripheral vision and subliminal awareness; and the result impacted ease of driving in complex traffic crowded with multiples of pedestrians, zooming bicycles, skateboarders, buses, and erratic cars. This minute skill did return, but only after several months. All these small things added up, and the net result was often exhaustion.

With Sophia's birth event getting closer, she had signed her eleven-year-old daughter up for six weeks of summer camps and asked me to do the transportation. Of course I welcomed the chance to spend time with my granddaughter, even if it meant many trips through city streets. I took it on as part of my reentry program, and in a way was happy just to be doing ordinary life. I began using a smart phone (oh yes, that!) to find out the least-congested routes. I caught up on some movies, and read a novel or two.

And every day I meditated.

Since the end of retreat I had been steeping on the idea of taking a road trip especially to visit some lamas in the Bay Area, and friends along the way. On a sunny day in September I set off on my own, heading south, camping gear and bags tucked into the back of my station wagon for an adventure of ten days.

As I traveled down, first I-5, then the coast highway, I was welcomed by friends, and fed and given a couch or a bed. It turned out that everyone on the trip was someone who had helped me in various ways on my retreat, so the sojourn turned out to be a lovely review, and an opportunity for me to express my gratitude. It felt luxurious to visit in informal circumstance, no longer rarefied, without restrictions or limitations.

Before I had arrived in California, one of my friends insisted that I make an appointment with her lama. I'd heard of him, an American dharma heir of Chagdud Rinpoche named Lama Drimed. My preference had been to attend one of his teachings since I didn't wish to request him as a personal teacher, but no teachings were scheduled. Spirit continued to urge me to see him for a formal consultation, and finally I agreed.

She and I drove out through the hot, dry, low hills of Marin County to the lama's small, modern house. When we knocked, a beautiful woman came out with Lama Drimed, both of them laughing, clearly having had a wonderful time. Lama Drimed, smiling, invited Spirit and me inside, where Spirit and he chatted for awhile. When she left, he invited me to stand in the kitchen and talk while he washed dishes, and he began to interview me—about my retreat, and my previous life helping and studying with Kilung Rinpoche.

As we sat down in his living room, I presented him formally with a khatak, and he continued to ask questions, deeper in, about my understanding and experiences with esoteric practice. Finding it difficult to express, but definitely interesting, I was often tongue-tied, and thought, he's just going ahead as if he's my teacher, shouldn't I be asking him questions? But ah well, it's good to be engaging with someone, a Westerner, who is forthright, who operates outside the box, someone whose knowledge of the dharma is clearly profound.

Then, he said, "Well, if I were your teacher, I would give you some advice about what to do now after your retreat." Oh! I thought, very good, that was the question I ultimately came here to ask. "You should do one more year of retreat." Oh darn, more retreat... "You've come a long way, but you have a bit more you need to do. You're at this point that often happens after the three years, where one is not quite stabilized enough in rigpa; and then the samsaric world exerts its inevitable pressure to rejoin... and then..." Here he drew his hands out in front of him as if holding an oversized balloon, "... the consciousness that has expanded through the three year retreat..." then his hands moved back toward each other, "... begins slowly to contract back to a samsaric state." I thought, oh yes, I have been sensing exactly this.

"If you delay this additional retreat year, you'll have to repeat the difficult adjustments of the psyche that normally occur in the first period, and which it sounds like you've gone through." Oh dear, he's right, I thought.

I asked, "So you really think one year would be enough time to make a difference?" He said he did. I then asked, "Is there something you 'see' in me that indicates it would actually be worthwhile?" He said that he did. I recalled Rinpoche's suggestion months before retreat ended, that an addi-

tional three-year retreat would be beneficial... followed by my immediate, not-on-your-life answer. Hmm, now I would have to think.

By the time Spirit and I returned to her home, I had decided. I thought: Three more years I cannot do, but one year I can, and it seems I should. What this lama said made sense. I kept this within, not discussing with Spirit. But late that night, lying outside on her patio, inside my little tent, I sent an email to Kilung Rinpoche telling him my plan. All the way from Tibet, his reply came instantly: "Wonderful!"

A sense of calm went with me, as I left Spirit's company, returning up I-5. The practicalities of pulling off another year began to turn over in my mind. How to break this to my family was another subject.

Back in Seattle, my family was not at all happy with the thought of another year, continuing my unavailability. In fact, my son's response was so full of anguish, I almost changed my mind. In the end I promised him that this would be my last long retreat... for this lifetime.

The next three months were full of more life, complexity, and preparations. And in mid-December 2015, I set off again, small boat, vast ocean.

Aspiration
written on retreat

My wish for all of us is that our imaginations of what is possible
expand in such a clear picture with such confidence,
that the pathways open up,
and we're drawn in, without effort,
like water mixing with water.

Like a Boat Drifting

Like a boat drifting,
sleep flows forward
    on the deep water of dreams.
Drifts and drifts . . .
until, finally
the bottom falls out of knowledge.

In the fragrant mist of dawn
the rower wakes,
    picks up the oars, sets them,
    and begins to row.
All night
he labored in his dream
    to be born
like a song in the mouth of God.

Robert Sund
from *Poems from Ish River Country*

Glossary

awakened mind – The mind of enlightenment. The idea in Buddhism is to wake up from our delusions, the fog—of concepts, attachments, afflictive emotions, fears—that has covered the seed of enlightened buddha nature within us and other sentient beings.

bardo (Tib) – In-between state, famously the stage between lifetimes where one searches for one's next rebirth. Bardo states also include the period of dying, the moment of death, of this life, meditation, and dreaming.

beyul (Tib) – A blessed, pure land, which exists as a parallel universe to the mundane one we ordinarily walk in. These are said to be passable through exceedingly hidden portals only by those who are enlightened, or, for those with a pure heart, tagging along with someone who is. See Ian Baker's book, *The Heart of the World: A Journey to Tibet's Lost Paradise, 2006.*

bodhisattva (Skt) – An enlightened person whose consistent, prime directive is motivated by bodhicitta, vast compassion. Also, a technical term for a class of deities.

buddha nature – All sentient beings carry buddha nature within, the capacity for enlightenment, our birthright. See "awakened mind."

chakra (Skt) – Wheel. Chakras are part of the system of channels that run throughout the subtle body. Innumerable channels come together at specific chakra points, each resembling a wheel with spokes, and each with a specific quality of energy.

chöpen (Tib) – Vajra performer. During a puja, this person conducts the ritual gestures and offerings, lighting of flames, incense, etc. During a traditional puja with many people, especially in monasteries, roles filled by others may include the lama leading the service, chant leader, musicians, discipline master, assistant chöpens.

cognizant luminosity – Attributes of the nature of mind, or intrinsic nature.

daka (Skt) – The male equivalent of a dakini.

dakini (Skt) – Manifestation of the sacred feminine, sometimes in physical form as a woman, sometimes as a female deity, as a catalyst to help beings on their path to enlightenment.

dedication – Essential element of any practice in Tibetan Buddhism, made at the end, to offer the merit generated in that practice for the benefit of all sentient beings.

dharma protector – Deities who protect the buddhadharma and buddhist practitioners.

dharmadhatu (Skt) – Space of truth, the basic space of phenomena in which anything may arise, which has the qualities of wisdom and compassion, and which is buddha nature.

dissolution – The stage during a sadhana, usually at the end, where one dissolves the meditational visualization.

dzogchen (Tib) – A level of teachings and practice found in the Nyingma School of Tibetan Buddhism, characterized by non-elaborate, natural methods and outlook. Its lack of ritual and iconography, along with its reputation as the quickest route to enlightenment, has attracted many in the West, although traditionally it is only introduced to students who have demonstrated commitment to and development on the Vajrayana path, and to bodhicitta. Dzogchen is very similar to Mahamudra in the Kagyu School, and parallels have been made with some schools of Zen.

empowerment – A transmission which empowers one for a specified practice, and gives permission on a spiritual level to do the practice. See "transmission."

emptiness – *Shunyata* in Sanskrit, meaning empty of intrinsic existence. A core principle of Buddhism: things exist on one level, but normal understanding loaded with concepts and associations leads us to delusion about their true nature; this then leads to attachment and then to suffering. "Emptiness" is considered to be an incomplete translation since it implies a nihilistic state where things do not exist at all. Contrary to this, they do arise, due to interdependency upon other factors, but are "empty" of the concepts that we usually attribute to them. Once we come to realize their empty quality, and that of all things, then vast compassion and wisdom naturally arise, and suffering and confusion dissolve.

Four Thoughts – A contemplative practice to increase motivation for dharma practice. They include: the preciousness of this human life; the fleeting nature of life; the unavoidable laws of karma; and the suffering of samsara.

Guru Rinpoche (Tib) – Enlightened master who brought Vajrayana to Tibet in the 9th c. Also known as Padmasambhava, he is revered by Tibetans and others as the second Buddha. He was invited to Tibet by King Trisong Detsen; then subjugated many local spirits, binding them by oath as protectors of the dharma; built Tibet's first monastery, Samye; and began the hidden treasure practice (terma). (See "terton.")

hung (Tib) – (pr. *hoong*) A sacred syllable meaning heart-mind of enlightenment. (Hum, Skt)

intrinsic nature – Refers to an inner core of being that defines us as sentient, not stained nor added onto by our psychology, habits, or cultural concepts; considered primordial, luminous, with vast understanding. Nature of mind is another term often used.

karma (Skt) – Cause and result; a cosmological understanding of how things work in the universe of sentient beings; in the West, similar to "as you sow, so shall you reap." In Buddhism this principle extends beyond one's present life, and also affects the circumstances of communities and nations. Karma is also changeable, depending upon current actions—of body, speech, and mind. Intention and motivation are key elements.

kaya (Skt) – Body of enlightened existence. Three kayas commonly referenced: Dharmakaya (see "dharmadhatu") is the formless aspect of enlightenment, beyond words or concept, all-pervasive; sambhogakaya is the energy aspect; and nirmanakaya (see "tulku") is the aspect of enlightenment which manifests in this material world.

khatak (Tib) – A special scarf, usually white and silken, used in ceremony or greeting. It's used in a variety of circumstances, for example, draped around the necks of those who are embarking on a journey, or returning from one; around those who have received a degree, or just gotten married, etc. In a buddhist context it's often presented to a teacher with the variation that the teacher receives the scarf into his or her hands and then drapes it around the neck of the student as a blessing.

koan (Jpn) – Poetic, paradoxical statements used in Japanese Zen Buddhism to stun the mind of the student out of mundane modes of thought. Ex: *What is the sound of one hand clapping?*

kora (Tib) – A circular path around a sacred shrine or place, covered by any mode of transport—foot, horse, car. A famous kora is a several-day pilgrimage by foot around Mt. Kailash in western Tibet. Kora is generally made in a clockwise direction.

Kuntuzangpo (Tib) – The primordial Buddha, according to the Nyingma School, depicted as naked because totally without elaboration, beyond concept, and deep blue, the color symbolizing space. This icon is used in dzogchen practice, symbolizing the Dharmakaya (see "kaya"), and depicts our pure true nature. (Samantabhadra, Skt)

lama (Tib) – Buddhist teacher, spiritual friend. (Guru, Skt)

lineage – Because the practice of devotion is centrally important in Tibetan Buddhism, lineage is a key element in order to develop strong confidence in the authenticity of one's teachers and the purity of their transmissions—confidence in the veracity of the teachings they give; of their bodhicitta; of the unspoken understandings that may be transmitted, mind-to-mind; and by becoming part of their community, of the sharing of their karma. If one's teacher has a strong lineage, then a spiritual connection to great masters of the past may also be available for the student.

Lojong (Tib) – Mind training, in the form of a set of contemplation slogans to aid in the development of compassion, developed in the 12th c, based on previous classic texts, *Way of the Bodhisattva*, and *37 Practices of a Bodhisattva*.

Longchen Nyingtik (Tib) – Literally, heart essence of the vast expanse, the lineage and cycle of teachings and practices established by Rigdzin Jigme Lingpa in the 18th c, based on revelations and teachings of 14th c Longchen Rabjam (Longchenpa). A major lineage of today's Nyingma School. Jigme Lingpa had four main disciples; the present reincarnation of one of them, Dza Kilung Jigme Rinpoche, is a central holder of and transmitter for this lineage, and appears in this book as the author's principal teacher. The author's buddhist practices derive from this cycle and lineage.

lung (Tib) – (pr. *loong*) Tibetan medicine identifies three basic bodily elements to be addressed for any ailment—bile, wind (*lung*), and phlegm. For health, balance between the three is needed. *Lung* is not the same word as in English, but is related—the air of the gross body that interacts with the subtle winds that move through the subtle body. Imbalances can be brought on by habitual emotional or mental patterns, including "too much *lung*," which can be caused by meditation done with too much striving or intensity. Practitioners in intensive retreat and their teachers have to be on the lookout for signs of this common imbalance, and take corrective action to avoid long-lasting mental and/or physical consequences.

mala (Skt) – Rosary, with 108 beads.

Mara, mara (Skt) – The famed demon(s) who attempted to defeat Shakyamuni Buddha in his quest to achieve enlightenment as he sat beneath the bodhi tree in Bodhgaya, India, around 450 BC. Of course, Shakyamuni triumphed and Mara, in that instant, dissolved. Mara is often thought of as a manifestation of one's own ego or self-interest, sallying forth to distract, tempt, or dissuade the higher self from the spiritual path.

mo (Tib) – Divination.

nature of mind – The true core of being human, without blockages, concepts, fabrications; pure and luminous, with vast wisdom and compassion. See "intrinsic nature" and "rigpa."

Ngöndro (Tib) – Foundation practices found in most schools of Tibetan Buddhism. Comprised of taking refuge; generating bodhicitta; purification; offering; guru yoga (connection). Also included are prostrations, mantras, supplication prayers, dedications, and aspirations. In a typical beginning, one commits to completing a large number of mantras, after which one may make this a lifelong centerpiece of practice.

nonduality – Nonduality is considered the true state of things in which there is interdependent union of all, from one's mind to all aspects of the universe. Its opposite, duality, is the common, samsaric way of viewing the world, a state of delusion in which we perceive that subject and object are separate, in which there seems to be an executive "I" that controls one's own thoughts and perceptions. Our human habit of attachment to dualistic perception keeps us in this fog, the lifting of which is one of our principal tasks on the buddhist path.

Nyingma School – Ancient school. Of the four main schools of Tibetan Buddhism, the Nyingma is the oldest, originating with Guru Rinpoche's appearance in Tibet in the 9th c.

om mani peme hung (Skt-Tib) – The mantra of Avalokiteshvara (Chenrezig), the Buddha of Compassion. Considered a kind of anthem of Tibetans, it's commonly chanted on a daily basis, printed on prayer flags, contained with spinning prayer wheels, carved into stone.

one hundred deities – A set of deities, peaceful and wrathful, at the center of the liturgies of the well-known *Tibetan Book of the Dead.*

Pema Kilaya – The sangha (community) of students and practitioners of Dza Kilung Rinpoche. Established in 2003 in Seattle, now with its center on Whidbey Island, Washington state, mainly practicing Dzogchen-Longchen Nyingtik of the Nyingma School.

phurba (Tib) – A ritual implement in the form of a three-sided dagger. (Kilaya, Skt)

prostration – In Tibetan Buddhism, prostrations are full-body gestures. As a practice, they are done to develop the physical and subtle bodies as a kind of yoga, and to develop humility and devotion, as an homage, an offering. In Tibet, adepts make a pilgrimage of prostrations, up to a thousand miles, across the plateau all the way to Lhasa.

puja (Skt) – Ceremony or practice based on a liturgy. See "sadhana."

rigpa (Tib) – Enlightened awareness, the mind of enlightenment, our ultimate nature. A state of awareness wherein we recognize our nature of mind.

Riwo Sangchöd (Tib) – Mountain incense offering ritual. Common in the Nyingma School, this practice is based on pre-buddhist shamanic elements. It utilizes singing and drumming with the burning of cedar, juniper, and mixtures of fragrant herbs (*sang*) from the Himalayas. The buddhas, bodhisattvas, and protectors are invoked, supplicated to, clouds of fragrant smoke offered, in order to dispel negativity in the world, to bring peace and harmony, and success for spiritual endeavors.

sadhana (Skt) – Liturgy. In the context of Vajrayana it is the text for a full practice, puja, which usually includes a specified set of prayers, visualizations, mantras, dedications, etc.

Saga Dawa (Tib) – Special springtime month in the Tibetan calendar in which three significant days in the life of Shakyamuni Buddha are observed: his birth, his enlightenment, and his parinirvana, passing out of the endless cycle of rebirth at the end of his life due to his complete enlightenment.

samadhi (Skt) – A state of deep meditation.

samaya (Skt) – A kind of spiritual oath or promise, which can be explicit or implicit. Often seen as being held on a mystical level, samaya is sometimes difficult to keep, if, for example, it includes continually keeping the principle of emptiness in the forefront of one's mind. Fortunately there are ways to repair broken samaya.

samsara (Skt) – The endless cycle of life based on delusion. Birth, old age, sickness, death, rebirth, and start again.

sang (Tib) – (pr. like *song* in English) Fragrant herbs from the Himalayas used in incense (smoke) offerings. See "Riwo Sangchöd."

sangha (Skt) – Community of Buddhist practitioners, similar to congregation; ordained Buddhist monks, nuns, teachers (lamas).

shunyata (Skt) – See "emptiness."

skandhas (Skt) – Aggregates. The five skandhas are invoked to explain the usually instantaneous and subtle comprehension process that our consciousness normally goes through when apprehending objects or other arising phenomena: form, feeling (sensation), perception, formation, and consciousness.

skillful means – Method. Vajrayana is sometimes referred to as the "path of skillful means" because it includes a plethora of methods that can be employed in one's spiritual development. It's also often paired with "wisdom," the idea being that the two are required in concert to make progress on the Vajrayana path.

smoke offering – See "Riwo Sangchöd."

tantra, tantric (Skt) – Texts of the Vajrayana from India and Tibet, emerging beginning in the third century; the perspective and practices deriving from those texts. The tantra vehicle, or tantrayana, is synonymous with Vajrayana (see below) and Tibetan Buddhism.

Tara (Skt) – Beloved female Buddha. Her most well-known form is the female Buddha of Compassion, born from a tear falling from the eye of Avalokiteshvara, the male Buddha of Compassion, when he found that, in spite of his efforts to dispel the suffering of the world, it would inevitably arise again. One of Tara's great powers is her responsiveness, to go immediately wherever she is needed, wherever she is called. In the Nyingma School, 21 different manifestations of Tara are revered, each with a different set of specialties and qualities, some peaceful, some wrathful.

tendrel (Tib) – Interconnected auspicious circumstances, especially as they contribute to causes for spiritual understanding and development.

terton (Tib) – Treasure revealer, one who reveals *terma* teachings hidden usually in the 9th c. by Guru Rinpoche or his consort, Yeshe Tsogyal. The purpose was to rejuvenate high-level dharma teachings, with the foresight that over time and for a variety of causes, they might degrade. Tertons are generally reincarnations of enlightened beings who have the qualities of vast wisdom and compassion to enable their comprehension and correct dissemination of the teachings. The treasures may be found, for example, in crevices in cliffs, or sometimes through mind transmission, and are still found today.

thangka (Tib) – Scroll paintings of Tibet, usually of iconography, unsigned by the artist.

Three Jewels – Buddha, Dharma, Sangha. This triad are what we make ultimate when we become Buddhists in the form of a vow, and continue to uphold in our heart throughout: Buddha as the enlightened guide, Dharma as the sacred teachings, and Sangha as the community sharing the path.

tiglei (Tib) – An orb of blessed light energy, essence. It can be thought of as containing a whole universe, a deity's sphere; also as the essence traveling through the channels of our subtle body system. (Bindu, Skt)

transmission – Transference of energy. In Tibetan Buddhism, teaching can be given verbally or by text, or by energy transference. This may also be a bestowal of blessing, healing of body or mind; and empowerment for a specified practice.

tsok (Tib) – A food-offering ritual, at times an elaborate puja, or very simple. Can refer to the food item that's being offered.

tulku (Tib) – Reincarnated enlightened being. This term is a translation of nirmanakaya (Skt), the physically manifested dimension of enlightenment (see "kaya") as a person or other physical arising. Commonly it's used as an honorific indicating the person is a recognized reincarnation, no matter his or her age.

vajra (Skt) – A ritual implement resembling a scepter, symbolizing the compassionate energy of the enlightened state, often paired with a bell, symbolizing the empty potentiality, or matrix, and wisdom of space. (Dorje, Tib)

Vajrayana (Skt) – Diamond Vehicle. Sometimes synonymous with Tibetan Buddhism, or tantric Buddhism, Vajrayana is technically one of several vehicles within the Tibetan tradition. It's characterized by the use of visualization, empowerment, devotion, and inner yoga. Rather than attempting to reject or suppress all-too-human states, such as afflictive emotions, suffering, concepts, and internal energies, this vehicle employs these as fuel for their transformation into pure states of wisdom and vast compassion. Tibetan Buddhism very much includes the other vehicles, as well: the Sutra Vehicle, the Great Vehicle (Mahayana), and Dzogchen.

Vajrayogini (Skt) – Primary female buddha deity in Vajrayana, a dakini.

wrathful deities – Common in Tibetan Buddhism, wrathfuls represent another side of compassion, where ultra-vividness, power, and energy are needed to break through inner or outer logjams. All wrathful, and semi-wrathful, deities have a peaceful buddha residing in their heart. Not to be confused with anger.

yidam (Tib) – A deity which one chooses as the main focus of one's tantric development through sadhana and meditation. Also referred to as a class of deities, which includes protectors.

Skt: Sanskrit; Tib: Tibetan; Jpn: Japanese

ACKNOWLEDGEMENTS

The beautiful flowering of offerings made for this retreat by dozens of friends, family, and fellow Buddhists still astounds me. My gratitude begins with deepest bow to my teacher, H.E. Kilung Jigme Rinpoche, who supported me in every way with great perfection—and kindness, wisdom, and intuition, from inception through to completion. He contributed with advice, teachings, and encouragement, as well as encouraging others to support this endeavor. It would never have happened without his confidence and efforts.

There were fifty others who, with great heart and generosity, donated housing, grocery shopping, driving, funding, skills, and/or supplies. Here are their names. Joanne Terry and Tom Metke; Barbara Berger; Margi Berger; Skip Berger and Carol Poole; Kari Berger and Gary Kelfner; Sophia Berger; Gus and Crystal Berger; Lama Jamie and Sara Kalfas; Brent Naylor and Kathy Gunderson; Dr. Karen Carbone; Dr. Tom Roberts; Diane and Keith Brintzenhofe; Bruce Dobson; Tracy Dickerson; Susan Campbell-Webster; Peggy Sue Mc-Crae; John Soderberg; Anne Gresham; Andy Ryan; Jeanne Lepisto; Diane and Cutty Hyde; Jim and Dana Belisle; Thrinley DiMarco; Katherine Witteman; Mully Mullally; Judy Patterson; Lila Wheeler; Spirit Wiseman; Jana Rae; Kari Holman; Josh and Susmita; Lucille Laurin; Lynn Hays and Nancy Nordhoff; Lene Gregersen and Preben Petersen; Frank and Susan Ryan; Ruth Yeomans; Gwendolyn Roush; Carmen Nantez; Lesley Tinker; Sarah Hood; Phyllis and Roland Krauss; Cary Peterson; Christina Porowski; and Sheila Belanger and Anne Hayden. Words cannot begin to express my gratitude.

My thanks also go to those who read this manuscript and gave indispensable advice and encouragement—to Brian Hodel, Diane Hyde, Barbara Berger, and Sandra Moreano. For the wonderful gift of professional proofreading and copyediting, enormous thanks to my longtime friend, Judy Gouldthorpe.

About the Author

Diane Berger is a native of the Pacific Northwest, where she graduated from The Evergreen State College in journalism and anthropology. She worked for a number of publications, from newspaper reporter-photographer to copy editor, including a stint with the book division of Rolling Stone. As a member of the press, Diane first encountered a reincarnated Tibetan lama, His Holiness the Dalai Lama, on his first trip to the West in 1978. A decade later she took refuge as a Buddhist and became a member of Rigpa Fellowship. She attended many retreats, including one with HH Dilgo Khyentse in 1990, whom she still considers her heart teacher.

On a one-year adventure with her teenage twins, Diane's life took a significant turn in the south of India when she met the reincarnated lama, Dza Kilung Rinpoche. Already an experienced Tibetan Buddhist practitioner, she began assisting this young lama, eventually bringing him to the West, to her city of Seattle. While initially the goal was to find funding to rebuild his monastery in Tibet, the work took off, and they created a thriving humanitarian foundation and Buddhist sangha. After 15 intense years of worldly accomplishment, Diane felt it was time to shift her focus inwardly, to direct spiritual practice, choosing traditional three-year retreat.

Diane completed her retreat in 2015, with an additional nine months in 2016. Since then she has been teaching meditation and Buddhism in Seattle. And thoroughly enjoying her family, as well as time in the wondrous sphere of nature.

dianerigdzinberger.com

Printed in the USA
CPSIA information can be obtained
at www.ICGtesting.com
LVHW040537311023
762560LV00003B/287